The Ultimate Book of
sex

The Ultimate Book of

sex

A handbook for sex education that is
- **Value Based**
- **Culture Specific**
- **Age Appropriate**

Dr. Rajan Bhonsle, MD
CONSULTANT IN SEXUAL MEDICINE & COUNSELLOR

Dr. Minnu Bhonsle, PhD
CONSULTING PSYCHOTHERAPIST & COUNSELLOR

JAICO PUBLISHING HOUSE
Ahmedabad Bangalore Bhopal Bhubaneswar Chennai
Delhi Hyderabad Kolkata Lucknow Mumbai

Published by Jaico Publishing House
A-2 Jash Chambers, 7-A Sir Phirozshah Mehta Road
Fort, Mumbai - 400 001
jaicopub@jaicobooks.com
www.jaicobooks.com

© Dr. Rajan Bhonsle & Dr. Minnu Bhonsle

THE ULTIMATE BOOK OF SEX
ISBN 978-81-8495-255-1

First Jaico Impression: 2012

No part of this book may be reproduced or utilized in
any form or by any means, electronic or
mechanical including photocopying, recording or by any
information storage and retrieval system,
without permission in writing from the publishers.

Printed by

PRAISE FOR
The Ultimate Book of Sex

We can no longer afford to sweep sex under the carpet and expect our children to 'educate' themselves. The several valuable guidelines in this book can help parents to confront sensitive sexual issues, understand them ... and start a fresh dialogue with their kids.

— Shobhaa De, author and columnist

Scientific yet simple, authentic yet not like a textbook, in a flowing, easy to understand language without being judgmental. I wish my teachers or at least I had a book like this while I was growing up. It is meant for everyone and not only academicians or professionals. Especially a must-read for all parents and adolescents.

— Padmashree Dr. Mohan Agashe, MD (Psychiatry), DPM Founding Director – Professor, Maharashtra Institute of Mental Health; former Director General, Film and Television Institute of India; Advisor, Government of Maharastra on Mental Health Education and Service

The writing is simple, clear and honest, the format a systematic unfolding of a subject difficult to handle at the best of times. Everyone needs to pick up this book, written for India and Indians, retaining a proper scientific approach while keeping in mind our culture and our values. After you pick it up, read it, discuss it and apply it. Each one of us needs to arm ourselves with the information required to warn our children of the pitfalls of living in an exaggeratedly sexual world.

— Carol Andrade, Senior Journalist & Editor, Afternoon Despatch and Courier

This book is not about sex. It is about the science behind sex, from the psychology to physiology, and manages to cover everything under the sun in a lucid, logical and extremely sensitive way, striking a fine balance between the scientific and social aspects of this issue, while stressing on values and ethical behavior. This book busts the myths and misconceptions of the adolescents to the aged, and has been a valuable learning experience for me in particular, and I congratulate the authors.

— Dr. Snehalata Deshmukh, MS, FRCS
Former Vice Chancellor, University of Mumbai,
Paediatric Surgeon and Dhanwantri Award winner

CONTENTS

	Preface	xi
1	The why and How of Sex Education	1
	A must-read for EVERY parent, teacher, counsellor and doctor	
2	Values in Human Sexuality	14
	Discussing the need for the educator to live the values s/he imparts to the other	
3	Key Principles of Sex Education	20
	Discussing the rules to be followed while talking to pre-pubertal children	
4	The What and When of Sex Education	25
	Discussing what children want to know and need to know at various ages	
5	Child Sexual Abuse: Breaking the Silence	40
	Empowering children against sexual predators	
6	Modelling Healthy Sexual Conduct	47
	Discussing how adult sexual behaviour affects kids	

7	**Low-Down on Date Rape**	52
	Discussing the modern-day phenomenon of date rape	
8	**Anatomy of the Reproductive System**	60
	A scientific discussion of the physiology of human sexuality	
9	**Hormones: The Chemical Drivers**	82
	The role of the endocrine system in sexual physiology	
10	**Adolescence: A Sexual Transition**	89
	Discussing adolescent changes in boys and girls	
11	**Menstruation Cycle: A Complete Guide**	120
	Discussing the importance of educating girls about the monthly period	
12	**Premarital Sex Education**	132
	Counselling young couples before they tie the knot	
13	**Importance of Communication in Intimacy**	150
	Teaching couples to freely and frankly talk about sex	
14	**Reproduction and Birth Control**	157
	Discussing various contraceptive measures	

Contents ix

| 15 | Sexual fantasies – The Pros and Cons | 173 |

Discussing how fantasies affect your 'real' relationships

| 16 | Pornography: A Dangerous Drug | 179 |

Discussing the ill effects of pornography

| 17 | Pregnancy and Intimacy | 188 |

Discussing sexual relationship during pregnancy

| 18 | The Sexual Journey | 195 |

Discussing sex at 20, 30, 40, 50 and beyond

| 19 | No sex | 202 |

Discussing when not to have sex

| 20 | Menopause: A Change of Life | 208 |

Discussing the movement from a reproductive to a non-reproductive age

| 21 | Aphrodisiacs | 214 |

Discussing the most popular sexual myth

| 22 | Paraphilias: Arousal beyond the Norms | 222 |

Discussing arousal variants

| 23 | Chromosomes and Genes | 232 |

Discussing the microscopic building blocks

| 24 | Sexual Orientation | 236 |

Discussing the variations in orientation

| 25 | De-stigmatising Sex Therapy | 256 |

Discussing when to consult a sex therapist

26	Unsafe Sex	262
	Discussing sexually transmitted diseases	
27	The AIDS pandemic	278
	A detailed discussion on HIV infection	
	Glossary	296
	About the Authors	311

PREFACE

We present this source book in sex education with the firm belief that sexual crimes, sexual exploitation, sexual ignorance, sexual dysfunctions and sexual diseases can all be prevented through sex education. Therefore, our motto for our sex education endeavour through this manual or through our numerous awareness programmes is, 'EDUCATE TO ERADICATE.'

This contemporary sex education manual is the culmination of our extensive study, ongoing research, and detailed interactions with thousands of people of both genders, all ages, various professions, and from different economic strata of society. We have counselled and educated people through our one-on-one counselling sessions, as well as through our training programmes and awareness workshops. Through our interactions we have realised, that so many problems that people face can be prevented through timely and scientifically accurate sex education.

Whether it is the scars of sexual molestation in the childhood or the angst of date rape, the turbulence while attaining puberty or the agony of gender bias, the trauma of an unwanted pregnancy or the horror of contracting a sexually transmitted disease or HIV. Or, whether it is the psychological impact of pornography, or the confusion and anxiety in teachers and parents regarding empowering children during this time and age when they are surrounded by incorrect, perverted and explicit sexual messages through internet and other media—the only way to address all these issues is value-based, age-appropriate and culture-specific sex education.

This manual endeavours to educate readers about the physiology and psychology of human sexuality. It also discusses social, behavioural, relational and even legal aspects of human sexuality. It is, therefore, a complete and holistic guide for sex educators who need a ready-reckoner to address all queries from curious children, teenagers as well as adults.

This manual is meant for the reference of adult sex-educators such as parents, teachers, doctors, counsellors, social workers etc., as well as for those adults who seek to educate themselves. Great care has been taken to respect the sensibilities of all communities/groups/schools of thought in India and to make it culture-specific yet contemporary, without compromising on the scientific accuracy of the subject.

All pictures/diagrams in this manual have been used with responsibility and maturity, taking into account that people of all ages and different sections of society would be learning from them.

The scientific information in this manual has been compiled from numerous sources over three decades of study and research. During our study, there was no intention of publishing this manual hence, no record was kept of the various study sources. Therefore, while there is no individual acknowledgement or bibliography in this manual, we would like to humbly acknowledge the contribution of all those, whose published material and research papers have greatly added value to making this a complete source book. We have minutely scrutinised and taken great care to ensure the scientific accuracy and authenticity of all sources of information.

While we have taken every care possible in making this manual a scientifically accurate and sensitive one, we welcome suggestions from those who are equally passionate about helping create a sexually healthy, responsible and sensitive future generation.

— Dr. Rajan Bhonsle, MD

— Dr. Minnu Bhonsle, PhD

Chapter 1

THE WHY AND HOW OF SEX EDUCATION

A must-read for EVERY parent, teacher, counsellor and doctor

Sex Education: The Need of the Day

There are certain issues, which even the most courageous people choose to avoid discussing, and society keeps suffering the repercussions of such an attitude. Sex education is one such issue.

Parents as well as teachers hesitate to provide sex education to children; while they are being pounded with sexual messages everywhere they look; from newspapers, magazines, television and films, to public toilet walls. Their young minds are more vulnerable to these corrupt messages as they are rarely prepared with healthy and legitimate information about sex and sexuality. This interferes with their development towards mature and healthy adulthood.

What Is Sexuality?

Sexuality is a powerful dimension of the personality. It implies intelligent thinking, sensitive feeling and behavioural reactions associated with maleness or femaleness of an individual. Sex is not a grimy secret between two ashamed individuals, but a divine impulse of life and love. Like all the other instincts, the sexual instinct also carries with it certain responsibilities, and the only way to prepare the young generation for being responsible sexually, is through sex education.

Sex education does not mean merely providing information on genital-centred sex; it implies transferring correct values, balanced attitudes and sound perceptions. It is important that we raise children to become adults who will use their sexuality in mature and responsible ways. It is our responsibility to keep the young generation adequately informed, so that correct scientific knowledge may lead to building healthy attitudes towards sex, high standards of conduct, responsible behaviour, and wholesome personalities.

Objectives of Sex Education

Why do children, adolescents and adults need to be formally educated about human sexuality?

Formal sex education is aimed at achieving specific objectives:

- To appreciate and accept one's own body in totality
- To be able to interact with both genders comfortably, respectfully and in appropriate ways
- To learn to prevent sexual abuse, rape and exploitation
- To prepare children for the physical, psychological, emotional and sexual changes that they undergo at adolescence
- To educate children in a way that leads to building healthy attitudes towards sex, high standards of conduct, responsible behaviour, and wholesome personalities

- To help children grow into adults, who will use their sexuality in mature and responsible ways. To be able to discriminate between life-enhancing sexual behaviours i.e. responsible sexual behaviour and behaviours that are harmful to self and others i.e. irresponsible sexual behaviour
- To be able to enjoy sexual feelings without guilt, shame or fear
- To have a happy married life and responsible parenthood
- To learn to develop and maintain meaningful intimate relationships and to be able to express love and intimacy in appropriate ways
- To learn to relate sexually with honesty, equality and responsibility
- To learn to express one's sexuality without inhibitions, while respecting the rights of others
- To learn to refrain from consulting exploitative quacks in matters of sexual medicine
- To acquire scientifically accurate knowledge about the reproductive system
- To learn to avoid unwanted pregnancy
- To learn to avoid contracting or transmitting Sexually Transmitted Diseases (STDs)
- To understand and abide by legislation dealing with sexual issues.

Dos & Don'ts of Sex Education in Schools

It is important to keep the following points in mind while introducing and executing a formal sex education programme in Indian schools

- Only that teacher, who has acquired scientifically accurate knowledge, who is at ease with this subject, who has a good command on language, who is comfortable with his/her own sexuality and has a non-judgmental attitude, should teach this subject.
- Sex education should be started formally in schools, before the onset of puberty.
- Teaching (information) should be scientifically accurate. Answers should be given honestly.
- The language used should be easy and scientifically precise. Begin with the language that they understand/use, but then take them to using more appropriate terminology/language.
- Teaching should have a social perspective. Strictly avoid religious and cultural criticism during teaching sessions.
- The group of students should be homogenous in age and cultural background. The age difference between the youngest and the oldest student in the group should never be more than three years.
- Whenever possible, the education module should be taught to boys and girls together, and not separately. This could be a good opportunity to create gender sensitisation and transmit a healthy message of both being complementary and not opposite sexes. Moreover, the high level of curiosity about the other gender is satisfied in a healthy

educative environment, thus reducing the need of satisfying this curiosity through access to unhealthy sources of information and inappropriate behaviours.

- Teaching should be supported by appropriate audio-visual aids e.g. charts, slides, transparencies, handouts, diagrams etc. Sketches and line diagrams are the best teaching aids. Strictly refrain from using nude photographs and pornography as a teaching aid. Also refrain from using live models.

- For the Question-Answer sessions, besides encouraging open dialogue, questions should also be allowed to be put in writing to encourage those who seek anonymity. Answer ALL questions; never avoid answering any query. If you are not sure about the answer, or if you do not know how to answer, ask for some time. Never say 'This is not for your age'. If the children are old enough to ask questions, they are old enough to get the answers. However, strictly avoid answering questions posed by students to you about your personal life.

- Strictly avoid sharing any personal sexual experience.

- Do not narrate vulgar jokes. Use humour with great care. The sex educator can speak in an informal, pleasant way, but should never turn anything into a laughing matter.

- Sex education is not a subject to be taught by the educator like a one-on-one tuition, but to be taught to a group of students in a formal setting.

- Preferably have classes during regular school hours and avoid after school hours for sex education classes.

Information Overload

Research has shown that over 90 per cent children get their information on sex from immature friends, pornographic literature, films, television and videos and less than 10 per cent from parents and teachers. The youth, therefore, are misinformed through unhealthy sources, rather than informed in a legitimate way, through the family and school.

In the present day, avenues of exposure to sexual information as well as misinformation are colossal, and the dangers come unassumingly disguised. The information, both forbidden and desirable, is available to our children for the taking, and it is practically impossible for parents and teachers to really monitor and control all our children's activities all the time.

The exposure is immense, the dangers enormous, and the price that could be paid, huge. The best approach in this scenario, is to be our children's confidantes, nudging and guiding them gently in the right direction, giving them correct and adequate scientific knowledge, teaching them logical reasoning and rational thinking, and providing them with a sound scale of values, which can see them through the challenges of the often perverse exposure they are faced with.

Studies on the effects of sex education in schools show that it actually encourages children to delay their sexual activity and to practice safer sex, once they are active. This is contrary to the belief that teaching children about sex and contraception encourages sexual experimentation. Furthermore, this makes them better equipped at protecting themselves against sexual abuse, incest, molestation, sexually transmitted infections and unwanted pregnancy.

The question today is no more whether sex education should be given or not, but how best to give this education, what exactly is to be taught, when, at what age, how to impart it, and finally, who should teach it. These questions need our serious consideration and attention to help meet the needs of this generation in these changing and challenging times. Giving children a realistic and practical outlook on sex is as important as giving them food, shelter, security and loving care. It is easier to answer their questions today, but difficult to solve their problems tomorrow.

Talking to Children about Sex

One of the most common questions parents ask is: "What should my children know about sexuality, and at what age should they know it?" Answering children's questions about sex is one of the responsibilities many parents dread the most. Otherwise confident parents often feel tongue-tied and awkward when it comes to talking about sex to their children.

Childhood is a period of utter innocence, but for adults sex is not so innocent a subject. Most parents go to almost an absurd extent to keep anything and everything, even remotely connected to sex, as unreachable and as far away and hidden from children as possible.

In the course of fostering and bringing up our children, we tend to prohibit certain behaviours or conduct of our children. A little child's innocent delight in his/her own natural nudity is one such act that makes parents uneasy. A child's curious discovery of his/her own body is another such act. Any attention that a child devotes to exploring different body parts that parents consider private, often promptly invites a harsh admonishment. This is not to say that parents should allow the child to romp around naked all the time or not teach him/her correct etiquette and manners. This is simply to say that parents must restrain the immediate tone of outrage and taboo that they tend to adopt.

Children learn an enormous amount about affection, the human body, communication and relationships from their first year of life.

It is extremely important to help children feel comfortable about their sexuality from the very beginning. This will prepare them and make it easier for them to ask any question about sex without inhibitions throughout their lives. As they grow, parents and teachers can give them correct and useful information to help them make healthy and responsible decisions about their sexuality. This will help them grow into sensitive and affectionate adults, who will be able to initiate and sustain warm and loving relationships.

When exactly do children start becoming curious about sex?

Children are human beings and therefore sexual beings. All human beings are normally sexual. From the very infancy children have a curiosity about their own bodies, which is absolutely normal and healthy. It is difficult for parents to acknowledge this, just as it is hard for children to think of their parents as sexually active.

When is the best time to start educating children about sex?

It is best to start as soon as children begin getting sexual messages. And they start getting them as soon as they are born. But do not worry if you have not started yet. It is never too late. Just do not try to catch up all at once. The most important thing is to be open and available whenever a child wants to talk.

Children's queries related to their own body and sex are utterly out of curiosity and a pure sense of wonder. They have not yet learnt to attach any sense of secrecy and privacy to these matters.

Young children often touch themselves when they are naked, such as in the bathtub or while being wiped and diapered. They have no modesty at this stage of their development. It is their parent's reaction that tells them whether their actions are acceptable or not. Children should never be berated or made to feel ashamed of being interested in their own bodies. While some parents may choose to casually ignore self-touching, others may choose to acknowledge that, while they know it feels good, it is a private matter. Parents can simply make it clear to children that they expect the child to keep that activity strictly private.

By the time a child is three years of age, parents must choose to use the correct anatomical words for all body parts including the genitals. They may sound clinical, but there is no reason why the proper label should not be used when the child is capable of saying it. The words – penis, vagina – should be stated matter-of-factly, with no implied awkwardness. That way, the child learns to use them in a direct manner, without embarrassment. Using awkward infantile terms for body parts or body functions only serves to make children think of these as bad or disgusting and something to hide behind such words.

Children between three to six years of age are most trusting of their parents. They hero-worship their fathers and adore their mothers. Their parent's word is law for them. Most of the times, what children really want is to know that they are normal. We can help them understand that it is normal for everyone to be different. In fact, the most important lesson we can share with our children is just that: Being different is normal. This helps them grow into adults who are comfortable in their own skin and have wholesome and mature personalities.

Learning about Touch

There is information that is more apt for children at particular ages. For instance, a five-year-old child should know the correct names for his/her body parts, including the genitals, and that his/her genitalia is a private part, which should never be touched by anyone. It is necessary to tell them that their body is their own and that they have the right to privacy, and that if anyone ever touches them in a way that feels strange and unusual, s/he should tell that person to stop it and then tell you about it, even if the person is a close relative, neighbour, teacher or even a doctor. Such training at an early age can help to prevent sexual abuse, which is widespread in the society today.

The Myth of Good Touch – Bad Touch

We would like to caution parents and teachers against using the good touch – bad touch explanation because young children tend to think of a 'bad touch' as one that causes physical pain or involves hitting.

> Many types of sexual contact are not painful, do not cause injury, and may even feel good to the child. So instead, tell your child exactly what an OK touch might be – a pat on the back, a rub on the head, a high five, and so on. Ask your child to name some touches and let them know whether they are OK.

Invariably parents are concerned that telling children too much, too soon will harm them in some manner, or will provoke and encourage them to become sexually active early in their life. It is necessary to understand that education and information do not encourage children to be sexually active prematurely. On the contrary, children make better decisions about sex when there are no restrictions on what they can ask and talk about at home and when they have all the necessary information they need. This helps prevent possible sexual abuse, incest and sexual harassment at work as they are empowered to stop it, freely talk about it and report it immediately.

■ What Do You Tell a Very Young Child Who Asks Where Do Babies Come From?

> Depending on the child's age, you can say that a baby grows from an egg in the mother's womb, pointing to your stomach, and comes out of a special place, called the vagina. There is no need to explain the act of intercourse because very young children will not understand the concept.
>
> For little more curious children, you can say that when a man and a woman love each other, they like

to be close to one another. Tell them that the man's sperm joins the woman's egg and then the baby begins to grow. Most children under the age of six will accept this answer. Answer your child's question in a straightforward manner, and you will probably find that s/he is satisfied with a little information at a time.

An Ongoing, Graded Process

Learning about sex should not occur in one all-or-nothing session with children. It ideally should be more of an unfolding and ongoing process, one in which the child learns over time, what is necessary for him/her to know. Questions should preferably be answered as and when they arise so that the child's natural curiosity is satisfied as s/he grows and matures.

As children grow, parents can give them all useful and age appropriate information to help them make healthy and responsible decisions related to their sexuality. Keep in mind that it is not necessary to have a major conversation with your children each time they ask a question about sexuality. They may just want the answer to one question for the time being, and that is perfectly fine. Always be sure that you are answering the specific question, rather than talking in general terms. You can always ask for clarification if you are not sure what your children are asking. Be sure that they know that they can always ask follow-up questions. **Ask for time, if you don't know the answer or if you know the answer but don't know how to frame it.**

If at all your child does not ask any questions about sex, do not just ignore the subject. At around age five, you can actively begin to introduce books that deal with sexuality on a developmentally appropriate level.

Chapter 2

VALUES IN HUMAN SEXUALITY

Discussing the need for the educator to live the values s/he imparts to the other

When a sex educator teaches the student about human sexuality, what he mainly needs to impart in the course of the education is values related to sexuality. These values can, of course, only be transmitted to the student if they are an intrinsic part of the educator's own personality and if the educator himself/herself lives by them. The emphasis is on creating a generation of young adults who have a healthy attitude towards sex based on a scientific understanding of this natural instinct for the continuity of life.

As a part of encouraging high standards of conduct, responsible behaviour, and well-rounded personalities, students will be helped to understand that men and women complement each other, and therefore have an equal status and that the relationship between both genders is healthy only if it is one of mutual respect and regard. Therefore, the main aim in imparting sex education to students is to help create a strong and unshakable foundation of appropriate values related to human sexuality based on a healthy relationship between the genders.

The values that need to be imbibed by the sex educator, and then imparted to the students during a sex education programme are as follows:

1 **Sexuality is a normal and natural part of human life.**

Nature has ensured the continuity of life on earth by giving the sexual instinct to all life forms, including humans. Therefore, it needs to be accepted as a natural and intrinsic part of our body-mind during our sexually reproductive stage. If not for the sexual instinct, life on this earth would have been extinct.

2 **Young people explore their sexuality as a natural process of achieving sexual maturity.**

Just as one is curious about any new change in the body-mind during the early growing years, like exploring and using one's different sense organs, so also during puberty when the body-mind experiences sexual attraction for the opposite sex, it gives rise to immense curiosity about this new phenomenon. Curiosity is a tool by which sexuality is explored, which leads to an understanding of sexual energy, which can then be harnessed for the continuity of life on earth.

3 **Individuals and society benefit when children are able to discuss sexuality uninhibitedly, with trusted adults such as parents, family doctors, teachers and educators.**

Curiosity necessarily makes children seek out information wherever it is available. Therefore, it becomes imperative that they get the information to satiate their curiosity from authentic, mature and responsible sources that will help them develop a healthy view and attitude towards sexuality. If they are deprived of such reliable sources, it will lead to their acquiring information regarding sex from ill-informed peers, irresponsible and exploitative adults, and pornography, which will corrupt their views on sexuality, and leave them with warped attitudes towards sex.

4 All people are normally sexual.

When children display curiosity towards sex and seek information, adults often view it as indecent, incorrect, perverted or abnormal, and shun or condemn the sexual enquiry. By doing this, they stigmatise the curious child, who is normally sexual, just as the adult from whom s/he is seeking answers. In fact, children who do not display such curiosity are often masked and are probably accessing the information elsewhere, as they are aware of the unhealthy stigma attached to sexual enquiry. Therefore, adults need to view such sexual curiosity in children with respect, as it is emerging from an existential need for the survival of life on earth. Sexual curiosity, if condemned, could lead to creating warped, unhealthy individuals who will access to this information from irresponsible sources. The guilt in them for feeling sexual, could lead to creating distorted personalities obsessed with sex, with low self-esteem and a negative self-image, as they are deeply self-condemnatory.

5 Men and women are not opposite sexes, but are complementary sexes.

Plus and minus sound like opposites mathematically, however, without positive and negative polarities, we cannot have electricity. Also, while North and South again sound like opposites, there cannot be a magnet without both poles. Therefore, it goes without saying that life on earth cannot exist without male and female. So, the two genders are viewed not as opposite but as complementary in order to ensure continuity of life.

6 All sexual decisions have effects and consequences.

According to the scientist Newton, every action has a reaction. So also, every sexual action has some reaction, whether physical, emotional, social or legal. Therefore, it goes without saying that sexual decisions/actions need to be responsible in order to eliminate any adverse reactions/consequences. Freedom and Responsibility go hand-in-hand. Thus, expression of sexuality brings with it the responsibility of the effects of such expression. It is important to take those sexual decisions for which one is ready to take the responsibility and face all the consequences.

7 Premature indulgence in sexual behaviour poses risks.

Sexual experimentation carries with it the risk of pregnancy when you are not physically, financially, emotionally and socially in the position of assuming responsibility of parenthood. Moreover, premature indulgence in sex could result in permanent damage to the reproductive system as the body may still be in the process of maturing. Sexually transmitted diseases is the greatest hazard in sexual experimentation, and can not only impair your reproductive system irreversibly, but also be fatal.

8 Sexual relationships should never be compelling, exploitative, or lead to physical or psychological harm.

Since man and woman complement each other to ensure continuity of life, the sexual relationship between them should be consensual, non-coercive with neither exploiting nor feeling exploited by the other. A sexual relationship should only take place between two responsible and committed adults, and not prematurely and casually, as it can leave the exploited as well as the exploiter, emotionally disturbed and/or psychologically destabilised.

9 Sexual relationships should be based on mutual trust, respect, honesty and commitment.

Because sex is an existential union of man and woman, it is acceptable and in accordance with nature, only if the sexual relationship is based on mutual trust and respect, and part of a committed relationship such as marriage, as both would need to assume responsibility of nurturing life if sex results in pregnancy. Moreover, a committed relationship ensures that both feel good about the union in sex, as they are together because they want to share their life together.

10 Pornography humiliates both men and women. It offers a distorted view of human sexuality.

A sexual relationship is a very private act, the details of which are not to be shared with others, except a doctor if needed. Pornography makes a private act public. Moreover, the nude bodies displayed disregard the human dignity of both the man and woman, and the acts engaged in are often perverted, unnatural and abnormal. If these acts are imitated/modelled by those viewing pornography, they could cause psychological disturbances and major problems in their intimate relationship.

11 Sexual behaviour must be responsible and self-disciplined.

One is free to express one's sexuality only if one is also willing and capable of assuming responsibility of such sexual expression. Any function of the human body such as eating, sleeping or maintaining hygiene needs to be disciplined so that it does not interfere with, but instead enhances our survival in society. Likewise, our sexual functioning too should be such that it does not interfere with our harmonious and happy existence as a social being.

12 Refraining from penetrative sexual intercourse (vaginal, oral or anal) is the most effective method of preventing pregnancy, STDs and HIV infection.

The only foolproof way of preventing pregnancy and sexually transmitted diseases, is abstinence from any form of penetrative sexual relating. No contraceptive device is foolproof. Condoms can tear or slip. Moreover, they do not cover the entire genitalia. Therefore, they do not totally prevent STDs or pregnancy, and thus cannot be relied on. Any exchange of body fluids i.e. semen, saliva and serum, can result in transmission of STDs, the most dangerous of them being HIV. Therefore, total abstinence from penetrative sex is the only sure way of being safe.

13 Sexuality has four dimensions – Physical (biological), Emotional (Psychological), Sociological (Ethical) and Spiritual.

Human sexuality is an all encompassing phenomenon of life, which includes the physical, the emotional, the relational, the social and the spiritual aspects of a human being. Therefore, sex education needs to be such that it imparts values related to all these aspects in the context of human sexuality so that we can help create mature and wholesome individuals who are socially responsible citizens of society.

Chapter 3

KEY PRINCIPLES OF
SEX EDUCATION

Discussing the rules to be followed while talking to pre-pubertal children

1 Children often ask so-called sexual questions more out of curiosity.

The questions that children ask adults at the pre-pubertal stage are more often than not, merely out of curiosity and are not sexual in nature. Very often, it is the adults who have an unhealthy view towards human sexuality, and who because of their own inhibitions and awkwardness, read more into an innocent question by a curious child, and see it as an immoral sexual question. Things like watching a commercial on sanitary napkins or seeing the growing belly of a pregnant female teacher makes children curious to know more about what they see and hear. The thumb rule for parents and teachers is – never kill a child's curiosity. It is curiosity that has provoked man to discover the secrets of the universe and develop science, and therefore there cannot be a bigger crime than curbing a curious mind, which has the ability to learn, explore and reason.

2 Never avoid answering.

Feel grateful that the child has approached you with a question related to sexuality, and not anyone else. However, if you avoid answering the question – out of your own awkwardness emerging from a prejudice towards such enquiries and the subject of sexuality in general – you will provoke him to seek the answer elsewhere. Moreover, your awkwardness and avoiding the question will give the child the wrong message that human sexuality is a dirty grimy secret, which is not to be spoken about, and that the question arising in him (the child) makes him a lesser person. It also creates a distance between the child and the adult, which has the dangerous fallout of the child approaching other sources for information, and these sources could not only give him incorrect information, but also mislead him. Ill-informed peers, illiterate servants, illegitimate sources like porn sites and porn literature can do irreversible harm to the child. This is because the information gleaned from these sources will form the foundation of the way he relates in his own man-woman relationships and his view of the opposite sex. It will dictate his sexual attitude and conduct as an adult.

3 Never give false answers.

When children ask questions on sexuality or reproduction never give fictitious answers like the stork brings the baby home, or babies are brought from hospitals. Such answers result in loss of trust in the adult as and when the child accesses the correct answer from another source later on. This can be detrimental as the child now distrusts the adult regarding information in other crucial areas of life, and this distrust and disbelief could result in the child making choices that are not in his best interest. E.g. If the adult who has spoken about the stork bringing babies home informs the adolescent about sexually transmitted diseases through intercourse, the adolescent might choose to disbelieve such accurate information because of his previous experience of fictitious information. And it could result in the adolescent contracting diseases like HIV. Also, use the correct scientific name for the genitals while referring to them right at the outset, so that there is a comfort level in the child while using the right terminology, and no shame or awkwardness related to referring to the sex organs. Moreover, in this way, the message is quite clearly given by the adult, that the sex organs, which are a part of the reproductive system, are just like any other organ of the body, which are parts of others systems of the body like the digestive, circulatory, respiratory or the nervous system.

4 Avoid giving excessive information.

Answer only what has been asked. Do not over enthusiastically give more information than necessary prematurely for that particular age. You cannot tell a child too much; they only take in what they need to know for that moment. Information should be age-specific and question-specific. Any unnecessary information could leave the person feeling confused, shocked, or plain disinterested e.g. If the child asks about how babies are born and if you give an elaborate description on lovemaking between a man and a woman to a 10 year old, it would most definitely be out of place.

5 Be at ease and appear at ease while answering.

Books on communication skills explain that 80 per cent communication is non-verbal. Therefore, you are communicating more through your body language than with your words. And children are continuously observing you and learning more from what they see than from what they hear. If you are uneasy and uncomfortable while talking on human sexuality, you are communicating non-verbally that this is a forbidden subject, to be kept under wraps. On the other hand, if you are extremely easy and comfortable with the subject, the terminology, and are matter-of-factly fielding all questions, you are communicating non-verbally that this subject is no different from any other subject, and therefore does not need to be either hidden or highlighted, but can casually be spoken about in the course of life. Non-verbally according human sexuality an ordinary status, and not an extraordinary status, is the most useful way of educating the child on human sexuality. Your ease communicates that this is just one more aspect of human life, nothing more or less.

6 Ask for time.

If either you do not know the answer to a question, or you do not know how to give the answer, ask for some time to get back. It is also perfectly appropriate to say to your child, "I don't know, but let's find out together." It is a myth that you must give the answer immediately, or else you are inadequate as an educator. It is better to give the correct answer in the correct way a little later, than to give an incorrect answer in an incorrect way immediately. Take the time to find out the scientifically accurate facts from the right sources, like a good value-based sex education manual, and rehearse the way you are going to answer the question till you reach a feeling of comfort, and then answer the question completely.

7 Don't scold/punish the child if he asks you a so-called sexual question or if you notice him touching/exploring/pleasuring his genitals.

Admonishing a child for his natural and existential curiosity, only leads to a heightened and excessive interest towards a perceived forbidden fruit. It is condemning a child for what is natural that often leads to the child leaning towards what is an unnatural expression of sexuality. Moreover, scolding a child could reinforce excessive preoccupation with sex, as it gets him attention – even though negative – from the adult. Also, the adult's disapproving of his question makes him feel like a lesser person thus affecting his sense of self-worth. Further, it makes him view sex as a subject which is taboo, and therefore, makes him go to other irresponsible sources to satiate his natural curiosity.

8 Don't be afraid!

It is a myth that information and education encourage early sexual experimentation. In fact, studies have shown that educating children early, can prevent so many social evils like sexual abuse, incest, molestation and rape, eve-teasing, sexual harassment on the job, and the transmission of HIV and other STDs. In addition, a valuebased sex education programme helps create responsible citizens of society who have equal respect for both genders, have a healthy attitude towards sex and engage in responsible sexual conduct.

9 Information about sexuality is as important as food, shelter, and loving care.

The foundation for a mutually respectful man-woman relationship is laid in a good value-based sex education programme in schools. Healthy interpersonal relationships between both genders at home and at the workplace, is the need of our society today. Therefore, for a conducive home and work environment, equality of the genders needs to be learned and taught early.

Chapter 4

THE WHAT AND WHEN OF SEX EDUCATION

Discussing what children want to know
and need to know at various ages

This section is devoted to discussing what and how you need to teach children about sexuality at various stages of their growing years, failing which, children can fall prey to misguided sex education through pornography, and become vulnerable to sexual abuse and other social evils.

Birth to Two (The age of self-exploration):

This is the stage of self-exploration for the child when he explores his entire body and gradually becomes aware of himself as a sentient being separate from his surroundings. The survival instinct functions in the child, because of which the child who is dependent on his caregiver for his survival, receives and imbibes verbal and non-verbal messages from the caregiver (usually the mother) in the form of dos and don'ts. These messages dictate his attitudes and behaviours in all areas including sexuality. If the mother is herself conscious about the child's sexual organs as something distinct from other parts of the body and not as just one more organ, while bathing, cleaning and generally touching the child, and if she is uncomfortable with it, her touch might change while cleaning the genitalia, as compared with cleaning other body parts. This altered touch and biased attitude will be transmitted to the child.

Also, in the process of exploring himself as a sentient being, when the child touches or fondles his genitals as innocently as playing with his big toe or hands, if the parent is viewing the genitals with discomfort, they might admonish the innocent child, and unwittingly create in him a fear, anxiety, permanent discomfort or unhealthy sense of shame related to the sex organs. This will lay the foundation of the way he views human sexuality. It is important to note that for the child, the sex organ is no different from any other part of the body and the parent therefore needs to deal with his or her own discomfort and unhealthy attitude towards sexuality, so as not to transmit the same unhealthy views to the child.

Moreover, if the child views the sex organs as a forbidden area, it might create problems much later on when, as an adult, he needs to talk about sex with his partner, in terms of what pleasures him.

Communication is key in all relationships, more so, in an intimate relationship between a man and a woman. Therefore, the comfort in communicating about sex is extremely important for a healthy sexual relationship. Even otherwise, communication between partners needs to be gentle in order to create emotional intimacy, which sets the stage for physical intimacy. Therefore, as early as infancy, the child needs to be surrounded by gentle handling and gentle words, which he unconsciously learns and which establishes his communication style in all areas including with his partner. During infancy, the child can perceive to communicate through touch and tone of voice, as the world of words is alien to him. Therefore, if the touch and the tone are both gentle, the child grows up to be gentle in the touch and tone of his communication. If however, the environment is loud and crude, the child will exhibit the same demeanour as an adult with his partner.

We give babies a sense of themselves from birth. We make them feel secure or insecure by:

- the way we hold and touch them
- the way we feed, wash, and diaper them
- the tone of our voices
- letting them feel comfortable with their bodies and emotions.

They can develop healthier feelings about their sexuality if we do all these things in a pleasant, loving, gentle and caring way.

Babies explore their bodies. They learn quickly that touching their sex organs feels good. They should be allowed to enjoy this. If we shout at them or slap their hands, they will do it anyway – but they will feel guilty about it. And they won't trust us later in life when they are looking for guidance about sex.

Three to Five (The age of curiosity):

This is the age of curiosity and children ask many questions arising out of their curiosity. Make sure that their questions are not avoided or stopped but are answered in the same spirit in which they are asked, i.e. innocent curiosity. Of course, while age appropriate answers should be given, if you notice that the child is asking the same question repeatedly, it is possible that the question may be more for attention seeking. In such cases, make the child answer his/her own question as you know that the answer has already been given. This is also the age when children pick up their mother tongue at a rapid pace, and learn new words and languages easily.

By the time they are three, children are ready to know that men and women have different private parts (genitalia). Talk about it the same way you talk about eyes, ears and noses, fingers and toes. **Make sure that you use the correct words while talking about the sex organs if they are used while educating the child, or while answering their questions.** Say penis, vagina and breasts instead of using slang, family or street words. Otherwise, children may get the idea that something is wrong with these parts of the body. Teaching correct words not only equips them with the right vocabulary, but also ensures that they are comfortable in the use of such words, and thus view sexuality in a healthy, normal and natural way. Moreover, it is extremely important that the child accepts his/her body as a whole entity without creating a divide in the mind. This feeling of unconditional self-acceptance preserves the sanctity of the whole (as gifted by nature) and can prevent the child from developing neurotic feelings like shame or guilt about any part of his body.

At this age, children are curious about the bodies of their parents and other children. It is normal for children to have curiosity to know about similarities and differences in each other. They may try to accomplish this through games (such as playing doctor-patient) and keen observation. It would not help to punish children for being normal if found engaged in such games and activities. Between the age three and five they are too young and innocent to cause any actual or real harm to each other through such games.

They may want to snuggle in bed with parents or caregivers. They may also want to see them without clothes on. We should set limits that make the family comfortable. But children should never be thrashed or punished for such desires.

It is possible that the child might have a younger sibling at this age. During pregnancy, the child might express curiosity about the growing belly of the mother. This is an important moment of sex education about how babies are born. Also, after the infant's birth, the mother should consciously allow the older child to be around the infant while bathing and changing the baby's clothes, and allow curiosity towards the infant's body parts (in the case infant is of the opposite sex) to be another sex education moment. Since children of this age are extremely curious about similarities and differences between each other's bodies, use this curiosity to enlighten them of the difference between the male and female body. If there is no opportunity in the form of a sibling of an opposite sex, then you may use simple books depicting the different body parts.

At this age, children also develop a curiosity about "Where do babies come from?" You need not describe sexual intercourse at this point. Keep your answers simple for now. You can say something like, "Babies grow in a special bag inside the mother." As the years pass, you can gradually add other details, as the child becomes capable of understanding them.

This is also the age when children are away from their parent's protective gaze, as they go to playschool, kindergarten, and to play in parks, possibly accompanied by relatives, friends or hired help. This is the moment to educate them about the concept of private parts, which no one is allowed to view or touch, and that any such violation of the rule should be bravely resisted and immediately reported to the parent without fear. This key education will go a long way in protecting the child from potential sexual abuse.

Four-year-olds may become attached to a parent – even an absent parent. They may even be jealous of the other parent. They can get attached to parents or caregivers of either gender. None of these attachments mean a child is homosexual or straight. We should let children be comfortable with whatever attachments they form.

Five to Seven (Age of sexual self-consciousness):

This is the age of gender-consciousness i.e. a consciousness of one's own boyness and girlness. During this period boys and girls like to play gender-specific games with friends of their own sex, and want to assume the role of their own gender while playing house-house with a mixed group of friends with girls wanting to play mother or any other female role and boys wanting to play father or any other male role. We should strictly refrain from teasing them about having boyfriends or girlfriends. Make sure you do not stretch their roles in the game beyond the game.

Children also tend to get clubby and start clinging to friends of their own gender and stay away from the opposite gender, to the point that sometimes they go to the extent of saying specifically that they hate boys or hate girls as the case may be. Again, it is better not to tease them about it.

Children at this age may start becoming less attached to parents and caregivers, and this too is normal.

They also start attending primary school and are away from

their comfort zone with their parents, where they freely asked questions. Children in primary school may be shy about asking questions. But that does not mean they do not have questions. Teachers and parents therefore need to be more sensitive to this fact, and either elicit questions from them, or then on their own educate the children further in an agespecific way.

Eight to Twelve i.e. Pre-Teens (Age of sexual awakening):

This is the age when formal sex education at the school level should begin. Girls need to know about menstruation and boys need to know about wet dreams, masturbation and other signs of maturing. Preparing girls about getting periods before they get one is mandatory, as it makes them physically and emotionally ready even in the absence of any help.

Pre-teens are fascinated with the way their bodies change. They also worry a lot about whether they are normal. Boys and girls both, worry about their changing bodies, and tend to compare their physical maturation process with others of their age. For example, girls worry about their breast size, and boys worry about their height, and the beginning of changes in the genitalia etc. This is the age of puberty. It is necessary to reassure them that no two people are the same. What they want most is to know that they are normal. We can help them understand that it is normal for everyone to be different. In fact, the most important lesson we can share at this age is just that: Being different is normal.

Being at the age of puberty, 12-year-olds must know about sex and reproduction so that they are equipped to deal with their awakening sexuality in a healthy way. They want to know about sexual and social relationships. They need to know about sexually transmitted infections, the importance of abstinence from sexual experimentation, and the consequences of teen pregnancy. They need to clearly be told how all of this can adversely affect and irreversibly impact their young lives.

While we need to let pre-teens fit in with their peers, we must also encourage them to think for themselves.

Teens (Age 13 to 19): (Age of rapid sexual development)

When it comes to adolescents, the influence of misinformed peer groups has set the trend of exploring relationships with a new kind of freedom. Their approach to sex is more reactionary. This is because our society has always been prohibitive and repressive in matters of sex. The result is a paradox in their young minds. They are either found feeling guilty for their natural sexual instinct, or they are found indulging in risky sexual experiments.

The rising rate of premarital indulgence and premarital abortions in early adulthood, and the increasing number of teenagers visiting STD and abortion clinics, is an eye-opener to the new attitudes of teenagers towards love, sex and commitment. In our consulting practice, we have so often come across teenagers confronted with an unexpected and unwanted pregnancy, and do not know how to face the situation or what to do about it... And this is because they are told nothing about the price that one has to pay for sexual freedom; and the potential damage to their emotional health and well-being.

Reassure them that while their sexuality and feelings are

normal, they need to make responsible decisions regarding their sexuality. Teens can be easy targets for peer pressure and bad advice. Therefore, we must encourage them to think for themselves in their own best interest. They must learn how to say no. They must know how to have relationships without getting hurt and without hurting other people. And they must know that they are responsible for their choices, and therefore, need to refrain from making impulsive decisions based on either peer pressure or their own urges. **Freedom of choice comes with the responsibility of the consequences of that choice, needs to be clearly explained in sex education programs.**

Guilt associated with sex is yet another area of great concern. Here again, incorrect inputs from misinformed elders work as slow poison in the psyche of growing children. Many elders too, need to look at sex and understand sex in a new light, with a fresh, unbiased attitude. The percentage of youngsters feeling self-condemnatory for having sexual thoughts and feelings is very large. Something as natural as wet dreams or something as harmless as masturbation, could play havoc in the body-mind of many teenagers, because of such misinformed elders.

Thus, value-based sex education can stop our children from accessing unreliable information from illegitimate sources, which will help them make responsible decisions regarding their own sexuality.

What to Say about the Risk of Pregnancy at Puberty

During puberty, most girls start having periods and most boys start having wet dreams. Girls and boys start thinking and feeling like sexual beings in an intense way. Sometimes they get uncontrollably sexually aroused.

Important changes happen inside the body by the time wet dreams and periods begin. These changes mean that the reproductive system is maturing. As boys mature, they begin producing sperms. Sperms are the male reproductive cells. As girls mature, the eggs (ova) in their ovaries begin to ripen. Ova are the female reproductive cells.

Conception takes place when a sperm unites with an egg (ovum). So, a girl or woman can get pregnant if a boy or man puts his penis in or near her vaginal opening. The sperms from his penis can swim up her vagina to unite with her ovum. Often our reproductive systems mature faster than we do. That is why girls can get pregnant and boys can impregnate before they are ready to assume responsibility for the pregnancy, and the parenting of a child.

Educating Teenagers about Postponing Partner Sex

Most parents wish that their teenagers wait to have sex till they are psychologically mature and have the emotional resources to manage relationships. It is important for parents to be able to convey this wish while communicating scientific information about sex and the consequences of partner sex. While we may encourage teenagers to postpone intercourse, the present reality is that some young people are tempted to become sexually active when their hormones are raging.

The decision of engaging in sex and losing your virginity is one such very important decision, which needs to be made based on empirically, logically and pragmatically verifiable information.

If you lose your virginity to someone with whom you have

casual sex you might lose out on the beauty and joy of sharing intimacy in a mutually loving, caring and committed relationship. This is something that cannot be undone. Moreover, if you are not with the same person subsequently in a committed relationship, the comparison of your previous sexual experiences with your present experience can adversely affect your present relationship.

Parents can further help their children understand the value of self-respect, assertiveness, and responsible decision-making, which could help the young adult to decide about postponing partner sex.

A mature person is one who can exercise freedom of choice and is also able and willing to bear the short-term and long-term consequence of that choice, whether good, bad or ugly. Maturity is also, making an aware and well-informed choice, which is not based on impulse and temptation, but on verifiable information, and only after weighing the pros and cons of the choice.

Everybody is doing it is an age-old peer pressure tactic that applies to experimenting with drugs and alcohol as much as it does to experimenting with sex. Encourage your children not to be taken in by it.

Many people give up their virginity because of peer pressure of so-called friends, or emotional blackmail from the boyfriend or girlfriend who might threaten to break off the relationship if sex is not a part of it. It is important to consider whether such friends are really friends who care about you, or whether they are provoking you to do what they probably do, so that they can justify to themselves that everyone does what they are doing when they engage in indiscriminate and irresponsible sexual behaviour. Emotional blackmail would indicate that the person who is forcing you does not respect your wishes, and therefore you should be vary of going ahead in such a relationship where the partner can go to any length to get one's way. Ask yourself whether you want to be in a relationship in which you are not respected, but are only used as a means to an end?

Teenagers often say they have intercourse the first time because they are curious. Free and frank communication within the family about sexuality, can satisfy a teenager's curiosity, and help him/her behave more responsibly while exploring his/her sexuality.

The age where boys and girls lose their virginity is much lower today. High school kids are found engaging in sex. At this age and stage of their life, neither are their minds nor their bodies ready for the repercussions of such sexual relating. Teenage pregnancy is a physically and psychologically traumatic consequence of sexual engagement at an early age, the scars of which remain forever.

Information about preventing pregnancy and sexually transmitted diseases, and the emotional repercussions of partner sex, are vital to help the young adult make informed decisions.

THINGS YOU MUST KNOW OF BEFORE YOU DECIDE TO LOSE YOUR VIRGINITY

- STDs including HIV can be transmitted through exchange of body fluids, which includes any form of penetrative intercourse, and even other acts such as oral sex and deep kissing. The condom DOES NOT fully protect you from STDs as it only covers the penis, with the area around the penis being exposed to infection. Cuts and abrasions in and around the genitalia area could allow the body fluids to be exchanged, thus resulting in transmission of infection.

- The male condom, or any female contraceptive is NOT 100 per cent safe. There is a failure rate for all contraceptives which is scientifically documented, and this failure rate is much more than one would be comfortable with premaritally. The morning after pill is utterly unreliable, has a high failure rate, and can cause complications with the hormone cycle of a girl.

- If you get pregnant you need to consider whether to continue or terminate the pregnancy. If you decide to continue with it, you need to consider the social, financial, psychological and relational consequences of the same at the age and stage of your life at which you get pregnant. Issues such as your sexual partner not wanting to be a part of your decision to keep the baby, might result in the consequences of being an unprepared single parent, or then giving the child up for adoption with the resulting psychological impact of the same on you. If you decide to terminate the pregnancy, you might have to deal with serious medical/surgical complications, and more than that, the painful memory of terminating your very first pregnancy because you and your sexual partner engaged in irresponsible sexual conduct.

Communicate to your teenager that anyone can have good

intentions of abstaining from intercourse; however, to translate this intent into responsible behaviour may not always be easy because of the high levels of arousal experienced due to raging hormones. Therefore, one needs to remember the consequences of irresponsible sexual behaviour at the right time, in order to practice responsible sexual behaviour.

Such free and frank discussions that acknowledge the sexual urges, and the fact that these urges can be managed healthily without engaging in sexual experimentation, go a long way in preventing teenage pregnancies, emotional disturbances and STDs including HIV/AIDS which is plaguing humanity.

Why do Parents Feel Uncomfortable Talking about Sex?

It is not surprising that most parents feel uncomfortable talking about sex. The reasons are as follows:

- They themselves usually have had no sex education as children
- They have learnt that sex is too dirty a word to be verbalised.
- They feel that talking about sex and sexuality is indecent, crude and uncultured.
- They are simply afraid that they might not have all the right answers and correct vocabulary.
- It is hard for them to accept that their children are sexual.
- It is even tougher to admit that they are sexual.

- Some fear possible sexual feelings between their children and themselves.

Parents need to be open with their children about their own hesitations. You can use an opening line like, "This is a little awkward for me to talk about, but essential. There is much you need to know about human sexuality, and I want to be the source of information about it. It is important that someone who cares about you gives you accurate information about sex, because this information will ensure your physical and emotional well-being. I will share some information and wisdom with you, and I want you to feel free to ask me anything you might want to know about sex."

Never avoid talking about sexual matters as it could lead to harmful consequences. However, if you still feel that despite being comfortable with the subject you do not have all the answers to your child's questions, then you could take your child for a sex education session to a trained sex educator.

Chapter 5

CHILD SEXUAL ABUSE:
BREAKING THE SILENCE

Empowering children against sexual predators

Sexual abuse is amongst the most sensitive and the most important topics parents need to discuss with their children. Some parents believe their children face little danger of being abused, that they are too young to be told about the possibility, and that discussing the subject will frighten them unnecessarily. Others want to deny the thought that it might happen in their families. The facts belie such attitudes. It is like a fire drill. You hope the real thing never happens, but if it does, the well-prepared child is more likely to survive. There is a misconception among adults that it is usually only the girl child who is the victim of sexual abuse. However, boys are not immune to it. They can also be sexually abused, and must be educated about this.

What Is Sexual Abuse?

Sexual abuse happens whenever a person's sexual privacy is not respected. It is a verbal or physical behaviour, which has a significant sexual element, which is directed by one person towards another (of same or opposite gender), and which can significantly harm, upset, demean or injure the person towards whom it is directed. It ranges from sending sexual messages to actual penetrative intercourse. Inappropriate touching, fondling, watching, talking, or being forced to look at another person's sex organs are all forms of sexual abuse. It also can be verbal, visual, audio, or any other form which forces a person to participate in unwanted sexual contact or attention. All forms of sexual abuse are crimes as per the Indian Penal Code (1860).

According to the U.S. Justice Department, one in six (16 per cent) of rape victims, are under the age of twelve. Nearly six out of ten (60 per cent) sexual assault incidents are reported by victims to have occurred in their own home or at the home of a friend, relative, or neighbour. Therefore, your child needs to know that there are some people in this world who force others to perform sexual acts against their will. The abusers, usually adults or older children whom the victim knows, will force, trick, bribe, threaten, or pressure the child into sexual activity. This is called sexual abuse. We may ourselves be responsible and stable adults, and we expect other people to be so too. But some people are not. They may try to force themselves on a child who finds it difficult to defend itself.

Most people think an abuser is a stranger, a sleazy character lurking near the school compound, luring children with sweets. On the contrary, 75 to 80 per cent of sex crimes against children, are committed by someone the child knows, trusts and loves. Some 45 per cent are relatives such as uncles, cousins, brothers and even fathers. Another 30 to 40 per cent are acquaintances such as friends, neighbours, servants, teachers, drivers and even doctors.

The idea of sexual abuse can be very confusing for kids. They are often taught to respect and obey their elders, a lesson that perpetrators can use to their advantage. Many children are made to promise to keep sexual abuse a secret. Because most children are trusting, and because they usually know the abuser, physical force is rarely needed. The parents are often completely unaware that their child is being sexually abused.

Sexual abuse has been termed the silent problem because children often are either afraid to tell, having been threatened by the abuser to keep quiet, or are too young or too ashamed to put what has happened into words. They may be confused by the feelings that accompany the abuse, and they may blame themselves for it. Abuse also may betray their sense of trust, because it often involves telling on a loved one.

Another problem is that at first, particularly if the abuser is a known person, some children may like the extra attention shown to them because it makes them feel special. And some children may feel guilty that they didn't initially resist. The child may also fear getting the abuser into trouble, or damaging or severing the relationship with an abusing loved one if she tells or resists – concerns that the perpetrator often play upon to continue to take advantage of the child.

Educating Children about Sexual Abuse

Sexual abuse of children is a 'social time bomb', with the potential for destroying many futures. To prevent victimisation of our children, we must educate them.

In a calm and caring manner, you will want to give your child ageappropriate information to ensure the child's safety and well-being. Before getting into specifics, though, it's important to tell children that they are loved, valued, and deserve to be safe. Also, never tell them to "do anything an adult tells you to do!"

When you are sure they understand, follow these guidelines with your child's level of understanding and maturity in mind.

- As a starting point, tell your children that no one has a right to touch them in a way that appears strange and unusual. Each one of us have a right to keep certain parts of our body private. Tell them that if anyone ever touches them in a way that feels strange and unusual, she should tell that person to stop it and then tell you about it, even if the person is a close relative, neighbour or even teacher.

- It is necessary to tell children that most people are good people who do not harm children; but there are also sick people with diseased minds who could harm them. Tell them that this applies to everyone they know, and not just strangers.

- Avoid using the conventional good touch – bad touch explanation because young children tend to think of a 'bad touch' as one that causes physical pain or involves hitting. Many types of sexual contact are not painful, do not cause injury, and may even 'feel good' to the child. So instead, tell your child exactly what an 'OK' touch might be—a pat on the back, a rub on the head, a high five, and so on. Ask your child to describe some touches and let him or her know which kind of touch is OK and which is not. It is like a fire drill: you hope and pray the real thing never happens. But if it does, the well-prepared child is likely to survive better.

- Stress to your child the importance of telling you about any improper, unusual advances made by anyone. Make sure your child knows it is OK to say NO to anything that instinctively makes her or him feel uncomfortable, even if the request is from a relative or friend.

- Tell them to tell you if any adult asks them to keep a secret.

- Question the motive of any adult – even a family member- who seems highly interested in your child and wants to spend a lot of time alone with them, especially overnight. Rely heavily on your instincts.

- Fun and Games lure is a very common decoy, where seemingly innocent games lead to intimate body contact. Games might include playing darkroom, hiding under a cover, playing doctor-doctor, hiding the coin. Common sense should prompt parents to realise that something is fishy when an adult consistently singles out a child for a playmate.

- Tell your children not to accept gifts, eatables, drinks from strangers and to report to you if such an offer has been made. Be alert to new toys, gadgets or money you cannot account for. Ask where the items come from.

- One of the very compelling lures used by molester is asking the child for 'help.' The request can include asking for directions to a popular landmark, or assistance in carrying an armload of packages to the car or house. Tell your child that adults should ask other adults for help or directions.

- Accompany your child on her talent pursuits and check the credentials of talent scouts.

- If your child tells you she has been sexually abused, believe her immediately and completely. In most cases, kids do not lie about sexual abuse. She may report it saying, "I don't like to be alone with him", or "He fools around with me and I don't like it." Believe her even if the person concerned is a close relative or a good friend.

- It is important to remember that the victims of these crimes are most of the times NOT responsible for what happened to them. They sometimes feel – and are sometimes made to feel – that it was their fault that they were abused. Make sure your kids know that. Tell them you will believe them and protect them if they tell you about abuse and that you will never blame or be angry with them for doing so. If a child's courage to confide about such an experience goes ignored, it is an ultimate betrayal. Nothing could be more wrong than adopting an ostrich-like attitude.

- Work on resolving conflicts, strains or any other dysfunctions within the family. Children from unhappy homes and dysfunctional families are easy targets. These children are so starved for attention and affection; they are easy pray to seduction.

FACTS AND FIGURES ABOUT SEXUAL ABUSE

• According to the U.S. Justice Department, 16 per cent of the rape victims, or one in six, are under the age of twelve.

• In the United States, a woman is sexually assaulted or raped every two minutes. One out of every three women will be sexually assaulted in her lifetime.

• Date Rape is the most common form of rape (78 per cent) with one in four girls expected to fall victim to rape or attempted rape before they reach 25, and three out of five rapes (60 per cent) occurring before a woman reaches age 18.

- 80-85 per cent victims are sexually assaulted by people known to them.

- Every woman, no matter where you live or who you are, is at risk. Thousands of abusers/molesters/rapists remain free and continue to attack because their victims don't report the rapes. 84 per cent rapes go unreported.

- Only 2 per cent of the women who are raped will ever see their rapist spend a day in jail.

- The average rapist/molester rapes/molests between eight and sixteen women before he is ever caught.

- A survivor of rape is nine times more likely than the average person to attempt suicide.

- Although girls are more often victims of rape, boys are not always safe – they can be raped too.

Chapter 6

MODELLING HEALTHY
SEXUAL CONDUCT

Discussing how adult sexual behaviour affects kids

Subtle Sexual Abuse

Sanjay Kumar's father would talk of how all the men in the Kumar family had always had women for the asking. He would be vulgar in his humour, and explicitly talk to the nine year old Sanjay about the female anatomy, and ask about every girl in Sanjay's class, "Is she your girlfriend?" One day the impressionable Sanjay touched a girl in his class inappropriately thinking it was okay to do so and he was pulled up by the school authorities. The mixed signals were a shock for Sanjay – what his father had encouraged, his teachers now disgraced him for. Sanjay developed an anxiety disorder as a result of this inner conflict, and suffered from feelings of inadequacy for years. He also compulsively engaged in promiscuity to live out the script dictated by his father that the Kumar men were proud of the record of their sexual exploits.

Kavita's parents had never bothered to check whether their daughter was asleep or awake in the same bedroom before engaging in sexual talk or sexual touching. Her mother had even walked out nude from the bathroom on a couple of occasions; six year old Kavita witnessed her father fondling her voluptuous mother, commenting on her breasts. As her mother sounded as if she was in pain, but also giggled intermittently, Kavita was confused and alarmed. As Kavita reached adolescence, and she naturally had small breasts at that age, she began to feel inferior, as she constantly compared her body to her mother's nude body, and found herself inadequate. Also, the vivid audio visual impact of the sexual interaction between her parents left her feeling confused about the pleasure element in sex. When she herself entered into a relationship, she found it difficult to let go completely with her sexual partner and therefore could not reach an orgasm.

In the case of Sanjay as well as Kavita, we can see how being a witness to inappropriate adult sexual behaviour adversely impacted their adolescent and adult lives, influencing both their attitudes and behaviours. This effect can be equalled to the adverse impact of pornography on young and impressionable minds. It leaves them confused as they are unable to process what they see and hear, resulting in warped perceptions, lopsided values, unhealthy beliefs, detrimental attitudes and dysfunctional behaviours.

When adults display sexual behaviour in front of young minds, they are in fact engaging in sexual abuse with the child. This subtle sexual abuse of the child's mind is not classically viewed as sexual abuse, but the damage is as grave as if the child had been physically sexually abused, and the effects as devastating and with long-lasting consequences.

Viewing of adult sexual behaviour can create arousal in a young child even before s/he is existentially ready to understand and process such feelings in a healthy manner. Thus, it is tampering with nature's timing, and interferes greatly with the natural growing up process of the child.

For a young adult, viewing of adult sexual behaviour may not interfere with the growing up process, but the stimulus can still result in an unmanageable level of arousal, leading to early sexual experimentation, which has its own set of problems such as teenage pregnancies, sexually transmitted diseases as well as leaving the young inexperienced teenager psychologically destabilised.

Verbally too, the use of sexual innuendos while talking, sexual jokes, and descriptions of sexual behaviour should be strictly avoided in front of children and young adults. Also, any form of touching with sexual overtones should be restricted to the bedroom or a more private place, away from the gaze of the child.

Ajit's elder sister was engaged to be married, and the young couple would often kiss and neck each other, and intimately touch each other with Ajit being around. Ajit, who was then 16 years old, would get aroused, and was not satisfied with self-pleasuring as he would view his sister and brother-in-law being openly sexual with each other. He started craving the touch of a woman, and so once when he was alone at home for the weekend, he arranged for a call girl to come home and had unprotected sex. She was HIV +, as he realised a year later when he developed immunity problems. He developed full blown AIDS a few years later, and died in his 20s.

Modelling Intimacy

However, we must clarify that if a child observes two adults of the opposite gender, either his parents or someone else, expressing warm and caring feelings, such as expression of appreciation, gratitude, admiration, encouragement and other kind and comforting words, s/he learns to model such emotional intimacy. Also, equally beneficial would be for the child to witness apologies being asked, and forgiveness being given, as it models humility and love in the relationship. Non-sexual touching such as holding hands, keeping your head on your partner's shoulder, or putting an arm around the shoulder, and a light and affectionate hug, are not only harmless, but also help in being a role model for a healthy and emotionally intimate man-woman relationship. When children see their parents affectionate in such a way, it creates in them a feeling of security knowing that all is well between the parents.

Seven year old Komal would force her parents to sit side by side and hold hands after they had an argument, which she had witnessed. After a few times, the parents realised that their arguments were making Komal insecure about the well-being of the family unit, and that she needed to feel secure, and hence she forced the togetherness. Parents need to know that if they express their differences in front of children, then it is their duty to also make up and make peace through words and acts of non-sexual affection with each other in front of the children. This helps them know that all is well.

Twelve year old Rohan was anxious about the state of the relationship between his parents, as in the midst of loud sounds he heard his mother refer to that woman, and his father using words such as "I'm fed up of your nagging". He was always watching from the corner of his eye as to how close or far they were sitting from each other, whether his dad was sleeping in the bedroom or on the sofa, and would breathe a sigh of relief when they held hands. In fact, on a vacation he became the family photographer, asking his parents to pose for the camera, instructing them on various affectionate postures like his father's arm around his mother's shoulders, asking them to sit very close to each other, to look at each other and smile, and even asked his father to plant a kiss on his mother's cheek for a photograph.

In conclusion, we can say that there is a clear demarcation between sexual and non-sexual yet affectionate behaviour, where the first if viewed is harmful, while the other is helpful. Therefore, adults should be alert and aware of the effects of both and make responsible choices while interacting with each other in front of children.

Chapter 7

LOW-DOWN ON
DATE RAPE

Discussing the modern-day
phenomenon of date rape

In 1999, an e-mail began circulating proclaiming that a new date rape drug had been introduced. This drug not only rendered the victims helpless to defend themselves against a would-be rapist, but also caused permanent infertility. The drug is **Progesterex**. It is said to be a veterinary medication, used for horses. The rumour is that some men had stolen it to use in combination with other stupefying drugs.

> **FOLLOWING IS A COPY OF THE HOAX E-MAIL STILL CIRCULATING**
>
> Ladies, be more alert and cautious when getting a drink offer from a guy. Good guys out there, please forward this message to your lady friends. And boyfriends, take heed. There is a new drug that has been out for less than a year. Progesterex that is essentially a small sterilisation pill. The drug is now being used by rapists at parties to rape AND sterilise their victims. Progesterex is available to vets to

sterilise large animals. Rumour has it that the Progesterex is being used together with Rohypnol, the date rape drug. As with Rohypnol, all they have to do is drop it into the woman's drink. The woman can't remember a thing the next morning, and all that had taken place the night before.

Progesterex, which dissolves in drinks just as easily, is such that the victim doesn't conceive from the rape and the rapist needn't worry about having a paternity test identifying him months later. The drug's effects AREN'T TEMPORARY. Progesterex was designed to sterilise horses. Any female that takes it WILL NEVER BE ABLE TO CONCEIVE. The crooks can get this drug from anyone who is in the vet school of any university. It's that easy, and Progesterex is about to break out big on campuses everywhere. Believe it or not, there is even a site on the internet telling people how to use it.

Please forward this to everyone you know, especially the gals.

Thorough investigations were carried out by various agencies subsequently to find out the truth behind this e-mail. They found that **there is no drug called Progesterex that has the** ability to turn a girl permanently infertile. There are indeed date rape drugs, such as Rohypnol (Flunitrazepam) and GHB (Gamma Hydroxybutyrate), and one would be wise to keep an eye out for those who might take advantage of a young woman at the many parties that are thrown on campus and elsewhere. However, Progesterex is one drug you can scratch off the list.

What Is Rohypnol?

Rohypnol (Flunitrazepam) is a popular and easily accessible date rape drug in the United States. It is not manufactured by any company in India. Rohypnol is similar to Diazepam (Calmpose or Valium) but about 10 times as strong. In Europe and South America, it is a prescription drug used as a pre-anaesthetic agent and as a potent sedative (sleeping pill).

The original tablets, marketed by the pharmaceutical company Hoffman La Roche, look like aspirin and dissolve rapidly in liquid. It is known by several street names: Roachies, La Roche, Rope, Rib, Rophies, Roofies, Ruffies, Mexican valium, or the 'forget (me) pill.' Rohypnol is especially dangerous because it is inexpensive. This makes it popular in college campuses, clubs, bars, and at private parties.

Originally, Rohypnol came as a small pill that dissolved in all kinds of drinks – alcoholic and non-alcoholic. The drug was odourless and tasteless.

Because of the widespread abuse of this drug, Hoffman La Roche changed the tablets; the new tablets take more time to dissolve and turn a drink blue.

Rohypnol takes 20-30 minutes to take effect. Initially, it causes muscle relaxation, dizziness, and headaches, slows psychomotor responses, and lowers inhibitions. Victims may have difficulty moving or speaking. They often remember the effects of the drug as a feeling of being drunk. Rohypnol has a synergistic effect with alcohol. Rohypnol became (in) famous because of its ability to cause memory blackouts – periods of memory loss that follow ingestion of the drug with alcohol. The blackouts typically last 8-12 hours. The victim may or may not appear awake during this time. Those who have been raped with the help of Rohypnol have reported waking up in strange rooms, with or without clothing, sometimes with a used condom on the bed, occasionally with bruises on their body… but they have no memory of the previous night.

Victims often feel nauseous the day after they have received Rohypnol.

What Is Sexual Assault?

Sexual assault is any type of sexual activity that you do not want or agree to. It happens whenever a person's sexual privacy is not respected. It ranges from inappropriate touching to penetration or intercourse. It also can be verbal, visual, audio, or any other form, which forces a person to participate in unwanted sexual contact or attention. Sexual assault includes rape and attempted rape, child molestation, voyeurism, exhibitionism, incest, and sexual harassment. All forms of sexual assault are crimes as per the Indian Penal Code (1860).

When someone is forced to have sexual intercourse, it is called rape. If a friend, relative or date forces you to have sexual intercourse, it is called acquaintance rape. Date rape is particularly common among adolescent victims. But rape is not the only kind of sexual abuse. Unwanted touching, fondling, watching, talking, or being forced to look at another person's sex organs are all forms of sexual abuse. Although the majority of sexual abusers are male, perpetrators can be of either gender. They are often friends, or even family members. In fact, 80 per cent of sexual abuse is committed by friends, intimate partners, acquaintances, or family members (Journal of Law and Medical Ethics, 1993). Nearly 6 out of 10 rape or sexual assault incidents are reported by victims to have occurred in their own home or at the home of a friend, relative, or neighbour. No matter who attacks you, sexual assault is a crime.

> Shivani's heart was pounding with excitement as she gave the finishing touches to her make-up. She was the envy of her friends. The most handsome guy on campus had asked her for a date. But that was not it. He had a swanky car to match his good looks. She heard the car horn and ran down for what she thought would be most beautiful evening of her life. But sadly that was not to be. She came back a broken soul with dishevelled hair and mascara mixed with tears rolling down her cheeks. She had been a victim of date rape.

Date rape is a serious crime. It's a betrayal of trust and can leave long-lasting emotional injuries.

Unfortunately, rape or sexual assault is a violent crime least reported to law enforcement. Only 16 per cent rapes are reported to the police. In a survey of victims who did not report rape or attempted rape to the police, victims gave the following reasons for not making a report: 43 per cent thought nothing could be done; 27 per cent thought it was a private matter; 12 per cent were afraid of police response; and 12 per cent thought it was not important enough. Remember, sexual assault is against the law. It is a crime. You have the right to report this crime to the police, and to be treated fairly.

Who Are the Victims?

An estimated 91 per cent of the victims of rape and sexual assault are female and 9 per cent are male. (Nearly 99 per cent of the reported offenders are male.) The National Violence Against Women Survey found that of the women who reported being raped, 54 per cent were under the age of 18 at the time of the first rape and 83 per cent were under the age of 25. However, sexual assault affects women, children, and men of all ages and racial, cultural and economic backgrounds.

How Can You Avoid becoming a Victim of Rape?

- Be wary about accepting drinks from anyone you don't know well or long enough to trust. If you are accepting a drink, make sure it is from an unopened container and that you open it yourself. Beverages that come in sealed containers (unopened cans or bottles) are much safer to consume than mixed drinks.

- Never leave your drink unattended. If you have to go to the bathroom, either finish your drink or throw it away.

- Don't take drugs or alcohol; it might cloud your judgment. If someone offers to buy you a drink, go up to the bar with them to accept the drink.

- Do not take any open beverages, including alcohol, from anyone.

- If you order a mixed drink, watch the person who mixes it.

- Never drink anything out of a common punch bowl.

- Subscribe to the buddy system: always party with one or more friends, and keep an eye on each other. If someone begins to appear too drunk, get that person to a safe place. More than one attempted Rohypnol rape has been prevented by watchful friends.

- Believe your intuition, and listen to your instinct. By the time we are adults we are good at ignoring our gut feeling. Reclaim that ability and acknowledge it. Give yourself permission to act on that bad feeling.

- Be very clear and firm with any person making advances. Most times that person has no intentions of being a rapist and he assumes that the woman is trying to protect her reputation or that she is playing games when she says no. Let him know that "This is unacceptable, it is rape, and you are breaking the law."

- When going out with someone new, who you don't really know, go to a public place so that you are not alone with your date.

- When out with friends at social events, never leave with someone you have just met.

- If possible, never let yourself be taken to a second location. This will give your attacker the opportunity to cause you more harm.

- Be wary of isolated spots, like underground garages, offices after business hours, terraces and apartment laundry rooms. Avoid walking alone, especially at night. Never hitchhike or pick up a hitchhiker.

- Park your car in well-lighted areas. Always lock your car and have your key ready to use before you reach the car.

- If you think you are being followed, run towards a lighted house, restaurant, store or some public place.

- At home, never open your door to strangers. Always check the identification of salespersons or service people before opening the door. It also is a good idea to have another adult at home with you when service people come, if you can arrange it.

- Take a self-defence class. If you appear stronger and assertive, you are less likely to be a target. Rapists are looking for someone who is not going to make waves and who is not going to fight back. If you look like someone whom they cannot mess with, they will probably move on to someone else.

Chapter 8

ANATOMY OF THE REPRODUCTIVE SYSTEM

A scientific discussion of the physiology of human sexuality

An understanding of the anatomy and the physiology of the sexual organs and reproductive system helps teachers educate students about their bodies and helps both students and teachers discuss sexual and reproductive health issues in a better way, with more clarity.

The sexual organs are also known as reproductive organs because they are the parts of our bodies that make us able to reproduce – that is, to have children. These organs are also called the genitals or genital organs.

When describing sexual anatomy to students, be sure to use language that they understand. Students may not use scientific (medical) terminology when discussing their genital features; they might use slang, or might even be too embarrassed to mention the correct terms. To communicate effectively with students, **learn their terminology as you share the scientific terms for body parts. Do not condemn, ridicule or look down upon their terminology** as you educate them about the correct terminology.

MALE SEXUAL AND REPRODUCTIVE ORGANS

External Male Genitalia

The external male genitals consist of the penis and the scrotum.

The penis is a cylindrical organ with the ability to be flaccid or erect. It provides a passage called the urethra for both urine and semen. It can be a source of pleasure in response to sexual stimulation and is the organ that penetrates the vaginal canal during sexual intercourse.

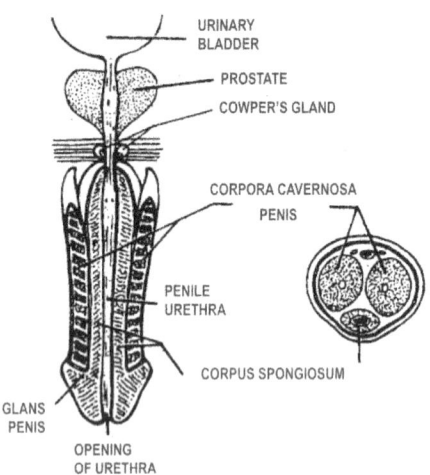

Male Sexual and Reproductive Organs

The penis is made up of three spongy tubes, each containing a sponge-like tissue that fills up with blood when the man is sexually excited. This is what causes an erection. The upper two tubes are called **corpora cavernosa** and the lower one is called **corpus spongiosum**. It is the corpus spongiosum through which the urethra passes out. All the three tubes are enveloped in a sheath called **Tunica Albuginea**.

The head of the penis i.e. the glans (glans penis), is the part that is most sensitive and has the most nerve endings (neuro-receptors). The ring, or ridge, of tissue that circles the lower edge of the glans is called the **corona**. The glans is covered by the **foreskin** (prepuce) in men who are not circumcised. A number of tiny **preputial glands** (Glands of Tyson) located here, discharge their secretions onto the glans penis. These secretions accumulate on the glans as a thick cheese-like substance called **smegma**. It has an offensive odour and therefore should be cleaned regularly by retracting the foreskin of the penis. A thin fold of skin is attached in a linear fashion underneath the glans in the midline. It is termed as **frenulum**.

Pearly Penile Papules (PPP)

Adolescents often observe and panic about the small, white, pinhead-sized spots that appear on the ridge of their glans penis. They are termed as pearly penile papules (PPP) and are completely harmless.

Pearly penile papules (PPP) are tiny skin-coloured papules that are typically found on the corona or sulcus of the glans penis. Usually, they are arranged circumferentially in one or many rows. They are often mistaken for a sexually transmitted disease such as venereal warts, but are in fact entirely innocuous. You can not contract them or spread them through sexual contact. They also do not itch, weep or bleed – but if they do, make sure you see your doctor.

It is believed that these papules are more common in men who are not circumcised, and that too in their twenties or thirties. However, the mechanism underlying their development remains unknown.

The truth is that no conclusive cause is known. No treatment is required, because PPP is not harmful to one's health and under no circumstances should one attempt to remove them oneself. Even so, if one is concerned in any way, one should not hesitate to get the penis examined by a qualified medical practitioner.

Normally, a man should be able to pull back his foreskin, enough to expose the whole of the glans penis. This may either happen on its own on full erection or one may have to do it manually before penetration. Both ways it is normal and fine. If the retraction of the foreskin is not possible or painful, then it is a medical condition known as **Phimosis**. This condition may require a minor surgery known as **Circumcision** which takes 20-30 minutes and is done under local anaesthesia. It is a small surgery in which the foreskin covering the glans-penis is removed.

There is always the concern of a person developing **paraphimosis**, if the foreskin is getting retracted incompletely.

▫ Paraphimosis

Paraphimosis is a medical condition where the foreskin gets entrapped behind the glans penis, and cannot be slid back to its usual flaccid position covering the glans penis. If the condition persists for a long time (for several hours) or there is any sign of a lack of blood supply, it should be treated as a medical emergency, as it can result in serious complications including gangrene.

Paraphimosis can be reduced by manipulation with the aid of a lubricant. This requires compressing the glans gently and moving the foreskin back to its normal position, using a lubricant. If manipulation fails, the foreskin may have to be cut (dorsal slit procedure) or excised by circumcision surgery. An alternative procedure, the Dundee technique, involves putting multiple superficial punctures in the swollen foreskin with a fine needle, and then extracting the edema fluid by manual pressure.

The scrotum is a pouch of loose skin hanging directly under the penis that contains the testes. It consists of several layers of tissue. Functionally, the most important of the scrotal layers is a muscular coat formed by the **cremasteric muscles**. This muscle coat acts as one of the thermoregulatory mechanisms that helps keep each testis at a constant temperature i.e. 1.5 to 2 degree centigrade lower than the body temperature, which is necessary for the production of sperms (spermatogenesis). Both fear and a cold environment cause the cremasteric muscles to contract in an action known as cremasteric reflex. Contraction elevates the testes to a position closer to the inguinal canal and thus closer to body heat.

The pampiniform plexus of veins that surrounds the artery supplying each testis also acts as a thermoregulatory mechanism. This plexus creates a counter-current system so that the heat of the artery can be lost in the veins. The temperature of the testis is thus kept lower than the body temperature, a temperature difference that is essential for spermatogenesis.

Internal Male Genitalia

The internal male genitals are: the Testes, the Epididymis, the Vasa deferentia, the Seminal vesicles, the Prostate gland, and the Cowper's (Bulbo-urethral) glands.

The testes: The paired egg-shaped glands that produce sperms and Testosterone are placed in the scrotum. Usually one testis hangs somewhat lower than the other one. Testes are highly innervated (supplied by nerves) and sensitive to touch and pressure.

- Before a boy is born, his testes are inside his abdomen. Once he is born, they come down (descend) through the inguinal canal, into his scrotal sac. In some cases one or both testes do not descend, and the boy has an undescended testis (cryptorchidism). About 3 per cent of full term and 30 per cent of premature infant boys are born with at least one undescended testis.

  An undescended testis is usually noticed when a male child is born or very early in life, and in 80 per cent cases it corrects itself by the first year of life. Once in a while, the absence of testis remains unnoticed until puberty, in which case the boy must have a surgery. This is necessary because there is a higher risk of cancer developing in a testis still undescended by the time of puberty.

The testes are made up of:

- **Interstitial cells** responsible for the production of testosterone (the male sex hormone), which is responsible for the development of male sexual characteristics and the sex drive (libido).

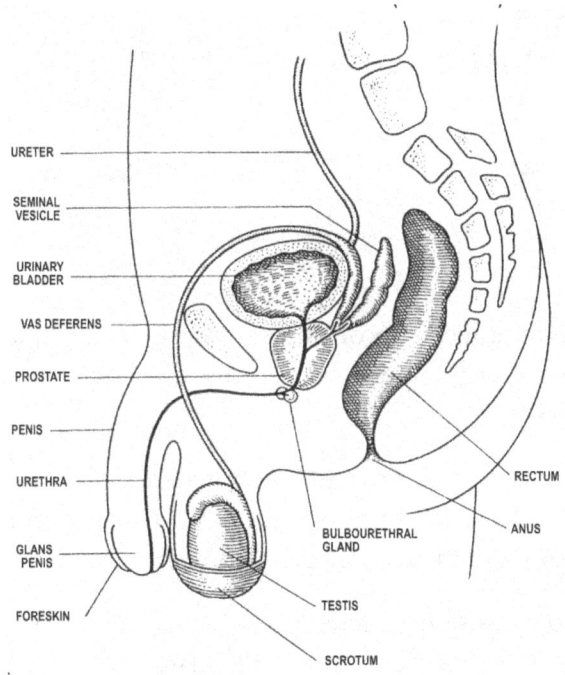

Male Reproductive System (side view)

- **Seminiferous tubules** responsible for the production of sperms (the male gamete or sex cell).

Spermatogenesis: Sperms are produced in the seminiferous tubules of the testes. The sperm takes about 74 days to be formed. Sperms have a life of about 25 to 40 days. Sperm production starts in boys at around 12 years of age and goes on for the rest of their life. Normally, at least 20,000 mature sperms are produced every minute. Each millilitre of semen contains around 20 to 120 million sperms. In each ejaculation a normal male releases around 60 to 360 million sperms. If sperm are not ejaculated, they are simply reabsorbed by the body.

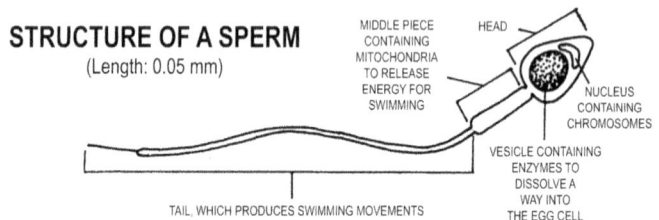

Each sperm is made up of an oval head, a middle piece and a tail. An average sperm measures 50 microns i.e. 0.05 millimetres.

The epididymis are the two comma shaped, highly coiled tubes against the hind side of the testes where sperms mature and are stored until they are released during ejaculation.

The vasa deferentia (plural: vas deferens) are the paired tubes 45 cms (18 inches) long that carry mature sperms from the epididymis to the urethra. Each vas deferens runs from the epididymis up into the body, and loops around the urinary bladder.

Surgical sterilisation in men (vasectomy) is performed on the vasa deferentia by cutting and tying them separately at the region before they enter the abdomen.

The seminal vesicles are a pair of glandular sacs that secrete about 60 per cent of the fluid that makes up the semen in which sperms are transported. Seminal fluid provides nourishment (fructose – a simple sugar) for sperms.

The vas deferens along with the duct from the seminal vesicle forms the **ejaculatory duct**. It is a short straight tube that passes into the prostate gland to open into the urethra.

The prostate gland is a walnut-sized gland. It lies just beneath the urinary bladder and secretes about 30 per cent of the fluid that makes up semen. The alkaline nature of the prostate secretions neutralizes the acidic environment of the male and female reproductive tracts. The prostate is sheathed in the muscles of the pelvic floor, which contract during the ejaculation. A muscle at the base of the prostate gland keeps sperms out of the urethra till the time of ejaculation. The prostate gland is quite sensitive to stimulation and can be a source of sexual pleasure for some men.

Benign Prostatic Hyperplasia (BPH)

The prostate gland is a compound, tubulo-alveolar exocrine gland of the male reproductive system. It often enlarges in elderly men to the point where urination becomes difficult. Symptoms include increased frequency of urination or hesitancy i.e. taking a while to get started. If the prostate grows too large, it may compress the urethra and hinder the flow of urine, making urination difficult and in some cases, completely impossible.

BPH can be treated with medications, a minimally invasive surgical procedure or, in advanced cases, surgical removal of the prostate. Minimally invasive surgical procedures include Transurethral microwave thermotherapy (TUMT) and Transurethral needle ablation of the prostate (TUNA).

The surgery most often preferred in such cases is called TransUrethral Resection of the Prostate (TURP). In TURP, an instrument is inserted through the urethra to scrape prostate tissue that is pressing against the upper part of the urethra and impeding the urine flow.

Prostate Cancer

It is one of the most common cancers affecting elderly men and a significant cause of death for older men (2-3 per cent). Regular measurement of Prostate Specific Antigen (PSA) and ultrasound examination of the prostate are strongly recommended for men above 50 for early detection of prostate cancer.

The Cowper's glands (Bulbourethral glands) are pea-sized glands in a pair at the base of the penis beneath the prostate gland. These glands secrete a transparent, alkaline, mucus-like fluid into the urethra during sexual arousal and before ejaculation (pre-ejaculatory fluid or pre-cum) that acts as a lubricant for the sperms and coats the urethra as semen flows out of the penis.

FEMALE SEXUAL AND REPRODUCTIVE ORGANS

External Female Genitalia

The external female genitals include the mons pubis, the clitoris, the labia majora and the labia minora. Together, along with the vaginal opening, they are known as the **vulva**.

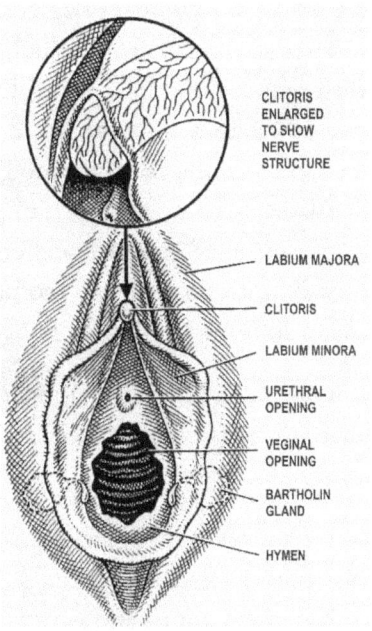

Female External Genitalia (Vulva)

The mons pubis (pubic mound) is a pad of fatty tissue covering the pubic bone. This structure, which gets covered with hair during puberty, protects the internal reproductive organs.

The labia majora (major lips) are two prominent longitudinal spongy folds of skin, one on either side of the vaginal opening, that cover the genital structures. They are the most visible parts of the female genitalia. Ordinarily, the labia majora touch each other along the midline and hence the labia minora and the clitoris may not be seen unless they are parted.

The labia minora (minor lips) are the two erectile folds of skin between the labia majora that extend from the clitoris on both sides of the urethral and vaginal openings. The size of the labia minora varies from woman to woman, and also in the same woman at different ages and stages of her life. The labia minora meet above to form a **clitoral hood** and their lower ends join each other to form the **fourchette**. They contain very little fat tissue. The labia minora are erectile in nature and are very sensitive to the sense of touch and hence they play an important role in sexual arousal of the woman. Between the labia majora and labia minora are the interlabial sulci.

The area covered by the labia minora that includes the openings to the vagina and urethra, as well as the Bartholin's glands, is called the **vestibule**.

The clitoris is an erectile hooded organ at the upper joining of the inner lips (labia minora) that contains a high concentration of blood vessels and nerve endings and is extremely sensitive to stimulation. It is a small, pea-like structure present at the top of the inner lips (labia minora) of the vagina, enfolded by the outer lips (labia majora). The size of the clitoris varies in different women. You may have to separate the outer lips of the vagina to be able to see it. It resembles a miniature male penis. Like the male glans penis, the clitoris is richly supplied by highly sensitive nerve receptors. The clitoris is the only anatomical organ in women whose sole function is providing sexual pleasure.

The clitoris is very sensitive to touch, even more than the labia minora, and hence many women do not like to be touched down there especially in the initial stages of arousal. This is a very important fact to be kept in mind, especially by men.

THE PERINEUM AND PUBO-COCCYGEAL MUSCLES

The perineum is a network of muscles located between and surrounding the vagina and the anus that support the pelvic cavity and help keep pelvic organs in place.

PC muscles is a commonly used term for the Pubo-Coccygeus or Pubo-Coccygeal muscle group. This muscle group runs from the pubic bone in front to the tailbone in the rear and supports the pelvic floor. In women, this is the muscle that contracts during orgasm and gives the vagina a feeling of tightness. In men, this is the muscle that contracts when ejaculation takes place.

A strong PC muscle contributes to your pleasure in sex in many ways. If you exercise it daily, you will build the muscle mass in the pelvic area, which will increase the amount of blood flowing to your genitals and allow for more pleasurable sensations during arousal. In addition, strong PC muscles can tighten the vagina and make intercourse, orgasm and ejaculation more enjoyable. An added benefit is that strong PC muscles often prevent bladder and prostate problems. In fact, correcting bladder problems in pregnant women was how this muscle was first discovered.

To exercise PC muscles, you must first learn to identify them.

Anatomy of the Reproductive System

To find these muscles, stop and start the flow of urine while urinating. The muscles that tighten as you do this are the PC muscles. To exercise the muscles, contract them for a count of five, and then relax. Start with six repetitions, and then gradually build up to twenty-five repetitions over three months. At first, holding the contraction for five seconds may be difficult, but like every muscle, the more you exercise, the stronger they will become. It takes about three weeks of daily exercise for your PC muscles to get in shape. Once they are in shape, you should still exercise every day to keep them strong, and enjoy the benefits.

The hymen is a thin membrane that covers the vagina. It may or may not be present at birth. In some women, the hymen only has some tiny openings through which menstrual blood can escape, but in others, the hymen is just a rim of tissue. Some times it just folds naturally along the walls of the vagina.

Not every virgin has a kind of hymen that could appear to pop with her first act of intercourse. It may get broken without one's knowledge while doing certain activities such as athletics, horseriding or some sports. It may also get broken if one masturbates or uses tampons. If it is unbroken, a little bleeding may take place at the first intercourse, however, it cannot be regarded as a test of one's virginity.

HYMENORRHAPHY

Hymenorrhaphy or hymen reconstruction surgery is the surgical restoration of the hymen. It is also referred as hymenoplasty. The most common intention is to cause bleeding during the first postmarital intercourse which in some cultures is considered a proof of virginity. This surgical procedure is not generally regarded as part of mainstream surgery, but is done at some plastic surgery centres.

Internal Female Genitalia

The internal female genitals include the vagina, the cervix, the uterus, the fallopian tubes, and the ovaries.

The vagina is the biggest of the three openings in the genital area. The other openings are the urethra (in front of the vagina) and the anus (behind the vagina). The vagina is a highly expandable, muscular, tubular cavity leading from the vestibule to the uterus. It is about 3.5 to 5 inches deep and 1.25 to 2 inches wide. It is made up of soft folds of skin. The vagina is the structure penetrated by the erect male penis during vaginal intercourse, and it also serves as an outlet channel for menstrual flow. During vaginal intercourse, contact with the vaginal wall generates sexual pleasure. The front wall of the vagina is more thickly innervated and more sensitive to stimulation than the posterior vaginal wall.

The vagina of an adult woman is very strong, extremely stretchy, elastic and muscular. During childbirth, the vagina

Anatomy of the Reproductive System

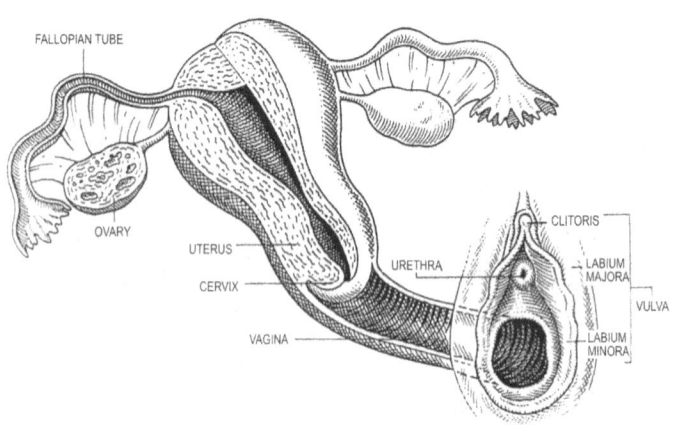

The Female Reproductive System

stretches to many times its usual size to allow the delivery of a baby through the mother. However, **a young adolescent girl's vagina is thinner and cannot stretch very much. This is one of the reasons why childbirth could be dangerous for young adolescent girls. The vagina of an adolescent girl can even tear during childbirth. This can cause very serious medical problems.**

At puberty, the walls of the vagina begin to secrete a fluid or discharge. This discharge is stickier and thicker than saliva. Its purpose is to keep the vagina clean, and to maintain the proper environment in which helpful bacteria (Doderlein bacilli) that prevent infections, can survive and grow. These bacteria are responsible for maintaining the acidic – hence the protective – nature of an adult vagina.

Many girls find increased vaginal discharge at different times of the month and also when they are feeling sexual. This is absolutely natural and normal.

The opening of the vagina is ordinarily enclosed by the labia majora and the labia minora, which are the outer and inner lips. Some people have a misconception that the vaginal canal is a continuous open tube. Ordinarily the vaginal walls, which have the capacity to elongate and expand, simply close upon one another. When the penis (or any similar object such as a tampon) is inserted inside the vaginal canal, the vaginal walls mould around its girth and accommodate the length of an erect penis.

The way the vaginal canal has the ability to stretch and expand during childbirth, allowing for the passage of a baby, it also has the capacity to elongate during sexual intercourse to accommodate an erect penis. For some women, the depth of the vaginal canal from the vaginal opening to the cervix (the mouth of the uterus) is three to four inches when they are not aroused sexually. Other women may have a vaginal canal length of five to seven inches. During sexual arousal, blood rushes to the genital region, and the sexual excitement causes the inner two-thirds of the vaginal canal to get longer by pulling the cervix and uterus upwards. The vaginal canal also gets lubricated, which facilitates penetration.

Sex and the Cervix

At times during deep penetration, an erect penis may touch the cervix. This may indicate that physically the woman is not adequately aroused. On proper arousal, her vaginal canal will elongate, and her cervix will get pulled up and move out of the way. At other times, if an erect penis is much longer than average or if the thrusting is deeper and aggressive, it may touch or even hit the cervix. At such times the woman should communicate to her partner about any discomfort so that he can be slower, gentler, and can adopt a more comfortable sexual position e.g. woman on-top.

The G-Spot

The 'G-spot' is an area of increased sensitivity within the vagina, with maximum potential for sexual arousal. It is supposed to be located on the upper vaginal wall about two inches from the external vaginal opening. However, as studies have shown, it may not be present in all women.

G-spot got its name after Ernest Grafenberg, a German gynaecologist, who discovered it in 1950. It has been described as a mass of tissue about the size of a small bean in the unstimulated state. If it is present in her, a woman will be able to exactly pinpoint it by inserting her finger(s) and sliding it in a forward-backward or side-to-side manner. With increased and intense stimulation, the tissue purportedly swells to the size of a mini ball and becomes firm. If the stimulation is continued, she climaxes.

There is not much information available about the G-spot simply because experts are not unable to pinpoint and label the area. They are also not able to locate the nerves that trigger the response. The existence of this spot is thus not accepted by all in the medical fraternity. Therefore, the G-spot is more for academic discussion than for practical knowledge.

There are conflicting results from studies done to locate the G-spot. Ladas, Perry and Whipper, authors of a book about the G-spot, state that examination of more than 400 women identified the G-spot in each one. But the studies at the Masters & Johnson Institute proved otherwise – less than 10 percent of a sample of over 100 women who were carefully examined had an area of heightened sensitivity in the front wall of the vagina or a tissue mass that fit the various descriptions of this area. Another study by Heli Alzate and M.L. Londono was also unable to find evidence supporting the existence of the G-spot, although many of the women studied showed signs of erotic sensitivity in the front wall of the vagina. Thus, at present, it seems that much more research is needed to establish whether the G-spot exists as a distinct anatomical structure.

The Bartholin's glands are two small, round glands, one on either side of the vaginal opening in the 4 o'clock and 8 o'clock positions. These glands secrete a sticky, transparent, mucus-like fluid during sexual arousal that provides lubrication at the vagina.

The cervix is the lower part of the uterus that protrudes into the vaginal canal. It has a narrow opening (orifice) that allows the passage of menstrual flow out from the uterus, and passage of sperms into the uterus. The orifice is so narrow that ordinarily it can allow only menstrual blood to come down and only sperms to swim in.

> Some women fear that during intercourse a condom could come off the penis and go up into the uterus or up in the body viscera. This is impossible as ordinarily the opening of the cervix is extremely narrow. If a condom does come off when a couple is having sexual intercourse and slips into the vagina, the woman can easily reach into her vagina with her clean fingers and pull it out. It does not enter the uterus or the body. The vagina is almost like a blind pouch with a very narrow collapsed passage into the uterus, which cannot allow the condom to go beyond that point. Moreover, a condom is too large an object to get lost in the vagina.

The cervix widens and opens only during childbirth so that the baby can come out from the uterus, into the vagina and out of the body.

The surface of the cervix is very delicate, especially in young girls and younger women. It can get injured or infected by organisms (bacteria, viruses, parasites and fungi) that may enter the vaginal canal during peno-vaginal intercourse. This could make the cervix extremely prone to cancer at a later age. **Girls who have sexual intercourse early in their life, or who have many sex partners, or who have HPV or HIV infections, are more at risk for developing cancer of the cervix than those girls who have a more guarded and restrained sex life and who refrain from early sexual experimentation. Clearly, delaying sexual intercourse protects the cervix.**

Vaccination to Prevent HPV

Vaccination for HPV infection is now available. It can help prevent cervical cancer before it occurs. This vaccination acts by producing antibodies against the Human Papilloma Virus. These antibodies then protect the cervix from an HPV infection, by fighting the virus. By protecting the cervix from an HPV infection, vaccination offers implied protection against cervical cancer.

The vaccine is given in three injections over a period of six months. It is best given as early as possible to teenage girls, as this is when the best immune response to the vaccine is achieved. However, since all women remain at risk of cervical cancer, the vaccination can be given at any age.

The uterus (the womb): It is a thick-walled, pear-shaped, hollow organ located between the urinary bladder and the rectum. Around 3 inches in length, it is made up of several layers of tissue and muscle. The inner layer is called the endometrium, and it is this that builds up, thickens and is then shed during menstruation. The next layer is called the myometrium – a powerful muscular tissue that twists, expands and contracts rhythmically during orgasm and childbirth. The uterus is the site for implantation of the zygote (fertilised ovum), this is where the foetus develops during pregnancy.

The fallopian tubes (oviducts): These are a pair of tubes that extend from the upper lateral corners of the uterus towards the ovaries but do not touch them. The ovum travels through these fallopian tubes, from the ovaries towards the uterus every month. It is in these tubes that fertilisation of the ovum takes place in most cases. The fallopian tubes are about 4 inches (10 cms.) in length.

The ovaries: These are two oval-shaped sex glands (gonads) located on either side of the uterus at the end of each fallopian tube. The ovaries produce ova, and release one ovum per month from menarche [first menstrual bleeding] to menopause. The ovary is made up of immature ova called **Graafian follicles**. At birth, these are two to four lakh in number. During the fertile span of a woman, only 350 to 500 follicles mature and the rest of them degenerate. Usually, every month one Graafian follicle matures and expels out one ovum. This process is called **ovulation**. The ovum is about 1-1.5 millimetre in size.

The ovaries produce the hormones oestrogen and progesterone, which are the hormones responsible for the development of the secondary sexual characteristics in females. These hormones are also responsible for the integrity of the vaginal lining, and the elasticity and lubrication of the genitalia. A small amount of testosterone is also produced by the ovaries, which is responsible for sexual desire in women.

Chapter 9

HORMONES:
THE CHEMICAL DRIVERS

The role of the endocrine system
in sexual physiology

An important part of our sexual physiology is under the control of the endocrine system, which consists of ductless glands that produce chemical substances called hormones. Hormones are secreted directly into the bloodstream (ductless), where they are carried to target tissues on which they act.

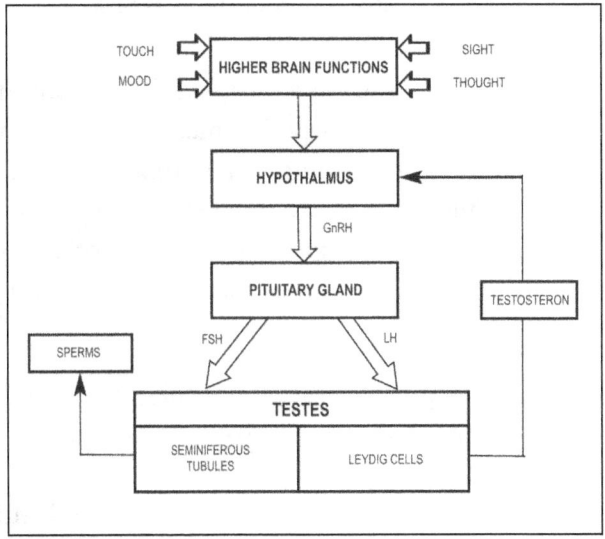

Endocrine Regulation in Adult Male

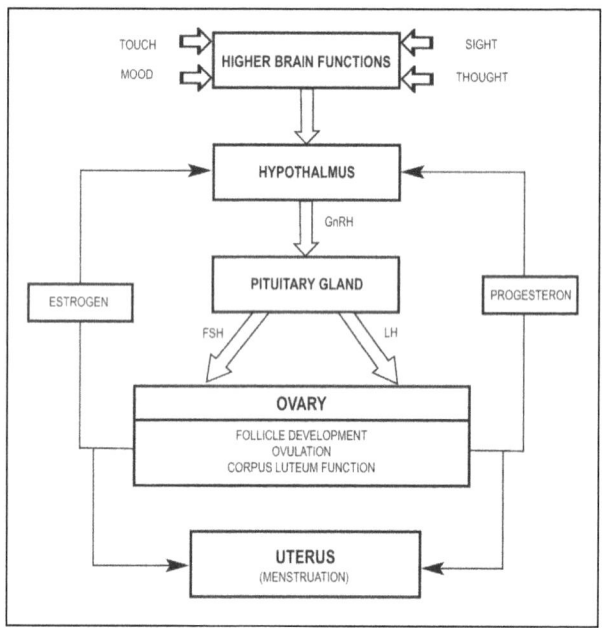

Endocrine Regulation in Adult Female

Higher brain functions such as touch, smell, sight and thought trigger the sex centre in the hypothalamus. The **hypothalamus** is a part of the brain that contains a number of small nuclei with a variety of functions. It is located at the base of the brain. One of the most important functions of the hypothalamus is to link the nervous system to the endocrine system through the pituitary gland.

The hypothalamus gets activated at adolescence, and starts producing a hormone called **Gonadotropin releasing hormone** (GnRH). GnRH controls the secretion of two hormones in the pituitary gland i.e. **Follicle stimulating hormone** (FSH) and **Luteinizing hormone** (LH).

In males **FSH** stimulates production of sperms (spermatogenesis) in the testes. In females FSH prepares the ovaries for ovulation. It stimulates the growth of the Graafian follicle in the ovary. It is in the Graafian follicle that the ovum (egg) develops.

LH stimulates the Leydig cells (interstitial cells) in the testes to produce **testosterone** in men. It also stimulates the adrenal glands to produce **androgens**. There are five different types of androgens, and testosterone is one of them.

Androgens are commonly considered the male hormones and oestrogens the female hormones, even though both sexes have both these hormones in different proportions circulating throughout their body. Women usually have higher levels of oestrogens than androgens.

In females, LH serves as a trigger for ovulation. It is responsible for the release of the mature ovum from the Graafian follicle. After the release of the ovum from the Graafian follicle, what remains is known as the Corpus luteum.

The Graafian follicle produces **oestrogen**. Oestrogen is responsible for the development and maintenance of the female sexual characteristics.

The Corpus luteum produces **progesterone**. Progesterone is another female sex hormone that along with oestrogen regulates the menstrual cycle.

Testosterone: It is also known as the male sex hormone; however, it is present in both sexes. In men, testosterone is responsible for the development and maintenance of the primary sexual characteristics as well as secondary sexual characteristics. It is also responsible for the sex drive and aggression. In a normal man, 6 to 8 mg of testosterone is produced every day: more than 95 per cent is produced by the testes and the remainder in the adrenal glands. In women, about 0.5 mg of testosterone is produced daily by the ovaries and the adrenal glands. **Testosterone is the principle biological determinant of the sex drive in both men and women.**

Starting at puberty, our bodies produce increased levels of testosterone, and it commands us to seek out a reproductive partner. This is not something we choose or have control over. This is true for both men and women. While women may have one-tenth to one-fifth (10-20 per cent) the amount of testosterone that men have flowing through their body, it still influences what they do to a significant degree. A woman's body is significantly more sensitive to testosterone, and therefore small changes in its level can have a major affect on their overall health and sexual desire. Without proper levels of testosterone one will not experience sexual desire.

After the testosterone is produced, most of it binds with a protein called Sex Hormone Binding Globulin (SHBG). Only 1-2 per cent of the total production of testosterone is considered free testosterone and affects the sexual function. When evaluating a person's testosterone levels, total testosterone, SHBG, and free androgen levels must be determined. This allows doctors to know how much testosterone is being produced and how much is available to affect sexual function.

Prolactin is yet another hormone (besides FSH and LH) that is secreted by the pituitary gland. Prolactin stimulates the breasts to produce milk (lactation) during pregnancy.

Prolactin in Pregnancy

Increased serum level of prolactin during pregnancy causes enlargement of the breasts and increases the milk production. However, the high levels of progesterone during pregnancy act directly on the breasts to stop ejection of milk. It is only when the levels of progesterone fall after childbirth that milk ejection becomes possible.

Sometimes, newborn babies (males as well as females) secrete a small amount of milky substance from their nipples. This substance is commonly referred as Witch's milk. This is caused by the foetus being affected by prolactin circulating in the mother just before birth. It usually stops soon after birth.

Prolactin also provides the body with a sense of sexual gratification after the sexual act. It counteracts the effect of dopamine, which is responsible for sexual arousal and is believed to trigger the refractory period i.e. the period between orgasm and the next arousal. The amount of prolactin can be an indicator for the amount of sexual satisfaction and relaxation. High levels of prolactin are believed to be responsible for the loss of libido.

Oxytocin (secreted by the pituitary gland) promotes the maternal instinct, feelings of love and attachment, and hence, bonding between mates. It stimulates the drive to nuzzle and the drive to protect one's offspring. It is also necessary for cervical dilatation prior to birth and causes the uterine contractions all mothers are familiar with. It plays some role in experiencing orgasm, for both males and females. In males, oxytocin is also said to facilitate the movement of sperms during ejaculation.

How Does the Hypothalamus Regulate Hormone Levels?

(Feedback mechanism)

The hypothalamus acts much like a thermostat in regulating the hormonal function. Instead of reacting to temperature as a thermostat does, the hypothalamus reacts to the concentrations of hormones in its own blood supply. For example, in adult males, the amount of testosterone registers in the hypothalamus. If the amount is high, production of GnRH is turned off, leading to a drop in LH secretion by the pituitary gland. The decrease in LH in the bloodstream quickly results in reduced production of testosterone in the testes, and therefore lower amounts of testosterone are secreted into the blood. When the amount of testosterone reaching the hypothalamus drops below a certain level, it triggers the secretion of GnRH into the pituitary. The pituitary responds to this signal by sending more LH into the blood, where it will soon reach the testes and cause an increased rate of testosterone production. This process is known as feedback mechanism of hormone regulation.

Hormones and Sexual Behaviour

In many animal species, patterns of sexual interaction are tightly regulated by hormonal events, which control both the sexual receptivity of the female (her willingness to mate), and the sexual interest of the male. Testosterone and oestrogen are found in mammals, birds, reptiles, amphibians and fish. In all of these groups, the actions of sex hormones on the brain, appears to be an important determinant of sexual behaviour.

In humans, however, there is a more complex relationship between hormones and sexual behaviour. Although a marked testosterone deficiency usually reduces sexual interest in men or women, there are cases where this effect is not seen. Similarly, although many men with subnormal testosterone levels have difficulty with an erection, others continue to have a completely normal sexual function.

Women who have low levels of oestrogen in their bodies do not usually lose their ability to be sexually aroused or to have orgasms. In human beings, their sex hormone levels alone do not predict their sexual interest or behaviour.

Chapter 10

ADOLESCENCE: A SEXUAL TRANSITION

Discussing adolescent changes in boys and girls

Adolescence

Adolescence is simply a transition stage – a bridge – between childhood and adulthood. It is derived from the French word adolescere, which means growing up. It is the time of life between puberty and adulthood. Scientifically, it is defined as a period of change, which everyone goes through from biological immaturity to maturity.

The period between 10 to 19 years is termed as adolescence. In boys, it starts around 12 or 13 years. In girls, it may begin as early as 9 or 10 years.

Puberty: The commencement of adolescence is known as puberty. It is the time when the sex glands begin to function.

Every individual has his/her own timetable for puberty to begin. Some boys/girls notice the first signs when they are only nine; others do not start puberty until they are fourteen or even older. However, boys/girls who enter puberty earlier or later than others do not remain ahead or behind forever. Within a few years, it all gets evened out. We all eventually end up in the same place – grown up!

Changes at Adolescence

At adolescence there are rapid physical as well as psychological (emotional) changes in boys as well as girls. Adolescent changes are triggered by hormones of the master endocrine gland known as the pituitary gland and gonads. Our bodies make chemicals called hormones that guide the changes in our bodies. Two of these hormones – oestrogen in girls and testosterone in boys – guide our growth into adulthood. These hormonal changes also cause abrupt changes in our moods.

Generally, girls start changing earlier than boys. Some of the changes are the same for girls and boys. The physical changes invariably precede psychological changes. We change from boys and girls into men and women. We all inevitably go through these changes, whether we are mentally ready or not; whether we want to or don't want to; and whether or not we know what is happening.

Our bodies change remarkably during these years. Our feelings – about ourselves, our families, and about other people – also change. Often puberty and adolescence make us feel like we are on an emotional roller coaster.

Sometimes, it seems the changes are happening too fast. Sometimes we feel that they are not happening fast enough. It can be very puzzling.

Even the words that are used to describe these stages of our lives – puberty or adolescence – seem a little strange. Whatever we may call this time of change, the more we know and understand about what is happening to us, the better, more confident and less confused we can feel about our growing up.

If you are thinking that these changes have something to do

with sex, you are absolutely right! For all of us, one of the most important things about growing up is to learn about our sexuality and how to deal with it. You must remember one very important fact – **when it comes to sexual development, it is normal for everyone to be different.**

ADOLESCENT CHANGES IN BOYS

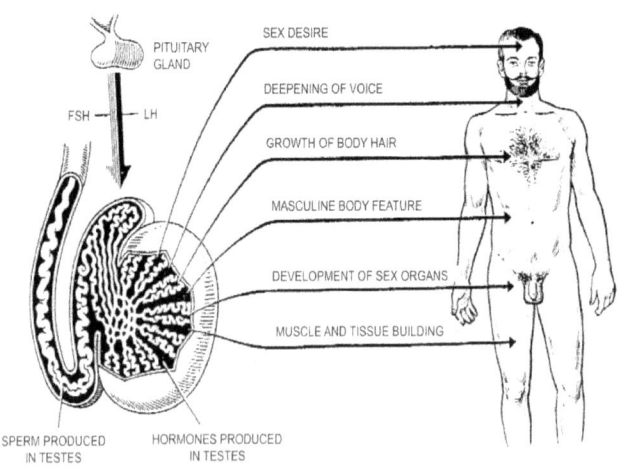

Male Secondary Sex Characteristics

Now let us understand what kinds of changes you can expect if you are a boy.

Body Shape and Size

Most boys get their first growth spurt between the ages of 11 and 13 years. Some boys start a little earlier, and some boys start a little later. During the growth spurt, you will start getting taller and bigger.

One of the first parts of your body to grow will be your feet. The bones in your feet grow much faster than the other bones in the body. Your feet may reach full size much before the rest of you. You may feel as if you are suddenly clumsy – it is because your feet are much larger than they were a while ago. Be patient! It will take some time for the rest of your body to catch up.

Some bones in your body will grow more and faster than others, and this will cause your body shape to change. For instance, your shoulders will grow a great deal, whereas your hips may only grow a little. In comparison to your broad shoulders, your hips may seem very narrow. Your arms and legs will grow faster than your vertebral column (backbone), so your legs may appear long compared to your chest or the trunk of your body. As a result of these changes, your body shape will be much different from that of a little boy.

Your muscles will also start developing, especially in your arms and legs. As these muscles develop, you will get stronger. Your chest will also get bigger and wider as muscles and some fat build up there. Many boys may notice that their breasts and nipples change during adolescence. The nipples may grow a little bit bigger and the rings around the nipples may get larger and darker.

Some boys find that their breasts swell and become tender. A few adolescent boys have a lot of swelling, which makes them feel worried that they are going to grow big breasts like women. Don't worry. This is perfectly normal. The hormones secreted by the endocrine glands in your body stimulate this swelling and tenderness. It may take a year or even a year and a half, but the swelling will diminish when your endocrine glands stop producing so many hormones. The body is mounting hormone production to transform a boy into a grown up adult man, and as a result, the nipple areas get slightly swollen and tender. The period when this normally happens is around the age 14 to 17.

While these changes are happening, be patient with yourself. Know that your body is just fine, and you are absolutely normal. Even if you are not growing as fast as many of your friends, there is nothing to worry about. You are definitely going to grow. It is just a matter of time. When and how much you grow is mainly determined by the characteristics you genetically inherit from your parents. Even if you start growing very late, you might land up being taller than many boys of your age who began their growth spurt earlier than you.

ACNE (Pimples)

During adolescence, sebaceous glands (oil glands) within the skin grow larger and begin producing more sebum, a white, oily substance that keeps the skin smooth, moist and elastic. The sebum can get backed up in the ducts of the enlarged sebaceous glands and cause pimples. Pimples can get infected, resulting in swollen, red, pus-filled glands. The infection may break through the walls of the ducts, causing a more severe acne problem.

Cracking of the Voice

Your changing voice is another definite sign that you are going through adolescence. The voice invariably starts changing after your growth spurt has begun, usually close to the age of 14 or 15.

The first sign that your voice is changing is often a sudden squeak or cracking of the voice while you are speaking. Some boys find it very embarrassing when their voice cracks, particularly because it is unpredictable. Their voice is normal one minute, but the next moment it is high-pitched and squeaky. Even if your voice cracks a lot, don't worry about it. This is just a passing phase. Like other changes during adolescence, it is absolutely normal.

Some boys do not notice very much when their voice starts changing. It happens more gradually in them.

Your voice becomes deeper and lower during adolescence because of a hormone called testosterone. Testosterone causes the larynx (voice box) to grow larger in size. As your vocal cords grow longer and thicker, your voice gets deeper and lower.

When the larynx grows larger during adolescence, it starts sticking out at the front of the throat. This is called an Adam's apple. A girl's larynx does not grow as much as a boy's does. That is why boys have Adam's apples. Most girls do not have Adam's apples, but some do. It is normal either way.

Once your voice has changed, you will probably start growing a mustache and beard. Beards grow rather slowly for the first few years, so the hair will appear light at first and grow heavier and darker as you get older.

Appearance of Body Hair, Pubic Hair and Facial Hair

At adolescence, the normal pattern of body hair growth starts with pubic and/or axillary hair. Boys will notice hair at the base of the penis. Some may detect pubic hair as early as nine and half years of age or as late as age fourteen. During this developmental stage, pubic hair may gradually darken and may become coarse and more curly.

When pubic hair begins to grow, boys may worry about small bumps that may appear at the base of the penis and on the scrotum. These bumps are normal. Boys will soon notice tiny hairs growing through these bumps. There may be other bumps as well, but these will consist of oil and perspiration, a sign that the sweat glands and sebaceous glands are active. These bumps are normal too.

The next area to grow hair is the legs, then the abdomen and the chest, one after the other. The area around the coccyx (tail end of the vertebral column) can grow hair quite early in adolescence, while hair on the rest of the back follows much later. Facial hair is variable in its growth pattern, usually growing after the first appearance of abdominal or chest hair. Upper arm hair grows quite late in the process and forearm hair is the most widely variable in the age at which growth occurs. Forearm hair can grow at any time from about the age of 14 to 25. It can grow before or after chest, abdominal or facial hair.

The first facial hairs usually appear between the ages of 14 and 16. Some boys develop facial hair at a younger age, while others do not do so until they are 20. Initially, they may be only slightly dark in colour, and there may not be very many of them. As you mature, your facial hair will get thicker, fuller and more deeply coloured. Men who hardly had any hair at the age of 20 may have a full beard and mustache by age 30. Also, the facial hair may or may not be the same colour as the hair on your head.

Your Private Parts

During adolescence, your penis will also begin to grow larger. You may wonder how large your penis will end up being. Soft (flaccid) adult penises are usually between 2.5 and 4 inches in length. Most erect adult penises vary from four to seven inches long, but some may be even shorter or longer.

A lot of adolescent boys spend a lot of time thinking and worrying about their penis size, such as – "Is it too small? Why does it curve that way? Is there something wrong with it?" Studies have shown that most adolescent boys either think their penises are too small or at least wish theirs were longer. The size is invariably thought to be the parameter for one's manliness and one's ability to satisfy his partner. First of all, the woman's satisfaction does not depend on the size of the penis. On the contrary, too big a penis can be a problem, as it could hurt the partner. Besides, only the outer 1/3rd of the woman's vagina (approximately two inches) is sensitive to sexual stimuli. So it doesn't matter to a woman how deep one reaches during the intercourse. If an erect penis is even two inches, which is usually the case with most men, it is enough to satisfy his woman. It is not the size, but what you do with what you have, that truly counts.

In men too, only the glans-penis (the front portion) is sensitive to erotic sensations. The shaft behind the glans is incapable of feeling erotic sensations. So the pleasure of the male partner too, does not depend on the entire length of the penis, but depends only on the sensitivity (and not the size) of the glans-penis.

A common mistaken belief that a flaccid penis gains in size on erection, in proportion to its flaccid size, causes this fear. The fact is that, though all penises are different in their flaccid state, they become much more similar in size, when they get erect. Also, one tends to find his penis small as it is always seen from above, as against that of others, which is observed from the side or from the front. The different angles from which the penis is viewed also makes the penis appear small or big, as the case may be.

> Peyronie's disease (also known as fibrous cavernositis or plastic induration of the penis), first described by French doctor Francois de la Peyronie in 1743, is characterised by the formation of an inflexible, fibrous plaque or hardened scar tissue (fibrosis) that develops beneath the skin of the penis (in the sheath of the corpus cavernosum) that causes pain, curvature, and distortion, usually during erection. Penile deformity may be severe enough to make penetration during sexual intercourse either difficult or even impossible.
>
> The treatment choices for patients with Peyronie's disease are very limited. The objective of treatment is mainly to maintain normal sexual function and relieve pain. Invariably, surgery is the only effectual treatment, and as Peyronie's disease may simply resolve by itself, doctors often suggest waiting for one or two years before going for this option. The non-surgical treatment should be implemented within six months of the onset of the symptoms and before the plaque has calcified.

Hanging behind and below your penis is the scrotum. The scrotum is like a sac or bag of a special skin that carries the testicles where sperms are produced from puberty to old age. During adolescence your testicles will get bigger and will hang lower. Usually, one testis hangs lower than the other. Testicles are very sensitive, that is why it is recommended to wear jock straps or protective cups while playing contact sports. The skin of the scrotum is a bit hairy and oily. It is prone to collect dirt, which may then start to emit foul smell if it is not washed on a regular basis.

During childhood, your scrotum is invariably drawn up close to your body. But, as you go through adolescence, the scrotum begins getting looser and starts hanging lower. The scrotum hangs down because the testicles need to be kept at a temperature lower than your body temperature in order to facilitate sperm production (spermatogenesis). However, whenever you are feeling cold or frightened or feeling sexual, your scrotum will again get tighter and draw up close to your body.

The more you inform yourself about the changes happening in your body, the more comfortable you will feel with all the changes you are going through. Furthermore, being well-informed will also enable you to help boys younger than you to understand what is happening to them as they approach puberty and go through adolescence.

Practicing Good Hygiene

Whether you are circumcised or not, it is very important to wash and clean the penis and scrotum every day while bathing; just as you wash every other part of your body. You should also wash the area between the scrotum and the thighs, and even in between your buttocks.

If you are not circumcised, you need to retract (roll back) the foreskin and gently clean the area underneath. You may notice that at the base of the glans penis there are tiny bumps. These bumps are glands that produce a whitish creamy substance called smegma. Smegma facilitates the prepuce (foreskin) to slide back smoothly over the glans. However, if excessive smegma collects beneath the foreskin, it can produce a foul smell and an infection. It is very important to keep the area under the foreskin clean at all times.

Erections

Ordinarily the penis is soft (flaccid) and hangs down. Erection happens when more blood flows into the penis than usual and less blood flows out. This makes the penis become bigger, harder and erect and it starts standing out from the body.

An erect penis may stand out at various angles, or it may stand nearly straight up. When erect, the penis may be straight or it may curve to the left, to the right, or some other way. No matter what the angle is, it is perfectly normal.

When your penis is erect, you will notice that you are not able to urinate easily because a muscle closes the bladder off. You may have to wait till the erection diminishes before you can urinate comfortably.

An erection can happen when you are aroused by a sexual thought, feeling, fantasy, or by the sight or memory of someone you find sexually attractive or when the penis is touched stroked or caressed. Though rarely, erection can also be caused by extreme fear or anxiety. It is also very common for adolescent boys to wake up from sleep with an erection in the morning. During your sleep in the night, your penis will possibly get erect and then go down about five to seven times. This may or may not be accompanied by a sexual dream or feelings. This is extremely common, normal and healthy.

Erection occurs in males of all ages, including newborn babies and even very old men. Sometimes adolescent boys worry that they are having erections too often. They may get disturbed by frequent erections in classrooms, while travelling or when they are watching a movie or television. Sometimes there could be an obvious reason for the erection to happen – probably you are sitting or standing next to someone you find attractive. At other times, however, there could be an erection for no obvious reason. There is nothing to worry! You are simply normal, healthy and under the influence of hormones. It can be embarrassing if you get an erection in the classroom or in any other public place, but remember, most of the time you are the only one who is aware of it.

Sometimes boys propagate that they must have sexual intercourse to control these erections. This is completely untrue. It is only a myth that some boys deliberately spread as an excuse for indulging in sex. Getting an erection is not at all a sign that you need to have sex!

Ejaculation

When you reach puberty, you may start noticing that a different fluid spurts out of the erect penis if you get sexually excited. It appears milky in colour and is sticky. This is semen. The sexual pleasure that you experience when you come (when the semen spurts out) is called orgasm or climax. The squirting of the semen is called ejaculation. It is not the same as urinating.

Semen contains sperms. The sticky transparent fluid that oozes out of the penis before ejaculation is called 'pre-ejaculate' or 'pre-cum'. Pre-cum can contain sperms and can cause pregnancy. Note that you cannot ejaculate and urinate at the same time.

Remember that you do not have to ejaculate every time you have an erection. If you simply wait, the erection can go down on its own, without causing any harm to you.

The ejaculate (semen) is made up of two things. About 10 per cent of the ejaculate are millions of sperms, which are the male reproductive cells. Sperms are so small (about 50 microns) i.e. 0.05 millimeter [1 millimeter = 1000 microns], that you cannot see them unless you have a microscope. If you see them under the microscope, you would see that each sperm has an oval head, a middle piece and a long tail.

The other 90 per cent of the ejaculate is a sticky, whitish liquid. 60 per cent of this are secretions of seminal vesicles, and 30 per cent are secretions of the prostate gland. These secretions provide the medium for sperms to swim, and it also provides nourishment for the sperms and keeps them alive and active.

Sperms are produced (spermatogenesis) in the seminiferous tubules inside the testicles. When a man ejaculates, the sperms (10 per cent) mix with secretions from the seminal vesicles (60 per cent) and prostate gland (30 per cent), and this combined fluid (semen) passes through the pair of tubes called the vas deferens, into the urethra, and comes out of the urethral opening at the tip of the penis.

It may seem that a lot of semen comes out of the penis during ejaculation. But in actuality, it is only about a teaspoonful

(3 to 5 ml.). In each ejaculation a normal male releases around 60 to 360 million sperms. Each one of those sperms can make a girl/woman pregnant. With about 60 to 360 million sperms being ejaculated in one ejaculation, you can see how easy it is to impregnate a girl.

Some boys worry that a condom may not be able to hold all these 60 to 360 million sperms. But sperms are extremely small, and therefore, a condom can hold them all, provided it is used correctly. Also remember that it is a myth that too much semen or sperms can accumulate or build pressure in your body. Your body is an impeccably tuned machine. Your body has it own ways to get rid of excess sperms and semen: one of them is nocturnal emissions (nightfall/wet dreams).

Some boys also worry that if they ejaculate semen too often, the amount of semen in their body will get diminished or finished. They worry that they may run out of sperms/semen and will not have an adequate amount when they require it for reproduction. This can never happen. A man is capable of producing sperms and semen from the start of puberty until his dying day.

If a boy/man is infected with HIV, a few drops of semen will also contain thousands of the HIVs (the virus that is responsible for AIDS).

Wet Dreams (Nocturnal Emission, Nightfall)

Boys/men sometimes release semen during sleep. This is commonly known as wet dreams, nightfall or nocturnal emission. It is a normal, natural and uncontrollable response to sexual tension that gets built up within the body. At the age of

12-13, the testes in boys start producing sperms. At this age boys start developing sexual attraction towards girls, and start discharging semen during sleep. This discharge is invariably accompanied by sexual dreams. This is a normal, natural, involuntary and uncontrollable response to sexual tension that gets built up within the body due to sex hormones. There is no reason to feel worried, frightened or guilty about a wet dream. It happens with all boys/men and is not a disease. It is completely harmless and has no ill effect on one's health or manhood.

A normal boy/man produces at least 20 thousand sperms every minute; and the same number of old sperms die every minute. With this rate of production (spermatogenesis), one needs an outlet. Either one can ejaculate (through intercourse or masturbation) or then a wet dream will take place through the body naturally.

For many adolescent boys, the first wet dream is the first time semen comes out of their penis. They may probably wake up and find a wet patch on their clothes or in the bed. If you do not know anything about wet dreams, this can be confusing and disturbing. You may think that you have wet your bed or that you are bleeding or ill. But you can see that the fluid is slimy and whitish, not like urine or blood.

Wet dreams happen only during sleep. During the day if you nap, you possibly may have a wet dream, but most adolescent boys get wet dreams at night when they are asleep. Many boys who wake up to notice that they have ejaculated, remember that they were dreaming about something sexual. But you can have a nocturnal emission even if there is no sexual dream.

Many adolescent boys find wet dreams embarrassing. But

remember that wet dreams are normal and extremely common during adolescence and nothing to feel ashamed about. Not every adolescent boy experiences wet dreams, but most do. For some boys, the start of wet dreams is a major event – something they feel good about. Other boys are not happy with the same. Once again, it is perfectly normal to feel differently about it.

Some adolescent boys have unkind friends who tease them or laugh at them about their wet dreams. It is incorrect to tease someone about it as wet dreams are normal and natural.

You cannot stop yourself from nocturnal emissions. They are a way for your body to make room for new sperms being produced in your testicles. Having wet dreams does not mean that you must have sex – it is a myth.

What You Must Know about Masturbation

Self-stimulation of the genital organs for sexual pleasure is called masturbation. It is a physiologically harmless activity. Contrary to common beliefs, it is not a hazardous, corrupt or sinful activity either for men or for women. It is natural and normal. Most boys and many girls discover masturbation during their adolescence and practice it frequently. It is harmless and has no ill effects on one's body (health) or sexuality – even though there are many myths and misconceptions that warn of dangers. As a matter of fact, it is a safe and simple method of relieving sexual tension. However, the feeling of guilt, shame, worry, and conflict associated with masturbation can be detrimental to one's emotional health and self-esteem.

There is absolutely no numerical safety limit to how many times in a day a person should or can practice masturbation. It is a matter of concern only when masturbation becomes a continuous preoccupation and is so frequent that it significantly starts interfering with other aspects of the person's life. For instance, if a young man/woman defocuses from his/her career or academics or stops socialising because all s/he wants to do is masturbate, s/he may lose out on career opportunities and/or become socially withdrawn, which can create its own problems. Otherwise, pleasuring oneself through masturbation is absolutely safe.

Some people do not want to masturbate for cultural, religious or even personal reasons. This is absolutely fine too. If one is not comfortable with masturbation, one can still have a normal, healthy and gratifying sex life.

Understanding Masturbation

There is absolutely nothing wrong if adolescent boys or girls masturbate. Practically all growing adolescent boys masturbate. It is an absolutely harmless act. It helps them to organise their sexual urges and patiently wait for a heterosexual encounter while they are still growing towards becoming responsible and mature men. **Medical science has proved that masturbation has no ill effects on one's health, growth, fertility or sexual strength. It is only when the child is made to feel either guilty or fearful about the act, that it weakens them psychologically and affects their self-image.**

Many adults have a certain bias about sexual expression, which fills them with disgust. There is nothing disgusting about selfpleasuring (through masturbation) in one's privacy without involving anyone else. At the age when secondary sexual characteristics are developing in boys as well as girls as an inevitable process of nature, they can find no better outlet than masturbation to vent their sexual urges. Such behaviour is a manifestation of them growing independent, which is a signal to parents that they are no more your baby-boys or baby-girls dependant on you for all their needs. Parents need to learn to respect their children's growing independence and individuality and love them for being normal, growing, independent individuals.

Masturbation Is Considered Abnormal or Harmful Only in the Following Situations:

- If it is done in front of others
- If proper hygiene is not maintained during or after the act
- If it is done in a manner that can cause injury to the organ
- If it becomes an obsession and starts affecting other aspects of one's life like career, education, relationships etc.
- If it is chosen over intercourse in married couples, even when the spouse is available and willing to have intercourse.

Masturbation is common during adolescence. It is necessary that we actively educate children about masturbation, while explaining to them that it is a natural form of release for pent-up sexual tension in the absence of a sexual partner. Boys need to be given the example of the pressure cooker mechanism, which requires the release of steam so that there is no explosion because of accumulated steam.

This can prevent irresponsible sexual experimentation, which results in unwanted pregnancies and sexually transmitted infections especially HIV, which leaves the teenager physically devastated and psychologically destabilised.

Benefits of Masturbation

- It helps to relieve sexual tension and helps individuals become more comfortable with their own sexuality.

- Masturbation gives the person sexual gratification while alone, without engaging in risky sexual activities with others. Thus, it does not carry the risks of unwanted pregnancy or sexually transmitted infections.

- Through masturbation, an individual can recognise and learn how s/he likes to be touched and pleasured. Once in a committed sexual relationship, the person can share this information with his/her partner to enhance pleasure and satisfy each other.

- Masturbation with the stop-start technique (withholding stimulation just prior to ejaculation, then stimulating oneself again once the orgasmic feeling is subsided) can help men improve their ejaculatory control.

NOTE: In adult committed couples, it is important that partner sex be the mutually accepted norm, and not individual masturbation, because penetrative physical intimacy is existentially the culmination of emotional intimacy, and thus crucial to sustain a mature and healthy man-woman relationship.

ADOLESCENT CHANGES IN GIRLS

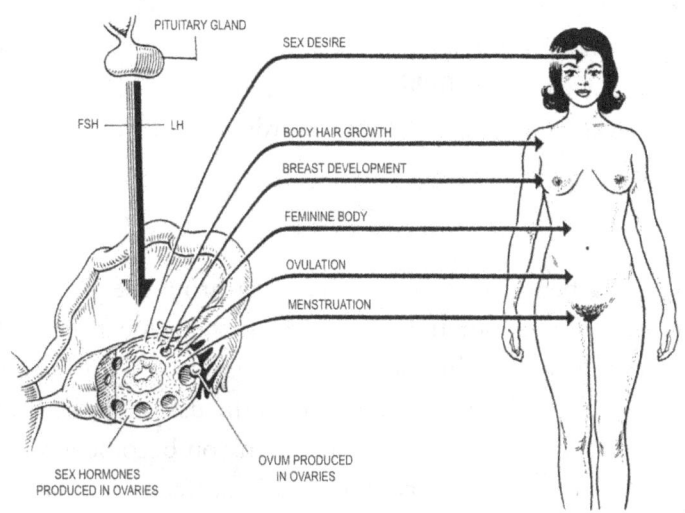

Female Secondary Sex Characteristics

The Changing Body

Most girls start growing rapidly around the age of 10 to 11 years old; however, a little earlier or later than this age is normal too.

One of the first parts of your body to grow will be your feet. The bones in your feet grow much faster than the other bones in the body. You may still be quite short, but find that your feet are suddenly quite large. There is no cause for worry, as the rest of your body catches up soon. The body grows at its own pace, in varying growth spurts.

Your arms and legs may start growing faster while your spine (vertebral column) grows more slowly.

Another noticeable change is that your hips start growing bigger. The hip bones get larger, and fatty tissue builds on the thighs, hips and buttocks. As your hips become wider, in comparison, your waist will start looking narrow and your body will have a rounder, fuller, more feminine (womanly) shape, thus indicating your movement towards being a young woman.

Breasts

Some girls begin to develop breasts at around eight or nine years of age, but others might develop them much later. The development of the breasts in girls is induced by a hormone called oestrogen. The oestrogen causes the tissues in the breasts to start growing so that some day, when you become a mother, you will be able to produce milk and breastfeed your baby.

Before your breasts begin to form, the nipples will start getting larger and stand out more prominently than before. Another change you may notice is that the ring of skin around the nipple (the areola) starts getting darker in colour and grows larger. You will also see tiny bumps appearing in the areola. These bumps are oil producing Montgomery's glands, which are normal. They are also referred to as areolar glands and tubercles. When a woman delivers a baby, the Montgomery's glands produce an oily substance that helps protect the nipple from prolonged exposure to wetness when the baby is breastfeeding.

As the nipples and areola get bigger and darker, the breasts start growing fuller and larger. While these changes are happening, you may notice that your breasts feel sore. It can even be painful if they are squeezed or touched roughly. This feeling of soreness is normal in the growing phase.

The skin surfaces of the nipples are richly supplied with special nerves that are sensitive to certain stimulus. On stimulation, these nerves quickly send messages to the smooth muscle in that region to contract. When the muscle contracts, the nipple gets stiffer, producing a nipple erection. The stimulus for nipple hardening can be physical – a loosely fitting garment that rubs or moves over the nipple, or it can be an exposure to a drop in outside temperature. It can also be a psychological stimulus, like thinking, imagining or fantasising about something sexual or sensual. If the erection of the nipples makes you self-conscious, then wearing a firmer, thicker, and more supportive brassiere and slightly warmer clothing could help.

Some girls' breasts grow very slowly, while for others the growth is pretty fast. On an average, for the breasts to develop fully, it takes around four years; but some girls' breasts develop amply in less than a year, while other girls' can take as many as six years to develop theirs. All these variations are normal, therefore, one must not be overconcerned about the pace of development.

Breasts can also vary in shape and size. The shape and size of your breasts are determined by the genetic traits that you have inherited from your parents. The size also depends on the amount of fatty tissue in the breasts. There is practically nothing you can do about the way your breasts appear. No exercise can actually augment or reduce your breast size. Exercises work by building up your muscles, and there are no muscles in the breasts. Furthermore, one must know that all breast sizes (big and small) are equally fine for feeding babies. Moreover, one must not connect one's self-esteem to breast size, as everyone's physical attributes are unique.

You must also know that invariably breasts grow unevenly. One breast may become a little bigger than the other one. In fact, no woman has both her breasts that are exactly the same size, but ordinarily this dissimilarity is not noticeable. The shapes of the nipples also vary widely. Some women's nipples instead of pointing out, turn inwards, and literally get sunk into the areola. This is known as inverted nipples.

Different cultures regard breasts differently. In some tribes and old cultures, it is acceptable for women to go bare breasted. In most of the other cultures, going bare breasted would be considered indecent and unacceptable.

Most girls come to like their breasts and see it as a sign of maturing. This is a healthy view towards one's body. However, there are some girls who feel embarrassed when their breasts begin to grow.

Some girls feel awkward about their growing breasts because none of their friends have started to develop breasts. They lose their upright posture and sink in their chests. Others feel awkward if their breasts are smaller than other girls around them. Remember, that the pace of growth varies, and one needs to welcome one's own unique pattern and enter gracefully into womanhood.

It would be prudent and sensible to not tease others about their breasts and any other physical attributes. People who tease others simply display their immaturity. It is best to ignore them!

Caring for your breasts: There are a few things you should know about taking care of your breasts. It is perfectly normal to have some hair around your nipples. You should never pluck the hair that grows around your nipples. This can cause an injury and infection. A few girls can sometimes have a little discharge coming from their nipples. Though not very common, this is normal. However, if the discharge has blood in it or is brownish or greenish in colour, you must see your doctor, as this could be a sign of an infection.

Remember, taking care of your breasts also consists of making sure no one touches them without your consent and against your wish. Boys and men commonly find women's breasts very appealing. But no one should be allowed to touch you against your wish. Also remember, touching and fondling your breasts can be sexually arousing and this might provoke you to go further than you really want to go at a very vulnerable age. Therefore, choose to say a firm 'NO' to touching of your breasts by anyone.

Brassiere (Bras): If you have very small or very firm breasts, you may not need to wear a brassier for a while. As your breasts grow bigger, you will feel more comfortable wearing a brassier that provides support to your growing breasts. Breasts tend to bounce when you walk, run, play or dance. A well fitting brassier can minimize this movement. Some adolescent girls feel self-conscious about their breasts. Wearing a brassier can help them to feel more comfortable, both physically and psychologically.

Many women discover their brassier size simply by trying on different sizes to see which one fits well and feels most comfortable. Other women take measurements to figure out the right size of the brassier.

To take the measurements for your brassier, you need to know your chest size and your cup size. First, measure around your chest, just under your breasts, to get the correct chest size.

Then measure around the fullest part of your breasts to know your cup size. If the difference between your chest and cup measurement is less than 2.5 cms, you need a Cup A. If the difference is between 2.5 to 5 cms, you need a Cup B, and if the difference is more than 5 cms, you need Cup C.

It is advisable to avoid using a brassier when you sleep at night for the health and hygiene of the breasts.

BREAST SELF-EXAMINATION

Breast cancer is the most common malignancy in women (current statistics estimate that one of every ten women in America will develop it). Amongst all cancers in women, the fatality rate in breast cancer is second highest. Since early detection makes it much easier to treat breast cancer successfully, breast self-examination is the first and best line of defence. Approximately four out of every five breast lumps so detected turn out to be a cyst or some other benign (non-cancerous) lesion. However, if a lump is detected, it is essential to determine as quickly as possible if it is cancerous or not.

Self-examination is recommended for all women from the age of 18 onwards. The best time to perform breast self-examination, is within a week after each menstrual period ends. Women who menstruate very irregularly, or who are pregnant, or who no longer menstruate, should select a particular day (the first, the fifteenth, payday) of each month to perform the examination, to maintain a regularity and discipline of the self examination to detect a lump early.

There are two parts to the self-examination: inspection (observing) and palpation (feeling). Inspection is performed in front of a mirror, first with the arms at the sides and then with both hands clasped behind the head and the hands pressed forward. Look for changes in size or shape, sores or scaling on the nipple or areola, discharge from the nipple, change in position of one or both nipples, redness or other skin discoloration, inward puckering or dimpling of the skin or nipple, enlargement of skin pores or any other change from the previous appearance. Next, place the hands on the hips and lean slightly towards the mirror, pulling shoulders and elbows forward; this contracts the muscles of the chest wall, making dimpling more obvious.

Palpation is done in two positions, first standing and then lying down. Standing-preferably in the bath or shower because it is easier to feel when the skin is wet and slippery. Raise the right arm high, and with the left hand, with fingers flat, gently explore the right breast in a clockwise motion. Feel for any unusual lump, mass, knot, thickening, area of tenderness, or any other change from the previous examination. Then repeat the process for the other breast. Gently squeeze each nipple and look for a discharge, if any.

Lying down, place the right hand behind the head and a small pillow or folded towel under the right shoulder. Then examine the right breast with the left hand, with fingers flat and close together, pressing gently in small circular motions around the breast as though it were the face of a clock. Begin at the outermost top edge of the breast and keep circling to examine every part of the breast, including the nipple. Then repeat the process for the other side.

Ideally, a systematic examination by a woman of her own breast in order to detect any abnormalities should be carried out every month, but if one forgets, it is better to do it occasionally than not at all.

Pubic Hair

As with breast development, the development of pubic hair occurs in stages. At the outset, fine, silky pubic hair grows along the midline of the outer labia. This is followed by hair growth that extends upward and sideways from the midline. Then the hair begins to cover the mons pubis (the layer of fatty tissue that protects the pubic bone). The adult stage consists of the growth of hair into a wider area. During development, pubic hair gradually thickens and may become coarse and curly.

Girls may begin to develop pubic hair around the age of 9, with the average age of development occurring around 11 years. Remember that a variation in the period when girls go through these stages, is normal.

Nature has provided pubic hair for a purpose. Pubic hair provides a protective cover on the genitalia. It acts like a cushion and helps to hold the genital odour. The genital odour may or may not be consciously perceived always and by everyone. However, irrespective of its conscious perception, it is present as a part of nature's mating instinct, and acts as a stimulus to arouse the mate.

It is not advisable to remove pubic hair permanently. Excessive growth of pubic hair is not helpful either, as it may cause excessive perspiration, keeping the genital area damp and unclean, causing fungal infections and parasitic infestations.

Removing pubic hair with the razor can cause injury. Using depilatory creams can cause skin irritation, burning and thus an invitation to skin infections. Therefore, the most recommended method is to simply trim the pubic hair once in three months with a pair of common household scissors, taking care to not injure yourself.

Genitals

During adolescence a girl's genitals go through a major transformation. Even before the noticeable breast development takes place, the tissues of the vulva start responding to increased hormonal (oestrogen) levels. Her labia majora, labia minora, clitoris and hymen often grow in size. Not only does the size of a girl's genitalia change, but also the color, shape and texture changes too.

If adolescent girls observe their genitals they may become concerned about these changes. They may feel that they have disfigured their genitals due to self-pleasuring, and now anyone who sees their genitals will know that they pleasure themselves. They may also feel that they are being punished for having sexual feelings, thoughts and sensations. It is for these reasons that adolescent girls should be made aware that these are normal changes. They must know that these changes (whether physical or psychological) are necessary, normal and natural in order to free them from any feelings of inadequacy or a negative self-image.

Hygiene for Girls

The vulva and anus should be washed regularly and kept dry.

After bathing, one should wear clean and dry cotton panties. Nylon panties are best avoided, as they retain moisture and heat, which causes the growth of bacteria, fungi and parasites. If you cannot find cotton panties, wear ones that have a cotton lining.

It is a good idea to avoid sharing towels with your friends or other family members as these can transmit infections from one person to another.

After you pass urine or defecate, you must always **clean yourself by starting from the front of your private parts backwards** towards the anus. Whether you use water or toilet tissue paper to clean yourself, make sure you **avoid wiping forwards**. If you wipe forwards, you risk pulling micro-organisms from the anus to the urethra and vagina. This can give you a urinary tract infection or vaginal infection.

One should **never try to wash inside the vaginal canal** unless a doctor instructs you to do so. Some girls and women try to wash inside the vagina with soaps. Some women spray the area with a perfume or deodorant. This is not only not necessary, but can actually be harmful, as soaps, perfumes and deodorants can alter the normal fluids inside the vaginal canal and can cause irritation to the lining inside the vagina.

All you need to do is gently wash the outer genital area daily with clean water and bath soap.

It is a good practice to observe your vaginal discharge regularly and notice how it changes during your monthly cycle, so that you can identify any unusual signs or changes. If you observe closely, you will notice that the vaginal discharge is not always the same. Sometimes it may be a bit whitish like egg white, and at other times it may be clear. When you are ovulating, it may become more clear and slippery. A woman's vaginal fluids also alter when she is sexually aroused.

If the vaginal discharge becomes thicker or heavier, changes colour to yellow, green or brown, or causes itching or a burning sensation in the genitalia, then it is suggestive of an infection. Foul smelling vaginal discharge, irritation, pain, burning, itching or bleeding, from the vagina, when you are not menstruating, are a sign that you need to be examined for infection. If you experience any of these signs and symptoms, you must consult a qualified gynaecologist.

Masturbation in Girls

Masturbation gives a girl/woman the opportunity to explore her body while giving her a sense of sexual independence. It allows a woman the opportunity to experience sexual pleasure without depending on a partner. It helps her to release pent up sexual tension whenever she wishes to. Masturbation can be really empowering for a woman as it gives her better control over her body and sexuality. For many healthy and normal women, masturbation is their primary and only means of experiencing sexual satisfaction, as they either do not have a partner for partner-sex, or their partner is not motivated to have sex in a way that the woman can enjoy sexual pleasure too. Some women experience their most intense orgasms while masturbating as they can provide to themselves the appropriate physical and mental stimulation they require without being overconcerned about the wants of their partner. Masturbation is extremely beneficial to women throughout their life. While a woman may not always have a sex partner, she will always have herself.

Female Nocturnal Orgasm

In 1953, Dr. Alfred Kinsey, PhD, the famous sexuality researcher, found that nearly 40 per cent of the 5,628 women he interviewed, experienced at least one 'nocturnal orgasm' (orgasms during sleep), or 'wet dream,' by the time they were forty-five years old. A smaller study published in the Journal of Sex Research in 1986 found that 85 per cent of the women who had experienced nocturnal orgasms had done so by the age of twenty-one. Women who experience orgasms during sleep usually have them several times a year.

Dr. Alfred Kinsey defined a female nocturnal orgasm as sexual arousal during sleep that awakens one to perceive the experience of orgasm. Women who do not experience orgasms in their sleep, or who do not know whether or not they have had them, are perfectly normal too. It is easier for men to identify their wet dreams because of the ejaculatory evidence. As against that, vaginal secretions could very well be a sign of sexual arousal even without orgasm.

Chapter 11

MENSTRUATION CYCLE: A COMPLETE GUIDE

Discussing the importance of educating girls about the monthly period

Most girls begin having menstrual periods (also called monthly periods) between the age of 10 and 16. Menarche (the beginning of menstruation) is a sign at puberty, that major hormonal changes have taken place inside a young woman's body. It is also a sign that she could now get pregnant if a man performs sexual intercourse with her.

During puberty, the Follicle Stimulating Hormone and Luteinizing hormone secreted in the pituitary gland causes the ovaries to mature and start releasing an ovum (egg) each month. Every girl is born with two to four lakh potential ova (eggs) in her ovaries. The ova (eggs) are so small that you cannot see them without a microscope.

As the ovaries mature, the uterus also matures, and a new soft lining starts to form in the uterus each month. This soft lining is the preparation to receive a fertilised ovum (zygote) in the uterus. This preparation takes place every month after puberty. If there is no zygote (fertilised ovum), the lining of the uterus breaks down and gets expelled out of the vagina through the cervix. This is called the menstrual period or menstruation. Because this new soft uterine lining is made of blood vessels, it is called menstrual blood.

For the first few months or even years, the menstruation cycle of most girls is quite irregular. They cannot estimate when they will get their periods. There appears to be no pattern to it, and they may also go several months without even getting their periods. This is normal too!

Even when the menstrual cycle is regular, its length varies for different girls and women. For some, the cycle is as short as 21 days or even shorter. For others, it is as long as 35 days or even longer. The average menstrual cycle is 28 days.

Let us look at the 28-day menstrual cycle of the average healthy woman –

On day **1** a woman begins to bleed. For the next three to five days her body will be shedding the lining from the walls of her uterus. At the same time, her body has perceived that there is going to be no conception (pregnancy) that month, and that it needs to start preparing another ovum (egg). One ovum now starts maturing in one of her ovaries. Shortly thereafter, her uterus starts to build up another fresh lining.

Sometime around day **14** or **2** weeks after she started bleeding i.e. halfway through the cycle – the ovum is released from the ovary (ovulation), and it starts to float down the fimbrial end of the fallopian tube. This is the most fertile period of her monthly cycle, when the possibility of getting pregnant is maximum. The ovum spends a few days inside the fallopian tube, and during this time if it unites with a sperm there, it can get fertilised and the woman could get pregnant.

If the ovum does not get fertilised, it goes into the uterine cavity, down through the cervix and vaginal canal, and passes out of her body. This happens around day 20. About a week later, when her body recognises that there has been no conception, the lining of her uterus will begin to shed as menstrual bleeding and the menstrual cycle begins all over again. This is how the menstrual cycle works.

Often girls/women presume that their most fertile period (unsafe period) is right in the middle of their cycle. This is true only for women with a 28-day menstrual cycle. For girls/women with shorter or longer cycles, the fertile period will not be in the middle of the cycle. This is because ovulation occurs about 14 days before the next menstrual bleeding starts. This means that a woman who has a 21-day menstrual cycle perhaps ovulates around day 7, whereas a woman with a 35-day cycle ovulates around day 21.

The menstruation cycle is particularly irregular during adolescence, and can also get affected by physical work, travel, stress, emotional disturbances and other changes in your life. Thus, it is difficult to assess when the safe period or unsafe period will occur. Often girls get pregnant by mistake because they have sexual intercourse during the period that they calculate and think should be their so-called 'safe days' (the days when they think that their risk of pregnancy is minimum).

Many girls and even boys have learned about 'safe days.' However, there are absolutely no 'safe days' for pregnancy. This is because the menstruation cycle is quite unpredictable and irregular during adolescence and may be even later. Even if you feel that your periods have been regular, they can at any time become irregular. Moreover, there are no 'safe days' against sexually transmitted diseases including HIV/AIDS. You can get infected with these infections every day of the month.

Waiting for the 'safe days' is not at all a reliable way to prevent pregnancy or to protect yourself against STDs. If a person is sexually active, she should never count on these so-called 'safe days' for protection against pregnancy and against STDs, including HIV/AIDS as they are not 'safe'.

In some cultures, menstruating girls/women are considered as dirty and impure – in reality, menstrual blood is normal clean blood. However, once the menstrual blood leaves the body, bacteria can grow in it, causing it to emit an unpleasant odour. That is why good hygiene is particularly important during menstruation. During menstruation, wash yourself properly at least once a day to keep your genital area clean and dry. Never use perfumes or deodorants on your genitals as they can cause irritation.

The First Menstruation

The first menstruation is a big event in a girl's life. Many girls can recollect the exact day they started menstruating.

Menstruation signifies that your body is maturing and functioning in a new way. It also means that you can get pregnant if you have sexual intercourse. However, **menstruation does not mean that your body is now ready for sexual intercourse or for having a baby.** The vagina remains immature and small till a young woman reaches the age of 18 to 20. Moreover, the hips and pelvic bones are still developing and are likely to be too small and narrow for a normal vaginal delivery. Therefore one should responsibly wait for the entire body to be ready for childbirth before getting pregnant.

Menstruation is a sign of good health, but many girls get shocked, disturbed and unhappy when they get their first menstrual bleeding; commonly because they were not prepared for it, did not know what it was, and felt that something was wrong with their bodies. Those girls who know what to expect and whose mothers have told them about menstruation in advance, often find it easier to accept this change.

You will know that you have started menstruating when a small amount of blood comes out of your vagina. The menstrual blood does not pour like water from a tap. It dribbles slowly. Commonly, by the time you notice a feeling of unusual wetness at your vagina, your panties would have absorbed any blood that has come out, but the rest of your clothes would remain unstained. However, sometimes there may be more blood, or it may come more suddenly, or it may take you a longer time to notice the blood. If this happens to you, stay calm, cool and collected! It is definitely not your fault! You simply did not know that the bleeding was going to start. It takes every girl a while to figure out how to deal with this situation.

Keeping a Calendar

For most girls, it takes some time to get mentally used to menstruation. If you feel disturbed and unhappy about menstruation, your feelings are understandable. However, always remember that menstruation is a sign of health and maturity. You should also know that it will not last forever. Most women stop having their periods when they are in their late 40s and 50s. This is called menopause.

Many girls find it helpful to keep a diary (calendar method) of when they get their menstrual bleeding each month. You can buy a small diary or a calendar and mark on it with an 'X' – the date you start bleeding. By counting the days between the X's, you will know how long your menstrual cycle is, and how regular or irregular it is.

- Manisha, aged 18, has a regular 28-day menstrual cycle. She started to bleed on January 1st. Her next period started on January 29th. In February she started menstruating on 26th. In March she menstruated on 26th. In April she started menstruating on 24th.

  Just notice that Manisha's period started on a different date each month – even though she has a perfectly regular 28-day menstrual cycle.

Keep in mind; the calendar method is a simple way to help you prepare for your periods. However, it is certainly not a method to know when your so-called 'safe days' will be.

Discomforts Associated with Menstruation

Some girls experience extra tenderness and swelling in their breasts just before their period begins or when they ovulate. This is normal. However, it may become physically uncomfortable sometimes. The soreness in the breasts is due to hormones, which make the breast tissue retain more water than usual. Wearing a well-fitting brassier can help you feel comfortable, and eating less salt in food can help reduce the amount of water that your body is retaining. Sometimes girls may feel irritable as their breasts feel sore or their body feels bloated.

Periods can also affect your mood. Some girls/women feel irritable, depressed and even tearful before their period starts every month. This moodiness is called 'Premenstrual Syndrome' (PMS) or 'Premenstrual Tension,' and is a common problem. Try not to let it disturb you too much. Systematic relaxation techniques can be practiced to provide some relief.

Many girls experience cramps or pain in their lower abdomen during their periods. These cramps are common, normal and can easily be managed. These cramps occur because the muscles of the uterus are contracting while the uterine lining is being shed. If the pain during this time is severe, simply lie down in a comfortable position and try to relax your body by breathing in slowly and deeply. You can also gently massage your lower abdomen and back. A hot water bag placed on the lower abdomen can also give relief. Medication can also reduce the pain of menstrual cramps. However, consult your doctor before taking any medication, and take it only if the pain is unbearable.

Light physical exercise also helps in some cases to ease menstrual cramps; even though this may not be your first instinct. You might feel like resting at these times, but taking a brisk walk actually helps some girls to deal with their cramps. Having your periods need not restrict you from doing things you enjoy, and you can remain normally active and follow your daily routine.

Menstrual cramps are normally a feature of adolescence and by the time you reach 18 years or so, they will probably not disturb you as much. Few girls have extremely painful periods. Usually these girls are the same ones who have very heavy periods.

Girls with heavy periods usually end up using many sanitary pads and yet they may stain their clothes or bed sheets. They often miss school because they bleed excessively or are in too much pain. If you are one of the few who have severe pain or bleed very heavily and if you are missing school because of your periods, you must consult a gynaecologist.

There is good medical treatment available for severe menstrual problems; so you need not continue to suffer unnecessarily. Some gynaecologists prescribe hormonal tablets to relieve painful and heavy periods. These tablets make the menstrual periods more predictable and regular, and they also control the amount of blood loss during periods each month. If your doctor chooses not to give hormonal tablets to you, ask what else you can do to reduce the distress you are going through month after month. Pain medication may be prescribed for you. You should not miss your school and studies because of a problem that can easily be solved.

Some valuable tips to make your periods easier and more comfortable to go through:

- Keep track of when your periods are due so that you are not caught unaware. Always be prepared
- Always carry a sanitary pad in your school bag or purse
- Salt causes your body to retain water, especially around the time of your periods. This can add to your feeling of heaviness, irritability and depression. Thus, avoid eating excessive salt
- Drink lot of water and/or fruit juices
- Eat whole grain cereals and/or take a Vitamin B complex (particularly vitamin B6) supplement every day
- Your diet should include foods that are rich in iron, like green vegetables and other iron-rich foods. This will help you replenish the iron lost in bleeding.

Is it true that sex cures menstrual pains? Does sex during menstruation have anything to do with developing and/or contracting STDs (Sexually Transmitted Diseases)?

There is no truth whatsoever to the belief that sexual intercourse cures menstrual pains. On the contrary, intercourse during menstruation can heighten the risk of contracting sexually transmitted diseases (STDs), including HIV/AIDS. Menstrual blood is a very rich medium in which micro-organisms can grow very rapidly.

If a menstruating female has sexual intercourse with a male who is infected with an STD, she is more likely to get infected than during other times of her monthly cycle. In addition, she is likely to get a more severe infection when she is menstruating. This is because the mouth of the uterus (cervix) is wider than usual at this time to provide for the menstrual blood to flow out easily. Because of this, the micro-organisms of STD can travel up into the uterus and fallopian tubes and can cause an infection high up in the female reproductive system. This can result in infertility.

For the male, having sexual intercourse with a menstruating female is also very risky. If she is infected with HIV, her menstrual blood will be very rich in viruses (HIV).

Sanitary Products for Use During Periods

Throughout history, in all countries and all cultures, women have always menstruated and coped with it, even when none of the sanitary products that you can buy today were available.

Sanitary pads are the most commonly used product during periods by urban women. They are designed to fit precisely between your underwear and the opening of the vagina. They have strips of tape that keep them firmly attached to your panties, and your panties hold the sanitary pads close to the vaginal opening. Pads have a plastic lining to restrict leakage. If you are using sanitary pads, remember to never flush them down the toilet, as they will cause a major blockage in the drainage system. The best way to dispose of them is to wrap them in an old news paper and throw them in a dust bin.

Toilet tissue paper is another alternative. It is not very expensive. You can buy about four rolls of toilet tissue paper for the cost of one pack of sanitary pads. You can make a thick long wad of toilet tissue and place it between your underwear and your vaginal opening.

In rural India, one of the most common and the cheapest material used during periods is clean cotton rags. It is necessary to make sure that the rags are clean. One can simply cut them to fit your panty area, folding or sewing several layers of rag on top of each other. After using them once, you must wash them well and dry them in a private but sunny place. Direct sunlight kills germs and is a very good disinfectant. So, even if one does not have the money to buy expensive sanitary pads, one can use inexpensive rags, that can be washed and re-used.

Some women use tampons. Tampons are small, hard, cotton objects that are inserted into the vagina during menstruation. The compressed cotton softens as it absorbs the blood that comes into the vagina from the uterus. Attached to the tampon is a little soft cotton thread, which hangs out of the vagina. You need to pull this thread to remove the tampon. A tampon cannot get lost inside your vagina or move to another part of your body. It stays inside your vagina until you pull it out.

When you first insert a tampon, let someone instruct you on how to put it in your vagina. Putting a tampon in your vagina should not be painful; but it may hurt if you are apprehensive and not relaxed.

One good thing about tampons is that once you place it in, you cannot feel them at all, so you can simply forget about the fact that you are having your periods. But tampons also require extra caution. Always wash your hands before and after inserting a tampon. You also need to change it often, because it could cause infection if it is left in your vagina for a long time. Women who use tampons change them every three or four hours, or even more often if the bleeding is heavy. Never leave a tampon inside for more than eight hours. Avoid using tampons at night because you may sleep more than eight hours.

Large amount of bacteria can develop if a tampon is left in the vagina for too long. This can cause a rare illness called 'Toxic Shock Syndrome' (TSS). Although TSS is very rare, it is very serious. If you develop high fever, vomiting, diarrhoea, and a sunburn-type skin rash while using a tampon, take the tampon out immediately and see your doctor without any delay. You can lower your risk of getting TSS by sleeping with a pad instead of a tampon.

Whatever you use (sanitary pads, toilet tissue, rags or tampons), change it frequently, as when menstrual blood gets in contact with air, it develops a musty odour. If your clothes get stained with blood, soak them in cool and salty water. Hot water causes the bloodstain to set and become permanent.

Your menstrual period is a normal and natural part of you. If you are physically and mentally prepared for it, you will not find it a big problem. You can still be active and have fun during your periods, and they need not cause you to miss school, work or play.

Some Important Instructions to Make Using Tampons Easier

- When you first use a tampon, have someone clearly instruct you on how to correctly place it in your vagina. You may ask your mother, elder sister, or another woman you trust to guide you.

- Putting a tampon in your vagina should not be painful. However, it may hurt if you are not relaxed.

- Do not use high absorbency tampons throughout your period. Do check the label to know how absorbent the tampon is.

- Change your tampon (or pad) every three to four hours to prevent an unpleasant odour and stains on your clothes.

- If you use tampons while swimming, there is less chance that the water will become tinged with menstrual flow.

- It is better to use pads instead of tampons while you sleep to avoid the risk of TSS.

- Never flush tampons (or pads) down the toilet. They will clog the toilet. Wrap them in old newspaper and put them in the dustbin.

Chapter 12

PREMARITAL SEX EDUCATION

Counselling young couples before they tie the knot

In India match making is still done on the basis of horoscopes, and religious and financial backgrounds of the two families. It is high time that we start ascertaining the compatibility of the couple on more practical and realistic grounds. This can be done by making the couple undergo premarital counselling and certain medical check-ups.

Like in Western countries, the divorce rate in our country too is steadily on the rise. On investigation, invariably the cause of divorce is found to be either a physical incompatibility or emotional incongruity between the partners. As counsellors, our personal observation has been that in 90 per cent cases the trauma of divorce can be avoided if couples undergo a counselling session and undertake certain medical investigations just before they get into matrimony. It is out of this concern that we started India's FIRST full-fledged Pre-Marriage Counselling Centre in 1997 at Mumbai.

The Necessity of Physical Check-Up before Marriage

It is necessary to know about the physical well-being of both partners before they marry, particularly about one's reproductive ability and diseases that could be transmitted sexually.

A simple semen examination of the groom-to-be, and a simple sonography examination of the uterus and ovaries of the bride-to-be, are recommended as screening tests to assess the reproductive ability of a couple.

People are fast becoming aware of HIV testing before marriage, however, the majority still does not know about the window period. If a person is infected with HIV, the blood test (Elisa test for HIV Antibodies) comes positive only after around three months. The period of initial three months, when the test comes negative is known as the Window Period. This is a dangerous period, as it gives the false impression that a person is HIV negative, and the infected person can pass on the infection to others through unprotected sex. We strongly recommend two HIV tests with a gap of three months before marriage. People are not very aware that pre-test counselling is necessary before every HIV testing, and that it is a responsible and sensitive task.

Besides HIV, it is also necessary to test for one more fatal disease that is transmitted sexually – Hepatitis-B. A carrier of Hepatitis-B appears healthy outwardly but could transmit the deadly disease to the partner through sexual contact. Syphilis, though fully treatable, is a dangerous sexually transmitted disease if undetected. It is particularly notorious as it plays hide-n-seek with the patient giving him/her false signs of self-recovery, while it is progressing in the body. Thus a VDRL test or TPHA test for syphilis is a must in all checkups before marriage.

Besides sexually transmitted diseases, it is also necessary to know whether both the partners are unknowingly carrying Thalassaemia minor traits, as it may manifest as a Thalassaemia Major child after marriage. Thalassaemia Major is a debilitating congenital disorder and no parent would like to face this nightmare.

Blood group matching before marriage is given undue importance by some ill-informed people. It carries importance only to the point, that if Rh factors of both the partners are not matching, it can be harmful for the second child of the couple. However, if such incompatibility is known beforehand, precaution could be taken to avoid any harm to the second child. An injection of **Anti D Immunoglobulin** to the mother immediately after the birth of her first child (or first abortion) is all that is required to prevent any harm to the subsequent pregnancy.

Besides the physical tests, pre-marital counselling includes helping the couple to discuss crucial issues that could become a bone of contention in their married life, e.g. family planning, religious practices and customs, beliefs, habits, financial and social values, role of in-laws, duties and responsibilities etc. During the counselling session, the couple also needs to be taught problem solving skills and the art of healthy communication.

Having done this, the couple will be able to tie the nuptial knot with more confidence and maturity, and start the new relationship on a more sound footing.

We need to have a very sincere approach towards marriage, as it is one of the most important decisions of our life. We need to prepare our young generation to tie this sacred knot with more awareness, clarity and understanding. We also need to prepare young individuals to be humanly loving, caring, respectful and considerate towards their partners. We need to give them correct and complete sex education, a healthy understanding of their new relationship and teach them the art of enjoying their freedom with responsibility. We need to make them understand the difference between male and female sexuality and feel comfortable with their own sexuality. A person can relate sexually with the other in a healthy manner only when he is comfortable with his/her own sexuality.

What Needs To Be Explained about the Sexual Relationship before Marriage

1. The necessity of sex in marriage.
2. The concept of Sexual Intercourse, that it is a peak response to sexual excitement when the erect male penis enters the female vagina and after reaching a climax of excitement ejects the semen into the vagina. This can result in conception (pregnancy).
3. Difference between male and female sexuality.
4. First night. What to expect! Myths and misconceptions about first night.
5. Addressing common concerns, anxieties, worries and misconceptions related to sex.
6. Importance of foreplay.
7. Importance of afterplay.
8. Hygiene. (Lack of proper Hygiene could be a great hindrance.)

9. Concept of male and female orgasm.
10. Contraception and planning your first child. (Lack of adequate and correct knowledge of contraception can greatly harm a sexual relationship.)
11. Importance of frank and open communication between husband and wife about their needs, preferences, likes and dislikes related to their sex life. (Love and physical desire wax and wane throughout a lifetime. This can not only be accepted but even enjoyed, if partners can communicate.)
12. Necessity of commitment of time and energy for intimacy.
13. Understanding sexual difficulties.
14. Guidelines for sex partners.
15. Pre-Menstrual Syndrome (PMS).

Importance of Sex in Marriage

Sex is one of the basic instincts in human beings, and it is powerful. Marriage is an arrangement we have created to discipline and channel this powerful instinct in us. Therefore, it is natural for us to think about our sex life, our sexual needs and fulfilment, particularly when we are married.

1. Sex is an **essential** aspect of marriage.
2. Both the partners need to be comfortable with each other. They need to **understand and value each other's sexual needs and communicate openly and clearly** about the feelings of pleasure or discomfort that the sexual activity causes.

3. Research shows that both men and women have strong and **equal sexual urges and it is the responsibility of both** to satisfy each other's needs and respect each other's moods and feelings.
4. The satisfaction or dissatisfaction in a sexual relationship between a couple contributes to the attitudes and behaviour of both partners towards each other.
5. Sexual activity is **not meant only for procreation.** It contributes to pleasure and enjoyment as well. It is also a means of intimate communication, bonding and expressing love for each other.

Physical intimacy is a significant relationship meter of a man-woman relationship. It is said that if the sex is good, then it forms only 10 per cent of the relationship, but if the sex is absent or bad then it forms 90 per cent of the relationship. In a healthy relationship, physical intimacy is built on the foundation of emotional intimacy, and there is an integration of love and sex.

It is also important for both, the man and the woman, to mutually enjoy the act of intimacy, with neither one compelling the other into any unnatural or unacceptable act. We advise you to either consult a sex counsellor to have a sex education session, or then read a reputed book on sex education, to be more informed. It is recommended to not rush into physical intimacy, but to get to know each other, feel comfortable and emotionally intimate with each other, so that such emotional intimacy naturally culminates into physical intimacy. Further, it is important for both you and your partner to freely and frankly communicate your likes and dislikes in the act of intimacy, so that it is mutually satisfying and fulfilling.

Essential Guidelines for Married Couples about their Sexual Relationship

1. Regard each other as 'equals'.
2. Always have each other's consent.
3. Never use direct or indirect force to get the consent.
4. Be clear in your communication with each other about what you want to do and do not want to do.
5. Be alert and attentive towards each other's pleasure.
6. Prevent and protect each other against any physical or emotional harm.
7. Safeguard adequately against unintended pregnancy and sexually transmitted infections.
8. Understand and accept each other's limits.
9. Be committed, faithful and honest with each other.
10. Accept responsibility for your actions.

Difference between Male and Female Sexuality

Male sexuality is body oriented. Men get sexually attracted to the body of a woman. They need not have any love for her. That is why some men go to prostitutes and are interested in seeing the woman's anatomy displayed in advertisements, movies, magazines and so on.

As against this, female sexuality is very heart oriented. The woman gets sexually attracted to a man only when she loves him. Just a handsome, muscular look may draw her attention, but is not enough for her to get sexually aroused or attracted to the man. It is said by someone that 'man gives love to get sex and woman gives sex to get love'.

However, it may be noted that all men do not carry male sexuality in them. They could be carrying a female sexuality i.e. such men would be heart centred and sensitive. They would need love as a base for a sexual relationship. Likewise, all women do not carry a female sexuality within them. Such women would be body-oriented and get sexually attracted merely by the physique of the man (thus the presence of gigolos i.e. male prostitutes and magazines displaying the bare male anatomy).

First Night

If you are getting married soon, you are probably as anxious as you are excited, especially about sex and the first night. If you know your partner well enough and have indulged in some kind of physical closeness, things might just be a smooth ride but if you are a virgin, a coy first timer, you might end up being a disaster in bed. On the other hand, if you are experienced in the art of love-making, you may have other kind of fears about being labelled loose or coming across as aggressive or having your own expectations remaining unfulfilled, especially if your partner turns out to be a virgin or has this holier-than-thou attitude and a thing about wanting a virgin bride. But, none of these can be a problem really, if you do a bit of homework, acquire all the knowledge you need to have and approach the issue with confidence, an open mind and the willingness to explore and enjoy.

In our country, 90 per cent of marriages are still arranged marriages where there is inadequate understanding, and lack of familiarity and romantic love between the partners right at the beginning. It is usually an arrangement done by two well-suited families to keep up a tradition. After such a marriage, the partners get the legal and moral permission to have sex with each other. A man with his body-oriented sexuality, who is eager to engage into sexual intercourse (as boys get sexually active around 12-14 years of age but get married almost after a decade), is likely to get blinded towards his new bride's feelings and state of mind, and might unconsciously end up forcing sex on her on the first night. The woman, feeling rather awkward, uncomfortable and exploited, might allow this forced act, as our orthodox teachings teach girls to be meek, submissive and tolerant.

The woman gets sexually aroused only if she feels emotionally close to the man, but here; he is giving her every reason to get repelled. And this is how their married life begins. Instead of love, a seed of hatred is sown. That is why we see so much pain, conflict and break-ups in marriages. We have seen many women, who have not felt loving towards their husband even once, even though they have borne children.

It is necessary for a woman to feel emotionally close to her partner to get sexually attracted to him. Arranged marriages, the way they are planned and executed, lack the opportunity and atmosphere for love to happen. Therefore, it is necessary that a couple gets adequate opportunity to get well acquainted with each other before marriage.

If you know each other well, there will be no need to tell each other that the most important thing is a good night's sleep at the end of an elaborate wedding ceremony as you are most likely to be utterly exhausted. If you are raring to go at the end of the ceremony, good for you, but the consent to consummate the marriage at that point has to be mutual. You have every right to tell your spouse if you are not up to it and it need not be a public issue. This is just between the two of you. Tradition may make it mandatory to have sex on the first night but it is better to wait and have fulfilling, love-filled sex than an awkward forced interaction, which leaves either or both partners dissatisfied and repelled.

Very often both are strangers to each other. Both are ignorant or have misconceptions about the sexual experience. Boys could carry an anxiety about their sexual performance. Girls could have the fear of pain and bleeding at the first intercourse. There is also often a fear of pregnancy. At the same time both feel that they have to live up to the first night fantasy as depicted in romantic novels and movies. With so many apprehensions, expectations and anxieties, it becomes impossible for a couple to enjoy one of the most profound experiences of their life. The best option, therefore, is to wait for a better emotional and physical state of readiness.

We strongly recommend that youngsters avoid sexual intercourse on the first night, particularly in arranged marriages. There is nothing wrong if the couple decides on their own to postpone their first sexual intercourse after the marriage till both of them are physically and emotionally relaxed, instead of rushing in to fulfil the common expectation of the first night (Suhaag Raat). They lose nothing, but they may gain a great deal of mutual love and respect, which can then become the foundation of a happy married life.

We also recommend that young couples refrain from planning their first child for at least one year after their marriage. It takes at least a year to know each other reasonably well, to get adequately adjusted to the new environment and the new family, and to assess one's physical, emotional and financial capability to parent a child.

COMMON FIRST NIGHT SEXUAL ANXIETIES

Performance Anxiety

Performance anxiety in men is common. Everyone experiences some level of performance anxiety during the first few attempts. However later on, it diminishes. If a man is in a relaxed environment and is physically and mentally at ease, and is with an equally involved and responsive partner, he will be able to engage in fulfilling sexual intercourse.

However, if a man is more focused on how well he is performing, rather than on enjoying the sensations during the sexual act, it may be difficult for him to attain or maintain an erection. This can become a vicious cycle, where the anxiety about whether or not he will have an erection becomes so severe that he is unable to have an erection, which causes more anxiety, and so forth. The way to remedy this problem is to stop spectatoring (focussing on himself), and to simply learn to relax. The more he relaxes and enjoys the experience of sensual touching, whether he has an erection or not, the more he is able to naturally get and sustain an erection.

Fear of Pain during the First Intercourse

Sex is not about performance. Sex is a continuation of the communication you have with your partner. A woman may or may not experience pain during her first sexual intercourse. Her experience depends on many factors, such as comfort level with each other, with the circumstances, the atmosphere, the level of relaxation one feels, the level of sexual arousal/excitement, the quality and duration of foreplay one has engaged in, the amount of lubrication at the vagina during penetration, the status of the hymen, the technique and position used during penetration/intromission etc.

It is not uncommon to experience some discomfort or pain during the first intercourse. It can be greatly minimised by helping each other relax, and by engaging in mutually arousing and satisfying foreplay to prepare each other for intercourse.

Anxieties Related to Hymen Rupture

Hymen is a thin membrane that covers the vagina. It may or may not be present at birth. In some women, the hymen only has some tiny openings through which menstrual blood can escape, but in others, the hymen is just a rim of tissue. Sometimes it just folds naturally along the walls of the vagina. Not every virgin has a kind of hymen that could appear to 'pop' with her first act of intercourse. It may get broken without one's knowledge while doing certain activities such as some sports or athletics. It may also get broken if one masturbates or uses tampons. If it is unbroken, a little bleeding may take place at the first intercourse, however, it cannot be regarded as a test of one's virginity. Bleeding may not happen in a virgin girl if the hymen is absent since birth or if it is ruptured without her knowledge during sports etc.

Myths about the First Night	Facts about the First Night
Sexual intercourse must happen on the very first night. If it does not happen, the marriage is invariably unsuccessful.	It is not necessary to have sexual intercourse on the first night. Success of the marriage depends on the love and understanding between the partners.
Women look forward to sexual intercourse on the very first night of the marriage.	Women look forward to understand and love their partner before being ready for sexual intercourse.
It is recommended to keep the lights on during the first night, as it helps to find the vagina during intercourse.	Women prefer to disrobe in the dark. The vagina can easily be located as a woman instinctively knows her body and can guide the man even in the dark.
Women judge the sexual prowess of a man on the basis of the size of his organ.	Women look forward to a loving and caring partner. They are least concerned about the size of the organ. Majority of women keep their eyes closed during the sexual encounter.
A woman must bleed during the first intercourse if she is virgin, as the hymen ruptures at that point.	Women may not bleed, even if it is the first experience of intercourse. The hymen may be absent since birth, or even get ruptured during sports or other physical activities.

Myths about the First Night	Facts about the First Night
Women experience pain during the first intercourse.	If there is love and understanding between the partners and if they engage in adequate, mutually pleasurable foreplay, there will not be any pain during the first intercourse.
The first intercourse needs to be performed with the man on top position. It is easier that way.	The easier way to engage in intercourse is with the woman on top position. This naturally ensures equal involvement of the woman.
Man suffers from premature ejaculation on the first night if he has masturbated before marriage.	Premature ejaculation is extremely common amongst newly married men because of the newness of the phenomenon, and not due to masturbation.
It is necessary to discuss your first night experience with either a parent, elder sibling or a married friend to check whether everything went off properly.	Never discuss your first night experience with anybody (except, a sex therapist or a counsellor, and that too only if you encounter difficulties). It is a private matter, and the sanctity of the experience must be maintained between you and your partner.

THE IDEAL SEXUAL ENCOUNTER

The ideal sexual encounter, which satisfies both man and woman, would be one in which there is adequate foreplay, and where the man does not penetrate unless the woman indicates that she is fully aroused.

Importance of Foreplay

There are three prerequisites for a satisfying foreplay. The first is genuine attraction for each other, the second is complete privacy, and the third is a state of relaxation and harmony with no negative emotions (such as fear, guilt, doubt, anxiety, anguish, distress, anger, despair or worry) clouding the moment. Besides these prerequisites, it is necessary that both the partners are in a state of good physical health without any pain, illness or malady.

Pain during intercourse is invariably due to a lack of lubrication...and a lack of lubrication is invariably due to inadequate and inappropriate foreplay before intercourse.

Foreplay is EXTREMELY important before intercourse. It should last till the partner is ready for intercourse and expresses such readiness. For those partners who are attracted to, and share affection for each other, 15-20 minutes of foreplay is usually adequate. If the relationship is strained due to any reason, any length of foreplay may not be adequate, as the prerequisite of relaxation and harmony between partners, is absent.

Remember to be gentle during foreplay. Involve your partner lovingly and sensually, and strictly avoid aggressive touching and squeezing. Only when she is ready and well-lubricated, should you engage in intercourse.

Erogenous Zones

Erogenous zones are areas of the body that are particularly sensitive to sexual stimulation if touched in a special manner. When touched by a loving partner at a willing moment in a special manner, erogenous zones can sexually arouse the person, giving him/her intense physical pleasure. However, if the same areas of the body are touched by a stranger at an unwelcome moment they do not feel pleasant and can actually be a put-off. So it is not just the sensitive areas on the body, but the willingness and the manner in which they are touched that make them erogenous.

Some obvious erogenous zones include the lips, breasts and genitals. Other erogenous zones could include the neck, ears, feet, and thighs, and usually vary from person to person. Do not hesitate to explore your own and your partner's body to find out exactly what the individual erogenous zones are, and then freely communicate about this to each other.

Simplest Approach/Position for Sexual Intercourse

The simplest position for intercourse is Female superior (Woman on top). This position has distinct advantages over the Missionary position (Man on top). With the man on top position, there is always a possibility that the man can attempt intercourse even before his partner is adequately aroused and ready for intercourse. In such situation, the inadequate lubrication may result in pain during intercourse making it unpleasant for both the partners. With the woman on top position, it is very difficult to force intercourse on a woman unless she is willing and ready for the act. This position ensures good lubrication during intercourse, making it enjoyable for both. It is also easier with the woman on top position to find the exact location of the vagina (even in the dark), as she is active and can manually guide the male penis into the vagina. It also ensures fearless and painless penetration for a woman, as and when she is ready. In the man on top position, very often, a woman anticipates pain and fails to relax her thighs and pelvic muscles, making it difficult for a nervous male partner to penetrate. In this position, the man finds his hands remaining engaged in supporting his body; however in the woman on top position, the hands of both the partners are free and caressing and fondling each other can continue even during the intercourse, keeping arousal levels high.

There is one more very important factor that needs to be understood. With the man on top position, invariably the contact between his penis and her clitoris does not occur, and therefore the right stimulation does not take place for her to reach her orgasm. The woman on top position ensures correct stimulation. This position in which the man is relatively passive and the woman active, ensures that the man remains aroused enough to maintain his erection till the woman is ready to climax (as opposed to the man-on-top position, where the man nears his ejaculation with every movement, but the woman may be still very far from climaxing because of lack of a correct stimulus). If the woman is on top and the man below, the woman will be able to move in a way that would give her clitoris the right stimulus, and she would then be able to climax fully and experience the pleasure of orgasm. This would, in turn, leave her feeling sexually satisfied, fulfilled and relaxed in her body and mind after the act. The man, of course, will reach his orgasm anyway, as he does not require a specific position or movement. Any movement is enough to stimulate his organ and bring him to his climax. It is easy for a man to penetrate and climax with the least effort, as his organ (glans penis) can be stimulated in any position; but it is not so for a woman. For her to be satisfied in the sexual act, she needs to climax too; and this is only possible if her clitoris (sensitive area) is stimulated in the right way for a clitoral orgasm or then a specific movement which would give her a vaginal orgasm. But the female orgasm happens only with certain movements and positions, (unlike the male orgasm) which only she is aware of.

In addition, as compared to a man, a woman takes longer to get aroused. But once she is aroused fully, if she is allowed to move in a way that stimulates her clitoris, she can climax with or even before her partner.

It is to be noted that once the man ejaculates, he loses his erection, and is then incapable of bringing the woman to her climax. Therefore, the key would be to prolong the male orgasm till the woman is nearing her orgasm. Then they can either climax together, or the woman first, immediately followed by the man. There should be some sort of a signal between the partners to indicate the nearing of the climax so that it can be timed in a way that the woman can reach her climax too. Once the woman reaches her orgasm (in certain cases even multiple orgasms), the sexual act can still continue (as there is nothing like loss of erection in women) till the man climaxes. This would provide complete sexual satisfaction to both the partners.

Chapter 13

IMPORTANCE OF COMMUNICATION IN INTIMACY

Teaching couples to freely and frankly talk about sex

Communication on sexual issues is one of the most difficult challenges faced by many couples. If we avoid discussing sexual issues openly with each other, we will never learn how to communicate in this matter, and not communicating in this area could be detrimental to the health of the relationship. It does not even occur to us to develop communication skills about sexual relating although it is not only extremely important, but also extremely essential for the relationship. Discomfort and embarrassment is a learned attitude about the subject of sex. Couples often engage in the sexual act, presuming and believing that they know what their spouse wants or likes based either on some random reading or pornographic viewing. This invariably results in an awkward, dissatisfying, hasty and clumsy sexual act.

Couples need to sincerely ask questions such as "Are you comfortable?", "What would you like me to do?", "Does this feel pleasurable?", "What can I do to make it better for you?", "Is there anything in particular that you enjoy more or something you do not enjoy at all?". If you are uneasy and uncomfortable asking such questions clearly, then probably you are not at a point in the relationship where you should explore sex at all. You can ask your spouse to signal to you, by squeezing your arm or any other non-verbal cue, to suggest if s/he wants any thing in particular.

A note for men: Refrain from presuming and pretending to know what a woman likes and wants, as she will figure out in no time that you actually do not know what pleasures her. To begin with, young women may not know what exactly they want during the early days of their sex life; however, soon they figure out what they really want and what they absolutely do not enjoy. They may participate in these activities mechanically thinking they should be enjoying what their spouse is doing. Men think that they are expected to know what to do, and women too expect them to know it all. However, the truth is that neither of them knows it all and communication is the only master key to explore sexual pleasure together.

David Reuben, author of *How to Get the Most out of Sex* writes: If sex is right, then everything is right. If sex is wrong then nothing else can be right.

Many people think about their sex life and some even talk about it, but find themselves completely at a loss when it comes to doing something constructive about making it mutually satisfying.

"How can my husband and I love each other so much, yet have such a dull and unexciting sex life?" asked a friend who is herself a clinical psychologist. Had she discussed the problem with her husband, a gynaecologist, to whom she has been married for over 11 years?

"I seem to be able to talk to him about everything but our sex life," she said at last. "I don't know how to tell him what I need without seeming to criticize."

Women from all walks of life, of all educational levels, and with varying sexual experiences, voice similar sentiments. Most married people lack the basic information about their spouses' sexual preferences. Our own informal survey of 70 wives found a myriad of needs they wanted to share with their husbands. But, as one woman told us, "It is difficult to know how to begin sharing it with him."

As relationship counsellors it is our continuous endeavour to make couples talk to each other openly about everything that matters to them. It is the first major lesson we teach, even to those who come to us for premarriage counselling. For everyone in a conjugal relationship, and at every stage of the relationship, communication is the life-line.

If you too wish to revitalise your sexual relationship, communication is critical. It is not the quantity or quality of sexual relations that makes or breaks a marriage, but rather the degree of the fit between partners' sexual needs and priorities. Such mutuality comes only with communication. Another essential ingredient is the commitment of time and energy for such communication, and then doing what has been shared with each other.

Try to define for yourself and your spouse what your complaints and pleasures are. Many people are uncomfortable and shy about making specific requests, but we must emphasise that open talk and experimentation are vital. No one can automatically know what pleases another, without communication.

Love does not make one a mind reader, but instead, love means, trusting each other enough, to ask openly and answer honestly.

Researchers William Masters and Virginia Johnson say something very insightful in this regard. They say, "Love and physical desire wax and wane throughout a lifetime. This need not only be accepted, but even enjoyed, if partners communicate."

CLEAR, CARING, COMPLETE AND CONTINUOUS COMMUNICATION

As a part of training in communication we emphasise four essential qualities (four 'C's) that one needs to bear in mind. Communication needs to be Clear, Caring, Complete and Continuous.

Clear: Clear communication is the one that conveys correct messages. Hints and gestures should be complemented with adequate verbal expression of your feelings.

Caring: You should communicate because you care for yourself, the other and for the relationship. Crass remarks, derisions, taunts, abuses and sarcasm are uncaring and toxic to any relationship. They do not communicate, but end all possibilities of communication and communion.

Complete: Incomplete communication is as good as no communication, or a miscommunication. It is only complete communication that helps. Abandoning the communication halfway due to frustration, shyness or other reservations is detrimental to a relationship.

Continuous: Communication should be a regular (on-going) feature in relationships and not occasional. A breakdown in communication lines should preferably never happen, but if it does happen, urgent efforts need to be made to re-establish communication lines as soon as possible.

CASES

Deepak came home from work and found his wife Sunita dressed in a long skirt. She greeted him with an enthusiastic hug and announced that she was serving one of his favourite meals – that too by candlelight. Instead of complimenting Sunita, Deepak responded to her efforts with an irritated frown.

When Linda remarked that she was tired and wanted to go to bed early, her husband Mark bade her good-night and settled down to watch television. The next morning there was no sign that Linda had benefited from her extra sleep. On the contrary, she snapped at Mark because he had forgotten to put the toothpaste back in the medicine cabinet.

What was wrong with Deepak and Linda? Their sex signals were mixed up. Deepak was receiving messages that weren't being sent, and Linda was sending messages that weren't being received.

Deepak assumed that Sunita's elaborate dinner was part of a plan to entice him into making love to her. That made him angry for two reasons: he had put in a hectic day at the office and was not in the mood for romance. He also disliked being manipulated. But Deepak's assumption was incorrect. The dinner was a thoughtful gesture, not an attempt at seduction. Sunita had noticed that Deepak had been looking down. She hoped his favourite meal would cheer him up.

Linda, on the other hand, wanted to make love to her husband, and her pretext of going to bed early was designed to tell him so. But Mark did not get the message. He thought Linda was really tired, and she ended up feeling hurt and angry.

It is not uncommon for couples to experience such breakdowns in their sexual communication system. Sex is an extremely sensitive and personal subject. Attitudes towards it vary, moods don't always match, and egos are generally at stake. Thus, it is not surprising that even the most compatible couples are sometimes tuned to different frequencies.

Most couples express sexual wishes with hints, code words and symbolic acts. There is nothing wrong with this. But husbands and wives who use such signals should be aware of how easily they can be misread, misinterpreted or simply missed. It is better to choose signals that can be clearly recognised as preludes to sexual activity – wearing particular nightwear, humming a special tune, talking about a previous romantic experience – anything that both partners will recognise and respect; but better than this, is clear verbal expression of your desire for intimacy.

It is strongly advised that husbands and wives do not conceal their desires out of the fear of incurring a partner's disapproval. Always take a chance. An invitation to make love is a compliment. Most partners will be flattered, and although they may not always acquiesce on the spot, they will undoubtedly return the compliment before long.

People who can't or won't send out recognisable sex signals are no less a problem than those who can't or won't recognise clear messages when they are sent. In some cases, the lack of recognition is deliberate. A partner may prefer to ignore a signal rather than give a negative response. Or he or she may be upset about something else and the missed cue is a way of venting wrath, i.e. a passive aggressive act.

Connecting Psychologically

The failure to connect psychologically is only one kind of sexual difficulty that can arise in an otherwise good marriage. Most couples find that their sexual encounters are influenced not only by how they feel about one another at the moment, but also by job pressure, financial worries, disruptive children, and above all, fatigue. Moving from a busy life into relaxed moments of intimacy often becomes extremely difficult, even for loving couples. Almost 50 percent of wives report that the 'inability to relax' is a significant problem in their sex lives. While lifelong inhibitions, fears and guilt may contribute to tension, it is also hard to adjust to instant intimacy when the bedroom door closes.

Can sex survive, let alone flourish, in a long-term relationship? We are pleased to report that the answer is a definite YES. For no matter how long two people have been together, they can still get better and better at connecting with each other, sharing intimacy, making plans, talking about feelings and fantasies and learning how to play and touch. Couples who never stop using their own intelligence, sense of humour and imagination to refresh their physical and emotional relationship, can have an enriching and meaningful sex life for a long, long time.

Chapter 14

REPRODUCTION AND BIRTH CONTROL

Discussing various contraceptive measures

Human Reproduction

A woman can become pregnant only during a small part of her monthly menstrual cycle. In addition, women are able to conceive only during a certain time in their lives – usually between the ages of 12 and 50 i.e. from Menarche (beginning of menstruation) to Menopause. About every four weeks, an egg (ovum) is released by one of the two ovaries in a woman's body. The ovum then passes through the fallopian tube. If it is not fertilised while in the fallopian tube, it goes into the uterus, where it disintegrates. The disintegrated ovum then passes out of the woman's body through the vagina as part of the normal monthly bleeding called menstruation.

During peno-vaginal sexual intercourse, millions of sperms are released by the male partner into the woman's vaginal canal. Some of the sperms swim through the uterus into the fallopian tubes. If an ovum and sperm unite in one of the fallopian tubes, conception takes place. If the fertilised ovum (Zygote) gets attached to the lining of the uterus, a new life begins to develop. About nine months and seven days later, a baby is born.

Parturition

Parturition is the act or process of giving birth to a baby (offspring). It is a less well-known term for labour and delivery or giving birth. For several weeks before parturition, the process of softening of the cervix begins through mini-contractions called Braxton-Hicks contractions. As labour nears, these contractions become more intense, though they are usually less difficult to bear than later contractions.

Parturition goes through three stages — the shortening and dilation of the cervix, descent and expulsion of the baby, and shedding of the placenta. During the first stage of **cervical dilation,** uterine contractions lasting about 40-60 seconds begin about 20-30 minutes apart and progress to severe labour pains about every three minutes. The opening of the cervix widens as contractions push the baby. These contractions work to help dilate the cervix to approximately three centimetres. It takes around 12-15 hours for cervical dilation in first-time mothers (primiparae), and less if a woman has had previous babies (multiparae). As the cervix reaches full dilation, the baby begins to move out of the uterus and into the birth canal. The amniotic sac breaks, and the woman needs to actively push the baby. This stage is called **Expulsion.** Expulsion lasts for 1-2 hours or less. Normally, the baby's head emerges first; other presentations (breech birth, feet first, face, brow or other) make childbirth more difficult and risky. The third stage of parturition is the **shedding of the placenta** or foetal membranes. In the third stage, the placenta is expelled, usually within 15 to 30 minutes.

Within six to eight weeks after childbirth, the mother's reproductive system returns to nearly the pre-pregnancy state.

Birth Control Intervention (Contraception)

Nature has an in-built mechanism to limit and space births, as a woman can become pregnant only during the ovulation period. All women and men should have control over their parenthood. They should be able to decide when and if they want to become parents. There are times when one may not want to conceive, especially for health reasons, inability to provide nurturance (physical, emotional and material) or even when one wants to space children in the process of planning one's family.

Birth control is a term that includes all methods used to prevent conception. Other terms with a similar meaning are contraception, family planning and planned parenthood.

There is no 'best' method of birth control. Each method has its own pros and cons. Some methods work better than others at preventing pregnancy. Researchers are continuing to work on improving or developing better and safer birth control methods.

Making decisions about birth control or contraception, is not very easy, as there are many things to be considered. Learning about various birth control methods and consulting your doctor are two good ways to get started.

You need to take the following aspects into consideration while choosing a suitable birth control method.

- Your overall health
- How often you engage in sexual intercourse
- If you wish to have a child in the near future or later at some point

- How effective each method is in preventing pregnancy
- Any potential (short term or long term) side effects
- Your comfort level with using a certain method.

Remember that any **birth control method can fail.** You can greatly increase a method's success rate by using it correctly and consistently. The only way of absolutely ensuring that pregnancy does not take place, is to not have peno-vaginal sexual intercourse i.e. abstinence, or else, surgical sterilisation.

Methods of Birth Control or Contraception

There are many methods of birth control that a woman or a man can use. Consult your doctor to help you decide which method is most suitable for you.

Remember that birth control methods DO NOT protect you from HIV or other sexually transmitted diseases (STDs), and that all the methods work best only if used correctly and consistently. Therefore, be sure that you know the correct way to use them. Discuss matters freely with your doctor and do not hesitate to clarify again if you do not understand or if you forget. Know that learning how to use some birth control methods can take some time and practice. Therefore, be patient with yourself and the method. The more you know about the correct way to use birth control, the more control you will have over planning parenthood. Sometimes doctors do not explain how to use a method because they presume that you already know the same. E.g. some men do not know when and how to put on a condom.

Let Us Learn about Various Birth Control Methods and How Well They Work in Preventing Pregnancy When Used Correctly

Continuous abstinence: This means not having sexual intercourse at any time. This method is 100 per cent effective at preventing pregnancy.

Periodic abstinence: A woman who has a regular menstrual cycle has about nine or more fertile days, or days when she is more likely to get pregnant, each month. Periodic abstinence means you do not have sexual intercourse on the days that you may be fertile. However, remember, you can never be absolutely sure about the exact days of fertility because the regular menstrual cycle could suddenly become irregular.

Barrier method of birth control: These methods prevent sperms from uniting with the ovum by creating an artificial barrier. Barrier methods include condoms, diaphragms, or cervical caps. If used together with spermicides (which kill sperms), these methods are 75 to 99 per cent effective at preventing pregnancy.

The male condom: Condoms are one of the barrier methods of birth control as they put up a barrier, which keeps the sperms from reaching the ovum. It is made of latex or polyurethane. Male condoms are 86 to 98 per cent effective at preventing pregnancy if used correctly. Condoms can be used only once. You can buy them at a chemist shop. Condoms come pre-lubricated, which helps to make sexual intercourse more comfortable and pleasurable. Condoms should always be kept in a cool and dry place. If you keep them in a warm place (like a wallet, or glove compartment of a car), the latex can break down, causing the condom to melt, tear or break. The condom is to be worn only on an erect penis, and just before intromission (penetration). It is packed with its borders rolled up. It is to be unrolled over the erect penis, till it is fully opened and covering the erect penis. There is a small pocket at the tip of the condom. It is given for the semen to get collected after ejaculation. This pocket may be pinched to avoid trapping of air at the time of wearing the condom. When putting the condom on the penis you must avoid tearing the condom or accidentally puncturing it with fingernails, a ring, or anything sharp like teeth, a blade or scissors.

A person infected with HIV or other STDs, or likely to be infected with the same, should be aware that a condom cannot completely eliminate the risk of transmission of HIV/STDs to themselves or to others.

Advantages

- Condoms are safe and effective (86 to 98 per cent) at preventing pregnancy when used correctly during each act of sexual intercourse.
- They are economical and freely available with a chemist, at general stores, and even vending machines. They come in many colours, sizes and even with or without ribbing.
- It helps some men to have better ejaculatory control and thus last longer during intercourse. Prolonging intercourse may make sex more pleasurable for both the partners.
- Condoms prevent spillage of semen in and around the vagina, making the act less messy.

Disadvantages

- You cannot use oil-based lubricants such as Vaseline or sun tan lotion along with a condom, as these products can damage the condom, making it unreliable.

- Some men either get nervous, or then lose the excitement/arousal while wearing a condom thus causing a loss of erection. Some others experience difficulty maintaining an erection with a condom on.

- The man needs to withdraw his penis soon after ejaculation before he loses the erection. If the penis loses its erection and becomes soft, the condom can be left in the vagina or slip off and spill the semen in and around the vagina.

- Some men and women are either sensitive or allergic to latex i.e. the material the condom is made of.

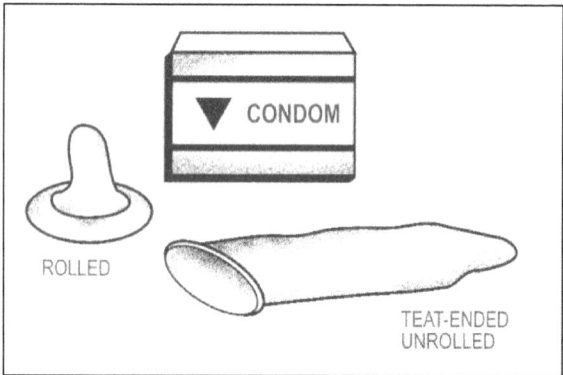

Diaphragm and cervical cap: These are old and outdated barrier methods of birth control. The diaphragm is shaped like a shallow latex cup. The cervical cap is a thimble-shaped latex cup. Both come in different sizes and you need a doctor's help to have them fitted. It is to be used with spermicidal jelly (to kill sperms) before sexual intercourse, and is to be placed up inside the vagina to cover the cervix. The diaphragm is 60 to 90 per cent effective at preventing pregnancy and the cervical cap is 80 to 90 per cent effective at preventing pregnancy for women who have not had a child, and 60 to 80 per cent effective for women who have had a child.

The female condom (Femidom): It is worn by the woman herself before sexual intercourse. This barrier method keeps sperms from entering into her vagina. It is made of polyurethane and is always packaged with a lubricant. It can be inserted up to 24 hours prior to sexual intercourse. Female condoms are 79 to 95 per cent effective at preventing pregnancy. They also provide a fair amount of protection from STDs.

Spermicidal gel or Pessaries: All spermicides have sperm-killing chemicals in them. They work by killing sperms. They come in several forms – foam, gel, cream or pessaries. Pessaries are to be inserted or placed in the vagina about 20 minutes before sexual intercourse (never more than one hour before intercourse) and left in place at least six to eight hours after the intercourse. Spermicides alone are about 74 per cent effective in preventing pregnancy. You may protect yourself more against getting pregnant if you use a spermicide with another barrier method such as the condom, diaphragm or cervical cap. Some spermicides have an ingredient called nonoxynol-9, which can protect you from STDs such as gonorrhea and chlamydia. However nonoxynol-9 does not protect you from HIV or other STDs. Some women are either sensitive or allergic to spermicides. In India, spermicidal pessaries are available at a chemist's shop.

Intra-Uterine contraceptive device (IUD or IUCD): An IUD is a small object made of plastic, copper or stainless steel. Your doctor places it inside the uterine cavity. It is 90-99 per cent effective at preventing pregnancy. Copper T is one such device that is shaped in the form of a 'T.' The arms of the Copper T contain some copper, which stops fertilisation by preventing sperms from making their way up through the uterus into the fallopian tubes. If fertilisation does occur, the IUD would then prevent the zygote (fertilised ovum) from getting implanted in the uterine lining. The IUD can be kept in your uterus for up to 2 to 10 years. It requires visits to your doctor to have it inserted and also to make sure that you are not having any problems. Remember, not all doctors are trained in fitting IUDs.

There are newer IUDs now available, which release hormones within the uterus to control conception.

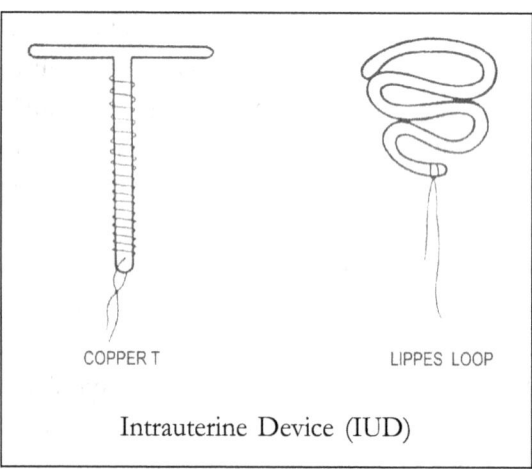

Intrauterine Device (IUD)

The upside of an IUD is that once a doctor places it inside your uterus, you cannot feel it and can forget about it for 2 to 10 years. Moreover, it is cost-effective. The downside of IUDs is that they can increase a woman's chances of pelvic infections, excessive menstrual bleeding and a higher risk of contracting STDs. The use of an IUD is avoided in nulliparus (a woman who has never conceived before) women. It is the best method after the birth of your first child. The IUD does not protect one against STDs or HIV.

Oral contraceptives (Combined birth control pills): Combined birth control pills contain two synthetic hormones - oestrogen and progesterone. They work by stopping ovulation (release of an egg), thickening the cervical mucus to block sperms and by making the lining of the uterus thinner – to prevent implantation of a zygote. The pill has to be taken from the fifth day of the menstrual cycle, one every night for 21 days.

The pill is 95 to 99 per cent effective at preventing pregnancy if used correctly. The birth control pill may add to your risk of ischemic heart disease, including hypertension (high blood pressure), thrombosis (blood clots) and blockage of the arteries. If you are over the age of 35 and a smoker, or have a history of thrombosis or breast cancer, your doctor may advise you not to take the oral contraceptive pill. You will need a prescription and visits to your doctor to make sure you are not having any problems. The pill does not protect a woman against STDs or HIV.

Advantages

- Many women enjoy sex more when on oral contraceptive pills, as they relax in the knowledge that they will not get pregnant.

- Oral contraceptive pills lower a woman's chances of having benign breast masses.
- Oral contraceptive pills decrease a woman's risk for cancer of the ovaries and cancer of the lining of the uterus (endometrial cancer).
- Oral contraceptive pills help to decrease a woman's menstrual cramps and pain.
- Oral contraceptive pills reduce excessive menstrual blood loss.
- Oral contraceptive pills may improve acne problems.

Disadvantages

- To be effective, oral contraceptive pills need to be taken regularly. Thus, a woman must remember to take the pill every day, at the same time of the day.
- Oral contraceptive pills may be expensive for some people and require a prescription from a qualified doctor.
- Women may experience nausea and spotting in the first month of taking oral contraceptive pills. Some women experience headaches, dullness, melancholy or decreased enjoyment of sex.
- Oral contraceptive pills tend to make periods very scanty and short. A woman may see no blood at all.
- Oral contraceptive pills may add to your risk of ischemic heart disease, including hypertension, thrombosis and blockage of the arteries.
- Oral contraceptive pills may promote growth of breast

cancer, though it does not cause breast cancer. It may also lead to higher rates of cervical cancer.

The mini-pill (Progestin-only pill): Unlike the combined birth control pill, the mini-pill has only one hormone – progesterone (instead of both oestrogen and progesterone). Taken daily, the mini-pill thickens the cervical mucus to prevent sperms from reaching the egg. It also prevents a fertilised egg from implanting in the uterus (womb) because of thinning of the uterine lining. The mini-pill is said to have lesser side effects. It causes lighter than normal periods, and the woman does not need to wait after stopping its intake, if she desires to get pregnant, unlike the combination birth control pill. Missing one pill even for a day can result in conception. Mothers who breastfeed can use the mini-pill because it does not affect milk secretion. The mini-pill is a good option for women who cannot take estrogen or for women who have a risk of thrombosis (blood clots). Mini-pills are 95 to 99 per cent effective at preventing pregnancy if taken correctly and regularly. You will need a prescription and visits to your doctor to make sure you are not having any problems. The mini-pill does not protect against STDs or HIV.

Monthly injections (Lunelle): Women can also take injections, or injectable shots of hormones once a month to prevent pregnancy. These injections are given in the arm, buttocks or thighs. The injections are more than 99 per cent effective at preventing pregnancy. This method requires visits to your doctor to make sure you are not having any problems.

Depo-Provera injections: This is a hormone (Medroxy-Progesteron), much like progesterone. The injection (150 mg/ml of Medroxy-Progesteron) is given deep intramuscularly in the buttocks within the first 5 days of the cycle or within 5 days of childbirth (if not breast feeding). If women receive their injections on time (every 14 weeks or three months), this method is very effective (99.7 per cent) in preventing pregnancy. Depo-Provera stops the woman's ovaries from releasing an ovum and also has other contraceptive effects. Nursing mothers can also take Depo-Provera injections. It is best to take the injection after the baby is six weeks old. It is okay for a woman to start another contraceptive method if it is less than 13 weeks since the last shot. It requires visits to your doctor to make sure you are not having any problems.

Advantages

- Nothing needs to be taken daily or used at the time of sexual intercourse. Thus, privacy is a major advantage. No one has to know a woman is using this method.
- Women lose less blood during menstruation when they are using Depo-Provera and have less menstrual cramps.
- Nursing mothers can also take Depo-Provera injections.
- The Depo-Provera injections may lead to improvement in PMS (premenstrual symptoms), depression or symptoms of endometriosis.

Disadvantages

- Depo-Provera injections can lead to very irregular periods. It may be a number of months before a woman's periods return to normal after her last shot. Depo-Provera may cause bone loss, although this is not fully ascertained.
- Some women may gain weight.

> In some women, depression and premenstrual symptoms may become worse.

Surgical sterilisation (Tubal ligation in women or vasectomy in men): These surgical methods are meant for people who want a permanent method of contraception, i.e. they who do not want more children or, never want to have a child. In the case of women, the method of tubal ligation (tying the fallopian tubes) is used, to stop ova (eggs) from travelling through the fallopian tubes to the uterus where they can be fertilised. The man has a vasectomy to keep the sperm from going to his penis, so that his ejaculate does not have any sperm in it.

Can Vasectomy Opertion Affect Man's Potency?

During a vasectomy (male sterilisation surgery), the tube that carries sperms (Vas Deferens) from each testicle is clamped, cut or sealed. This prevents sperms from mixing with the semen that is ejaculated from the penis. An ovum (egg) cannot be fertilised when there are no sperms in the semen. The testicles continue to produce sperms, but the sperms are re-absorbed by the body. Because the tubes are blocked before the seminal vesicles and prostate, one still ejaculates about the same amount of semen. Sexual desire and erectile function remain unaffected after this surgery.

Sexual desire originates in the sex centre situated at the base of the brain. The sex centre is activated by the senses of touch, sight, smell and thought. None of these things are affected by the sterilisation surgery. Sexual desire is also controlled by hormones, which remain intact after a vasectomy. The hormone Testosterone though secreted in the testes enters directly into the blood and not through the vas deferens. Therefore, we reiterate that neither the sexual desire nor the erectile ability (potency) is affected by a vasectomy.

Emergency contraception: The 'Morning after pill' is not a regular method of contraception and should never be used as one. It is also known as an Emergency contraception or emergency birth control pill. It is used to prevent a woman from getting pregnant when she has had 'unprotected' peno-vaginal intercourse. Unprotected implies that no method of contraception was used during intercourse. It can also mean that a contraceptive method was used during sex but it did not work, for example, a condom breaking or slipping during intercourse; or a woman may have forgotten to take her regular contraceptive pill, or may have been raped or forced to have intercourse when she did not want to. Emergency birth control consists of taking two doses of regular contraceptive pills twelve hours apart, and started within 72 hours after having unprotected intercourse. The pills are 75 to 90 per cent effective at preventing pregnancy if taken within 72 hours of unprotected intercourse. However, if conception has already taken place, the emergency contraception pill will NOT work.

Another type of emergency contraception is having the Copper T (IUD) inserted in the uterus within seven days of unprotected sex. This method is 99.9 per cent effective at preventing pregnancy. You will need to visit your doctor for either a prescription of the pills or for the insertion of the IUD.

If a woman has an ectopic pregnancy i.e. where the pregnancy develops outside the uterus, the emergency contraceptive pill will not work. An ectopic pregnancy can be a serious life threatening condition. Signs of ectopic pregnancy include severe pain on one or both sides of the lower abdomen, spotting of blood, and giddiness.

Chapter 15

SEXUAL FANTASIES –
THE PROS AND CONS

Discussing how fantasies affect
your real relationships

Mahesh was from a religious family, and his father was the head priest of a temple. On entering adolescence he was groomed to be a good boy who was not to make eye contact with girls. His surging sexuality conflicting with his upbringing, caused him to go totally berserk in his fantasies. He fantasised about orgies and deviant sexual behaviour, and pleasured himself for several years in his private world. He was married through an arranged match and the problems began from the first night. His shy wife was unwilling to engage in deviant sexual behaviour, and therefore, did not match up to his wild fantasies. He would ask her to invite her sister for a sexual orgy with them and would constantly find flaws with her physical appearance. His distressed wife went back to her parents within the first three months of marriage.

On hearing her story she was asked whether she could empathise with the fact that it was the rigid upbringing that had resulted in Mahesh's sexual repression, which had in turn resulted in wild fantasies, leading to the current intimacy problems in the marriage. Once she understood it entirely, she agreed to give her marriage a second chance only if her husband would engage in counselling. Mahesh came across as a decent young man and was fortunately open to one session with us. During the course of the session, he was helped to see the connections of his upbringing, his past and his fantasies, with the current marital problems. Gradually he was able to disengage from his dysfunctional past and fantasy world and find fulfilment in the real relationship. He established a normal healthy sexual relationship with his wife, and the marriage was saved.

From adolescence onwards, most people have sexual fantasies that serve a variety of functions and result in a wide range of responses within the individual. Some are pleasant or stimulating; others are confusing, embarrassing or even shocking.

Sexual fantasies occur in an astonishingly wide variety of circumstances and settings. Sometimes these imaginative interludes are intentionally called forth to enliven a boring experience, to pass time, or to provide a sense of excitement. At other times, sexual fantasies float into awareness in a seemingly random fashion, perhaps triggered by feelings and thoughts of which we have little or no awareness.

Fantasising allows individuals to escape from the frustrations and limits of everyday living. A phenomenon that is found extremely prevalent with fantasising is that the person returns to a particular preferred fantasy again and again, and gets comfortable with or even addicted to it. Occasionally, minor variations may be played out in such a preferred fantasy, but by and large the central theme remains fixed.

There are situations in which preferential fantasies may become troublesome. For some people, the repeated and exclusive use of such a fantasy may lead to a situation in which the fantasy becomes mandatory for sexual arousal. The person no longer responds sexually to one's partner since sexual arousal depends on fantasy alone. Sometimes, preferential fantasies can become obsessions that may interfere with behaviour or the thinking-feeling process.

Not all sexual fantasies are willfully conjured up or pleasurable. Some fantasies recur over and over again despite being unwanted; other fantasies flood into the individual's awareness in a frightening fashion, producing inner turmoil or conflict and feelings of guilt and shame. Fantasies of this sort may either result in sexual arousal or may be so distressing that sexual feelings may shut off.

Where It All Begins…

During adolescence (Age 10 to 19 years), boys and girls start becoming sexually mature and start developing secondary sexual characteristics. During this phase of life, besides physically growing to become adults, a lot of psychological and emotional changes start taking place rather rapidly. Strong sexual feelings and thoughts start crossing the mind rather erratically. Unusual and unexpected sexual dreams, strong physical attraction for the opposite sex, overwhelming urges to associate, relate, connect and impress the opposite sex start occurring. These psychological and emotional changes are more body and sex oriented for boys and more heart and romance oriented for girls. During the initial three to four years of adolescence when boys are around 12 to 16 years old, they find themselves getting sexually attracted to every other woman. This age is so peculiar that the sexually growing man in them is getting attracted to women who are in their twenties and thirties. Actresses, models and every other attractive woman around, is age wise elder to them. In spite of strong sexual urges they find themselves helpless, as these elder women show little or no sexual interest in them. Even girls of 18 and 19 years of age who are just two or three years elder to them ignore these adolescent boys of 15 and 16, as they find themselves getting attracted to men elder to them. This frustrates adolescent boys. They find themselves helpless. It is this stage that provokes fantasies, which come handy in taking care of the sexual upsurges. In this case, fantasies appear safe, can be elicited at any time and place, come for free, and can be modified at will to suit one's fancies.

The desire to know about something not yet experienced, forbidden or seemingly unattainable is often a key feature of sexual fantasies. Although it is only a make-believe excursion of the mind, fantasies do help young adults find temporary relief, excitement, adventure, self-confidence and pleasure. Through fantasy, the real, unfavourable world can be transformed into whatever he or she likes, no matter how brief or improbable it might be. In this sense, in the growing years of early adulthood, it could be a useful mechanism. However, with every pleasure comes the very real possibility of a person getting obsessed with or addicted to it, and thus losing conscious control over the phenomenon. The same device that was so useful when single can become an impediment and an obstacle once he or she is in a committed relationship.

Generally, imagination, creativity and playfulness are part of the act of fantasising. However if a fantasy becomes the controlling force in a person's life, the play element may get completely lost. This situation is not different from the person who gets so caught up in a competitive sport that the playful side of the sport activity is totally lost.

Mental Health Implications

Fantasies have been viewed as having implications for mental health. For almost half a century, psychoanalysts studied fantasies in depth. They viewed deviant sexual fantasies, i.e. those fantasies portraying anything other than heterosexual acts that led to intercourse, as immature expressions of the sex drive, and as blocks to the development of more mature sexuality. Many psychoanalysts strongly believed that such fantasies were most likely to be forerunners of actual deviant sexual behaviour.

A California psychoanalyst, Bernard Apfelbaum describes fantasies as "cut-off parts of us signalling wildly to get back in". He believes that sexual fantasies arise from dissatisfaction with reality and have a high potential for creating relationship conflicts. For example, if one partner feels that the other's turn-on comes from a fantasy rather than from personal involvement, an instinctive sense of being disregarded intrudes, and blocks sexual responsiveness. Apfelbaum also suggests that having unshared private fantasies, lessens intimacy and trust in a relationship, and says that "sexual fantasies always offer us precious clues about what needs to be done to strengthen our relationship."

Robert Stoller, a psychoanalyst in America, believes that sexual fantasies are a private pornography that allow us to gain revenge over a previously painful situation. He says that there is a flame of hostility at the core of all sexual fantasies.

Another psychoanalyst from New York Avodah Offit thinks, that if reality and fantasy are closely matching, it indicates a well-integrated personality, or a kind of psychological togetherness. If fantasy strays too far away from our personal realities, the inconsistencies point to potential personality problems. Offit also regards sexual fantasies as "a pale substitute for the complexities of joy and pain which are requisites for loving a real person."

Psychiatrist Dr. Ms. Natalie Shainess thinks that fantasies during intercourse are 'symptomatic of sexual difficulty' and 'signs of sexual alienation.' She also believes that healthy women do not fantasise very much except when they are young and inexperienced, and if fantasy persists, "you can assume there is a greater pathology."

Alan Rapaport, a clinical psychologist, takes the viewpoint that any fantasy that occurs during person-to-person sexual encounter is debasing because it reduces personal involvement. If a person is caught up in a private fantasy while making love, it interferes with a more sharing and intimate relationship.

Some popular magazines and even books written by sexologists suggest that if you are not turned on by your partner, you should fantasise about someone else while having sex. We personally believe that this suggestion is not always helpful. These things may work to improve one's sex life on a temporary and superficial level. But beware of the great danger in superficial sexual remedies. As one becomes more and more dependent on outside stimulation, one decreases his/her natural ability to feel turned on by one's partner. You may feel turned on while being with your partner but not by her or him. **Two individuals who are turned on by themselves, but not by the other person, are two individuals who are having sex, but not making love.**

Chapter 16

PORNOGRAPHY: A DANGEROUS DRUG

Discussing the ill effects of pornography

Suhas and Shilpa were married for two years, when Suhas first suggested to his wife that they see some blue films together. Shilpa consented, not anticipating how it would change their otherwise healthy and mutually satisfying sexual relationship. What started off as a casual fun activity, shortly turned into a nightmare for Shilpa, when Suhas started acting out in an abnormally aggressive manner in bed just like those blue film actors and started expecting acts such as fellatio and sodomy from her. Suhas, who was a gentle and romantic lover earlier, had turned into a ruthless and over-demanding husband after seeing just few of those blue films. He started compelling her to get new video cassettes from a nearby library, as he would find it embarrassing to get them himself.

Anita was married to Anil for eight years. After the initial few weeks of marriage, Anil started compelling Anita to watch blue films together, and had sex with her only after getting adequately aroused on seeing pornography. He would fail to get aroused and attain an erection whenever they were away on a holiday and could not get to see such films.

Milind and Maya had a turbulent marriage from the very beginning. They had differences of opinion in practically every aspect of their married life. To add fuel to fire, Milind got friendly with a group of his office colleagues, who would get together for drinks and blue-film shows. Maya even threatened to divorce Milind, but things did not change. She walked out on him the day he invited his friends for such a party at their house.

Pradip and Priya were married for ten months, when Priya was brought by her mother to me for the non-consummation of her marriage. What we heard from Priya was shocking. Her husband Pradip, was addicted to watching blue films every night till late and had not touched Priya sexually even once since their marriage. He would masturbate a couple of times while watching those films right in front of his wife, but would not attempt any intimacy with her.

These are four different examples where blue films or pornography became the epicentre of a painful marital storm. Besides serious situations such as the above, many couples go through less severe forms of conflicts over viewing pornography.

Many people think that pornography is just harmless fun and that it has no ill effects. However, it is virtually impossible not to be affected by pornography.

Research has shown that pornography and its messages are involved in shaping attitudes and encouraging behaviour that can harm individuals and their families. Pornography is often viewed in secret, which creates deception within marriages that can lead to even divorce in some cases. In addition, pornography promotes the allure of adultery, prostitution and unreal expectations that can result in dangerous promiscuous behaviour.

Let us try to understand various psycho-relational dimensions of this problem.

Sexual Problems or Relationship Problems?

Sexual excitement is a natural reaction to certain conditions. When those conditions are absent or inhibited, so is your natural sexual response. Sex is a great barometer for telling you how well your relationship is working, and when it needs more attention.

Some books say that if you are not turned on by your partner, you should fantasise about someone else while having sex, or watch blue films. These things may work to improve your sex life on a temporary and superficial level. But beware of the great danger in superficial sexual remedies. As you become more and more dependent on outside stimulation, you decrease your natural ability to feel turned on by your partner. You may feel turned on while being with your partner but not **by** her or him. Like we said earlier, two individuals who are turned on by themselves, but not by the other person, are two individuals who are having sex, but not making love.

If you feel you have sexual problems in your relationship, and your sexual functions were normal, healthy and exciting in the beginning of your relationship, then your problem most likely have little or nothing to do with sex. They are symptoms of something deeper in the relationship, such as unexpressed anger or disappointment, unresolved conflicts, lack of trust or fear of failure. By discovering the real problem and working together with your partner to heal them, you will see your sexual problems diminish and eventually disappear.

If you think that the biggest problem in your relationships has a lot to do with sex, you are probably mistaken. One of the serious mistakes most people make in their relationships, is attempting to isolate a part of the relationship, like sex, from the whole, thinking that when that one part is fixed, the whole relationship will get better. This is the **cover-up** approach to dealing with problems.

The real problem always lies in the relationship, and not in the bed.

Most sexual problems are just symptoms of problems in other areas of the relationship. If you try to hide or suppress the problems or weaknesses in your relationship, they will emerge in bed. Yes, many things could be suggested to create more excitement in the sex life, but they will not work. **Sex is just a mirror of the rest of your relationship.**

Blue Films As Stimulants

Many people have come to rely on using pornography to become sexually stimulated. This is often because they have spent so much energy numbing themselves emotionally that they cannot really feel unless they have a huge amount of stimulation. In our work with couples, we have found innumerable sexual problems and resentments stemming from the use of pornography. The wife cannot open up to her husband in bed because she knows that he has a collection of erotic videos, which he sees frequently. It makes her feel like she is not enough for him.

It is definitely a sign of sexual immaturity when one looks for excitement in pornographic films. For such a person sex is only skin deep. He is not adequately sensitive to the psychological and emotional components of sex.

Let us add that outside inputs are necessary when there is a lack of 'love' between partners... when sex is merely a physical activity. This lack of love cannot be blamed on only one partner. Love happens between two sensitive human beings. Both the partners need to deeply examine their relationship, either on their own individually, or with the help of a good counsellor.

Very often wives look down upon the husband and simply engage into the blame game. As counsellors, we advise them to change their focus from the other to oneself. They are told to ask themselves 'what can I do to bring more depth into my relationship and make it more than sex – a sharing of intimacy?'

Pornography: A Form of Sex Addiction

Pornography is a special class of sex addiction distinct from promiscuity, compulsive masturbation, anonymous sex, paedophilia, phone sex, fetishes, voyeurism etc. Sex addiction is not like any other addiction because sex involves your most personal and complex emotions. For some sexually-addicted people, pornography has little appeal. For others, their entire sex addiction revolves around pornography. It can best be described as an obsessive relationship with a fantasy. For many others, pornography simply adds to their otherwise sexually addictive behaviour.

Pornography, like any other sex addiction, becomes the user's fix. The user becomes so enraptured, s/he ends up destroying good relationships, spending hours and sometimes days surfing the Internet for porn and throwing out thousands of rupees on illusions.

At first it is almost impossible for someone caught up in a pornography addiction to believe that he or she can find real sexual enjoyment and better sexual pleasure with a person instead of a fantasy. However, with effective counselling, a genuine relationship does become the preferred sexual interest of the pornography addicted person.

Some people addicted to pornography would rather have sex with their partner than with a pornographic fantasy. Yet, they keep returning to pornography because they don't know how to overcome their addiction. For them, learning and applying the principles of overcoming addiction is the issue.

Some pornography addicts believe they have the best of both worlds: their relationship and their addiction. Their belief is mistaken. In fact, they live with a severely limited relationship and a hidden addiction. One of the great rewards of overcoming a pornography addiction is the ability to be fully committed to another person in a loving way, having nothing to hide and enjoying great sex.

Dr Victor Cline, noted researcher and professor of psychology said as early as the mid 1980s: "I have treated about 225 individuals over the past years who have had their lives disrupted one way or another because of their involvement with pornography. I have found a special syndrome associated with immersion in the world of pornography that repeats itself again and again." He found that there is a four-step progression among many who consume pornography.

Pornography Progresses through the Following Four Stages

1. **Addiction:** Pornography provides a powerful sexual stimulant or aphrodisiac effect, followed by sexual release, most often through masturbation.

2. **Escalation:** Over time, addicts require more explicit and deviant material to meet their sexual needs.

3. **Desensitisation:** What was first perceived as gross, shocking and disturbing, in time becomes common and acceptable.

4. **Acting out sexually:** There is an increasing tendency to act out behaviours viewed in pornography.

Where It All Begins...

Some therapists say that pornography or any form of sexual addiction is simply an excuse to justify lack of control (low frustration tolerance) and unwillingness to conform to acceptable norms. Other psychologists and psychiatrists maintain that it is a compulsive behaviour that has its roots in early childhood and can afflict both males and females. It is believed that people who suffer from this disorder come from dysfunctional families that failed to provide security and to reinforce the child's self-concept and self-esteem, and in which there was an absence of trust. The child could experience an empty feeling and also feel abandoned and vulnerable. There is evidence that a high percentage of people who experience the need to have a continuous compulsive urge to watch pornography, were physically or emotionally abused (either overtly or subtly) as children. These children could have been brought up to believe that sex was shameful, and that fantasising and masturbation were unacceptable. They also often display undeveloped social or dating skills. An intricate psychological pattern seems to emerge when they become adults. These people are usually involved in watching blue films, which provides a temporary relief. However, that feeling soon turns into disgust, resulting in more shame and anxiety. Then they become determined to and obsessed with controlling their urge, which results in over-control that cannot be sustained, and more shame and anxiety. They experience an inability to cope, the result of which is that they seek a sexual fix again, bringing them back to square one.

Pornography and the Community

The general content of pornography supports abuse and the rape myth (that women enjoy forceful sex) and serves as a how to for sex crimes. For example, in America, in the Phoenix neighbourhoods where adult businesses were located, the number of sex offences was 506 per cent greater than in areas without such businesses.

Dr Mary Anne Layden, director of education, University of Pennsylvania Health System, pointed out, "I have been treating sexual violence victims and perpetrators for 13 years. I have not treated a single case of sexual violence that did not involve pornography."

We can therefore safely conclude, that viewing of pornography/blue films can in no way truly enhance the quality of sexual relating. In fact, it has the distinct possibility of causing deep hurt in the partner, and grave harm to the relationship as a whole.

Chapter 17

PREGNANCY AND INTIMACY

Discussing sexual relationship during pregnancy

"Doctor, I got married just six months ago. My wife is three-months pregnant now. Is it okay for us to have sex during her pregnancy? I feel embarrassed to ask this question to our family doctor. Since we don't know anything about this, we are avoiding sexual contact; but I do feel the urge and desire for sex, and I don't know what to do about it. Can you please give us some guidance?"

This is a question that people have asked us innumerable times during the several years of our practice – either personally or through letters. This is such a delicate matter, that most people are afraid that their family doctor will react angrily and think badly of them if they were to bring it up at all. 'Should one have sexual intercourse during pregnancy?' 'If yes, then how, with what frequency, and when?' All these questions will be addressed in this chapter.

Nature has arranged it so that, for conception to occur, both man and woman must participate in the sexual act. Neither man nor woman can produce a child on his or her own. Only when they have sexual intercourse, can they procreate. After this, it is the responsibility of both man and woman to nurture the foetus (pregnancy) and then the child who is born. A lot of men think: 'Once I have got my wife pregnant, my responsibility is over.' Some men do take on a few responsibilities, but these are usually limited to taking the wife to the gynaecologist for check-ups, providing her with medicines, etc. A lot of men are quite unaware of a whole lot of other aspects that they must be involved in during the pregnancy – understanding the wife's psychological state and emotional needs, giving her love and support, joyfully sharing in preparations for the arrival of the baby. These are key supportive roles that a man can and must play.

During pregnancy, a woman's mental make-up undergoes a dramatic change. She becomes emotional and sometimes over-sensitive. She can be very sentimental and get hurt easily. She experiences intense feelings of anticipation, tenderness and motherly yearning.

At this time, she keenly feels the need for her husband's understanding, for his participation, for him to spend time with her, be close to her. These needs being met or being ignored directly affects her mental state and affects the foetus too. If she feels that her husband is not adequately responsive to her needs, she gets saddened and anxious. She can become irritable and fall prey to a bewildering mix of emotions and symptoms – strange thoughts, sudden tears, insomnia, loss of appetite or over-stimulated hunger...many such imbalances appear.

Most men are unaware of the fact that their behaviour may have caused some of these emotional upheavals. Many men take the easy way out and simply take their wife to the doctor, without realising that it is not a doctor or any medicines that she needs at this time. What she needs is her husband's involvement and co-operation, an understanding of her moods, feelings and anxieties.

Nature intends that every man and woman jointly participate in the nurturing of a pregnancy; and thus every man must participate in and be aware of each and every change that occurs in his wife during this time.

Motherly yearnings are a natural and integral part of every woman's psyche. This is why she experiences a deep, new sense of fulfilment when she conceives a child, a feeling that grows at every stage of the pregnancy. When she gives birth, this sense of completeness reaches its peak. This is the source of her inner strength that helps her to undergo the extremely painful process of labour and delivery. Once the child is born, she simply overflows with love and tenderness; she becomes completely wrapped up in nurturing and cherishing the new baby.

These changes in a woman's being (psyche) during pregnancy and child birth are part of the Grand Plan of Nature. This is evident, not just in the human race, but throughout the entire animal kingdom too.

The changes that take place in the mother-to-be are part of a woman's biological make-up. Hormonal and chemical changes in her body prepare her for conception, pregnancy and childbearing. There is, however, no such biological change in the father-to-be. A man has to become consciously aware of the physical, mental and emotional demands of fatherhood. This awareness does not come to him naturally or biologically.

For a woman, the knowledge 'I am pregnant, a new life is being created in my body' brings a new awakening of feelings. Long-dormant feelings of motherhood are now awakened. Her aspirations, her thought-processes, her emotional world, all begin to undergo a transformation. Now, for her, sexual relations take a lower priority. A completely new aspect of life begins to emerge for her.

Nature has basically intended the sex drive to be a means for procreation. Quite naturally, when a woman conceives, her urge for sexual intercourse reduces, and remains diminished for a while.

In men, however, this does not happen. A man does not naturally experience a reduced sex drive when his wife is pregnant; he continues to feel the urge and desire for intercourse. In this situation, it is absolutely essential that he does not force this one-sided need on his pregnant wife.

Though a woman may not have strong sexual urges during this time, she does need and appreciate warm and gentle physical contact and caressing, which husband and wife can engage into. In the process of such closeness, if she is aroused and willing, they can have intercourse too. However, the man must at all times be aware that he should not force himself on her in any way. Avoid the missionary (man superior) position during pregnancy. It is advisable at this time that the woman be positioned on top (woman superior position) and the man below, or that they both are in a sitting position, so that there is no pressure on her abdomen and that movement is gentle.

Spoon position is yet another good way. The spoon position is when the couple lie on their sides, their legs bent upwards, both facing in the same direction, with the man at the back of the woman. It is called the spoon because it is like two spoons, one nestling inside the other. In that position the man can enter the woman's vagina with his penis from behind. This is a very gentle position as neither partner is putting any weight on the other, and it is particularly good for making love to a pregnant woman.

If the man is on top (missionary position), his weight bears down on the woman, and without realising it, his movements can become rough. This can disturb the foetus. Doctors advise that intercourse should be avoided from the sixth to the twelfth week of the pregnancy; as it can cause a miscarriage. Sexual abstinence is recommended during the last two months of pregnancy too. At this time, there is a risk of the essential amniotic fluid leaking out during intercourse.

In short, intercourse during the first three months and last two months of pregnancy is not advisable. During the fourth to seventh month of pregnancy, intercourse is allowed unless you are otherwise advised for medical reasons.

However, husband and wife can and should engage in gentle lovemaking, fondling and caressing. Sexual acts such as oral and anal sex should be strictly avoided.

Motherhood is a deep and intense part of a woman's life. With the birth of a child, a mother is born too. Earlier she was a wife or a daughter-in-law, now suddenly she is a Mother. Her husband is now a Father. A first-time mother pours her heart and soul into her new-born. This is what gives her utmost satisfaction and a sense of fulfilment. This is the way nature has meant it to be. During this time, therefore, she is not just far removed from any sexual urges, but from almost every other aspect of life. Nurturing her baby becomes her primary pre-occupation, her world. This is nature's special arrangement in a woman's psyche.

As her baby becomes five or six months old, a woman begins to return to her pre-pregnancy state. She begins to menstruate again and her sexual desire returns too.

Just as a woman enjoys the pleasures of motherhood, a man too can derive much joy from becoming a father. If during this period he has to abstain from sex for a while, it should not constitute a very serious problem. In fact, at this time, a couple has the opportunity to experience a new kind of intimacy, a closeness and a bonding. This is a great opportunity indeed, which should not be wasted. It can provide the basis for an emotionally solid and sustainable marital relationship.

During pregnancy, a woman does not retain a shapely figure. It is possible that a man, at this time, may be sexually drawn to other women. It is known that men are tempted to have extra-marital affairs during this time. A woman's needs during pregnancy, as we have seen earlier, change completely. If during this period her husband, instead of understanding her and being there for her, indulges in a relationship outside the marriage, surely this is not right. While this is common and natural in the animal world, it is not so for humans. Man is the one creature who does not exist only for his bodily needs; he aspires for loving bonds, a sense of belonging and for the finer aspects of life.

If the couple has bonds with each other which go deeper than the body, then physical attraction towards another woman during the wife's pregnancy will not be an issue, because both of them will get closer, sharing the joys of their baby growing in her womb. Men are nowadays routinely involved in lamaze classes, which prepare the parents-to-be for the delivery and the post-delivery period. Men are also encouraged to be present during sonography examinations, thus emotionally preparing him for his new role. Sharing time with each other, picking out the baby's name, and planning the baby's room, all help him to grow in his new role.

The bottom line is, do you as a couple have a relationship which is meaningful, and extends beyond physical relating? If you do, there is no cause for concern.

Chapter 18

THE
SEXUAL JOURNEY

Discussing sex at 20, 30, 40, 50 and beyond

Sex, can provoke excitement, passion, love, intimacy, and ecstasy as well as anxiety, guilt, depression, anger and agony. The way we view sex, largely depends on our culture and upbringing, the source of our sex education (if any), exposure to peers (healthy or unhealthy), our experiences, and also our age. Let us explore sex for both men and women at various stages of their life.

Sex at 20

In the 20s the sex hormones are raging, and there is an eagerness to explore one's sexuality with an urgency, if one has not already experimented in their teens as is the increasing unhealthy trend in our youth today. If one has waited for a committed relationship/marriage, then the curiosity and impatience is evident especially in men. Girls too, are eagerly responsive. The quality of sex for girls at such times is largely dependent on the kind and duration of foreplay, romance, sensuality and emotional intimacy. Contaminants at this age could be pornography viewing, which creates unrealistic expectations in the way of the physical form of the sexual partner as well as sexual attitudes and behaviours, which may not be acceptable to the partner.

Certain myths and misconceptions about human sexuality, due to a lack of healthy sex education, could create unnecessary anxiety when the eagerness in men causes premature ejaculation making them worry about satisfying their partner, or when wrong information from peers about expectations of a girl, creates performance anxiety, creating a psychological impotence in them till they are told to relax in the relationship, and let sex be the natural outcome of emotional intimacy. Girls often come with their own set of unrealistic expectations of a Mills and Boon/Hollywood type romance, and expect their sexual partners to know exactly how to have the perfect first encounter. However, it is most likely that the first encounter will be far from perfect and not at all like an on screen couple. The transition from reel to real is the first rude shock for both, and they have to come to terms with reality if they are to truly enjoy the pleasures of physical intimacy.

However, the fact remains that this age is very focused on creating excitement in sex, and wanting to experiment. Couples need to know that ONLY such sexual behaviour that is mutually acceptable, can be fulfilling for both. Contraception should be used in order to freely relate sexually, without the fear of a pregnancy at a stage in your relationship when you are still getting to know each other. The fear of pregnancy when you are not ready for it, can impede sexual pleasure in both. It is important to explore each other's personalities and bodies and get comfortable with each other emotionally and physically, and relax in the knowledge that sharing of intimacy needs to be much more than biological sex to remain exciting for a long time.

Sex at 30

During the 30s, while the frequency of sexual encounters might reduce compared to the 20s, the quality of love making more than makes up for the reduction in frequency. As both have already got comfortable with each other's bodies and the sexual act, and hopefully know what are the likes and dislikes of both, intimacy can be more pleasurable.

Women have usually transcended their initial hesitation, shyness and amateurishness, and are more uninhibited and actively participating in the sexual act. They often take the lead and initiate intimacy as an indicator of their feeling liberated. This proactive stance helps enhance their own as well as their partner's pleasure, as they have discovered what pleasures both. It is claimed in certain studies that a woman reaches her sexual peak in her late thirties. However, this is also the time when men and even working women are focused on climbing the ladder of success in their careers, and therefore a lot of time and energy is invested in furthering careers. If a child is born by this time, then the period of pregnancy, post-delivery, and early years of the baby, sees a marked maternal involvement of the woman, which could take away time and energy from being together.

However, it is important for both to make sure that togetherness time is consciously planned, so that the all-important connect remains in spite of busy schedules and other preoccupations. Sharing an activity that both like, enjoying the milestones of the child, arranging weekend getaways etc. keeps the emotional intimacy alive, which automatically translates into physical intimacy. Those couples who fail to do so, find themselves drifting apart straight into affairs at the workplace/

gym/chatrooms etc. Men find it easier to let off sexual steam by self-pleasuring with the easily accessible porn sites. It is also important for both to recognise the love language of the other, and do small but meaningful gestures for each other to demonstrate that you care and want to make the other feel special. Also, remaining physically fit not only keeps you healthy and attractive, but makes sure that your sexual life is not impeded by obesity, diabetes, hypertension etc.

Sex at 40

By the 40s, both are sexually experienced with each other, and know how to enhance the pleasure for oneself and the other whenever there is an intimate encounter. The frequency, however, is much lesser, as men are usually at the peak of their career graph and therefore extremely preoccupied, and women could be juggling careers and the difficult teenage years of their children. Men and women could also show the first signs of the aging process if they are not having a fitness regime, and women being at the peri-menopausal stage of their life, could display physical and emotional signs related to the irregularity of the menstrual cycle, hot flushes, mood swings etc. which could disrupt sexual encounters at times.

Medically, the percentage of men developing hypertension, diabetes and dyslipidemia is highest during this period, which affects their ability to have and sustain an erection, and unfortunately the medications used to counter hypertension and diabetes also contribute towards many of the sexual dysfunctions. A fitness regime and a keen watch on one's health are therefore advised, to have a healthy sexual life during this stage. Urban statistics show that many financially successful men in their 40s tend to have flings with younger women, to reassure themselves of their attractiveness to women. Many men also believe that they deserve to celebrate their hard-earned success with sexual pleasure, and want to now fulfil every sexual fantasy of theirs with sex outside marriage, in flings or with commercial sex workers, instead of their wives. This can lead to not only a major contaminant in the sexual life of the couple, but also a downward spiral in the relationship itself. Therefore, being in a relationship which is more holistic, and not only body-centric, is the correct foundation for couples, so that sex is not only sex, but a sharing of deep intimacy and companionship, which never grows stale, but only ripens and gets better with age, like vintage wine.

Sex at 50 and Beyond

Women are invariably through with menopause in this decade, and since their oestrogen levels have fallen, they experience symptoms such as vaginal dryness, therefore taking much longer to be aroused, with a resultant difficulty in climaxing. Of course, artificial lubricants can be used to easily counter this problem. Post-menopausal abdominal weight gain is common, and the skin shows signs of aging. This could affect the esteem of those women who are focused on the outer beauty and thus affect their sexual life too. The empty nest syndrome, with children having grown up and moved out or married with families of their own, could leave the woman feeling a sense of loss with a resultant depression, if her life has mainly revolved around child-rearing. This is when she needs gentle, loving companionship with her spouse, and the reassurance that she is attractive to him as a person and loved dearly, and he wants nothing more than to grow old with her just the way she is. Such a reassurance could keep the passion alive, and sexual encounters, though infrequent, could have the new found flavour of a relaxed intimate touching which may or may not end up in intercourse.

Men at this age may have problems with their prostrate glands and other age-related wear and tear of the body parts that affect his sexual life. They also find it difficult to maintain their erection long enough to complete the sexual act. However, this can now easily be countered with the use of modern medications. The reduction of testosterone during this period does reduce the sexual desire in men and women, but the hot passion is replaced with a warm companionship, if the relationship has evolved and has been more holistic from the beginning. Again, it cannot be stressed enough that both men and women should strive as much as humanly possible to maintain a lifestyle of appropriate exercise, healthy diet, and emotional well-being, so that they can not only enjoy a longer and more healthy life generally, but can enjoy physical intimacy, though qualitatively different, for a longer period in their relationship.

Ways to Better Your Sex Life

- *Base your relationship on more than each other's body, and let sex be more than biology i.e. a sharing and culmination of emotional intimacy.*

- *Access scientific and value-based sex education to help address all your concerns related to sexual relating as well as to remove misconceptions, if any, before engaging sexually. Refrain from pornography or taking advice from peers who dole out misinformation.*

- *Recognise the love language of the other and make small special gestures to show you care.*

- *Remain physically and emotionally fit, with a regular fitness regime, because the lifestyle that keeps you generally healthy, is the same lifestyle that keeps you sexually healthy.*
- *Consciously plan togetherness time e.g. weekend getaways or dates.*
- *Whisper or SMS sweet nothings to each other.*
- *Dress to feel sensual and attractive to yourself and your partner.*
- *Celebrate special moments, plan holidays together, and see family albums to reminisce on joyful times.*
- *Be supportive during challenging times at home or at work.*
- *Touch each other non-sexually in passing, to keep the intimate connect.*
- *Engage in mutually pleasurable foreplay in the form of non-verbal suggestions and physical touching till both are ready to go ahead.*
- *Communicate freely and frankly about your likes and dislikes so that intimacy is mutually pleasurable.*
- *Strictly avoid visual stimuli in the form of pornographic viewing, so that reality is not contaminated by fantasy.*
- *Use effective contraceptives for family planning, so that sexual relating is more spontaneous and uninhibited.*
- *Both should freely and uninhibitedly initiate intimacy and gradually involve the other through gentle foreplay.*

Note: Sex should never be forced on the other.

Chapter 19

NO SEX

Discussing when not to have sex

The most important tenet about human sexuality is: Never force one's desires on another, or in other words do not force sex on your partner directly or indirectly, if s/he is not **willing**.

Willingness plays a major role in all aspects of sexual relationships, be it arousal, actual pleasure and even orgasm during the sexual act. Reluctant consent invariable results in a cold, one-sided sexual act. A willing partner can induce desire, make the sexual act passionate and enjoyable and can even heighten the possibility of experiencing orgasm. However there are situations when in spite of the willingness of both the partners, sex is not allowed on moral and even legal grounds.

1 With a minor:

When the female partner is legally minor (below the age of 15 if married and below 16 if not married), in spite of her willingness, sex is a criminal offence as per sections 375 of the Indian Penal Code (1860).

2 Incest:

Sexual activity among blood-related family members such as

brother-sister, father-daughter, mother-son, is called incest and is not permitted morally as well as legally in most of the countries irrespective of their willingness.

3 Adultery:

Sexual relationship by a married person with another partner outside marriage, even though a consensual relationship, is termed as adultery and is not permitted as per the section 497 of Indian Penal Code.

4 Acts against nature:

A sexual act such as anal sex, which is considered to be against the law of nature, is also legally punishable as per section 377 of the Indian Penal Code even when it happens between a willing married couple.

5 In public:

A sexual act in public places (where others witness it) is also prohibited as per the law. Privacy during sexual act is of prime importance while living in a civilised society. Besides not being able to experience the much needed let go during the sexual act that gets hampered if there is no privacy, our social structure very rightly does not permit us to get intimate in the presence of others even legally.

6 Group sex:

Sexual acts such as Group-Sex or Orgies may not fit as illegal into any of the sections of penal code, if the involved people are adults and willing, however it is definitely not accepted by the moral standards of most of the societies and therefore prohibited. Even medically, group sex is considered as high-risk behaviour with very high chances of transmission of Sexually Transmitted Diseases including HIV.

RELIGIOUS RESTRICTIONS THAT ARE FADING

Most of the legal restrictions on sexual behaviour have their roots in religious teachings; however, some religious ideas related to sexual behaviour have not been able to find place in law books. Modern societies have been able to discard some of the religious tenets related to sexual behaviour permanently after finding no logic in observing them.

E.g.

- No sex for anyone on certain religious days, weeks or months.
- No sex after certain age limit or menopause even for a willing married couple.
- No sex if you are a widow.
- No sex ever, if you have taken the oath of celibacy (Bramhacharya) or Sannyas.

Medical Science Prescribes 'No Sex' in the Following Conditions

1 Physical illness:

During any physical illness for which bed rest is advised, sex is not permitted for obvious medical reasons. In some (not all) cases of Ischemic Heart disease where actual bed rest may not be advised, penetrative sexual activity is still not advisable as such sexual act puts undue pressure on heart.

2 Post surgery:

After ANY surgery how-so-ever minor it is, sex is prohibited until the operating surgeon has examined the person and confirmed complete healing of the surgical wound. Major surgeries prevent sex for at least three months but even minor surgeries require some time for the complete recovery before which sex is not advisable.

3 Sexually Transmitted Diseases [STD]:

When either of the partners is carrying a STD, sex is absolutely prohibited to avoid transmission. Even mere suspicion of STDs such as HIV/AIDS, Hepatitis-B, Syphilis prompts doctors to advise 'no sex' till the suspicion is ruled out through laboratory tests.

4 Other communicable infections:

Besides sexually transmitted venereal infections, there are many other communicable infections such as Pulmonary Tuberculosis and all respiratory infections, skin infections such as Herpes, chickenpox or other bacterial and parasitic skin infections which can also be transmitted during intimate physical contact. Sex is prohibited in all such cases till the infection is cured and is no more communicable.

5 Mental illness:

Mental illness in oneself or in the partner becomes a major barrier in the sexual relationships of many couples. Some mental illnesses such as depression, anxiety neurosis, severe mental stress or nervous breakdown themselves finish sexual desire in a person.

Pain – An Alarm

Pain during intercourse is one of the important causes to abandon the act, till the cause is found, treated and eliminated. Pain is like an alarm, which alerts you to investigating into the cause of the problem. Painful intercourse could lead to physical as well as psychological problems and complications affecting sexual relationship severely. It is absolutely not advisable to tolerate pain during sex.

During Pregnancy and After Childbirth

Gynaecologists advise that intercourse should be avoided from the sixth to the twelfth week of pregnancy; as it can cause a miscarriage. Sexual abstinence is recommended during the last two months of pregnancy too. At this time, there is a risk of the essential amniotic fluid leaking out during intercourse. However, the couple can and should engage in gentle lovemaking, fondling and caressing.

In short, intercourse during the first three months and the last two months of pregnancy is not advisable. During the fourth to seventh month of pregnancy, intercourse is allowed unless you are otherwise advised for medical reasons.

After childbirth usually intercourse is not advisable for about six weeks. After that it is advisable to get oneself examined by a gynaecologist before resuming sexual intercourse. Anytime between when her baby becomes three to six months old, a woman begins to return to her pre-pregnancy state. She begins to menstruate again and her sexual desire returns too.

Emotional Issues

Very often couples fail to have mutually satisfying sexual encounters when there are unresolved emotional issues between them. At such times, it is best to not have sex for a while as either one, or both, may not feel intimate, and it could be detrimental to the relationship in the long run, if they have forced sex or sex as a ritual. Working towards resolving all issues and having an emotional closure then needs to be the number one priority, after which the emotional intimacy, if re-established, will naturally lead to mutually fulfilling physical intimacy.

Thus, sex should be seen as a mind-body phenomenon, and if either the mind or the body is not in homeostasis, then sex can only be a mechanical act, and should be refrained from, for the long-term well-being of the relationship.

Chapter 20

MENOPAUSE: A CHANGE OF LIFE

Discussing the movement from a reproductive to a nonreproductive age

Menopause, climacteric, or change of life are all terms used to describe that part of the aging process during which a **woman passes from the reproductive to the non-reproductive years.** The change of life can begin up to ten years prior to actual menopause, i.e. the time that menstruation stops. Many women experience changes in their menstrual cycles during this period.

There are two types of menopause: natural and surgical. The natural menopause starts somewhere between the 42nd and 45th year of life and lasts for about eight to ten years. The average age at which natural menopause occurs is fifty years. **Menopause before the age of 40 is considered premature.** Surgical menopause is a result of removal of the uterus (hysterectomy) or ovaries (oophorectomy), or both.

Physical Signs of Menopause

Many women experience physical changes during and after menopause. One of the first changes is missed periods. Some women just stop having periods, while others skip some months. **Pregnancy can still occur during this time.**

Contraception should be continued for one year following the last menstrual period. If there is any bleeding, after six months have lapsed without menstrual periods, it should be reported to a doctor.

Hot flushes are the most common characteristics of menopause. The hot flush is a sudden flushing and sweating of the skin, usually from the neck up. Some women experience a simple warming sensation throughout the body. Others feel acute flushes that begin with a sensation of pressure in the head similar to a headache, which then leads to a feeling of heat or burning in the face, neck, and chest, followed immediately by an outbreak of sweating. Episodes may last 20 to 60 seconds and occur up to every hour. The frequency can vary from one or two a week to one or two per hour. In most cases, hot flushes are mild and disappear after a year or two. Some women could experience them acutely for as long as two or three years.

Some women also experience night sweats. This symptom can disturb a woman's sleep and contribute to fatigue during the day. Another common change is vaginal dryness. Some women may begin to find sexual stimulation uncomfortable because of decreased lubrication.

Emotional Aspects of Menopause

Many women have heard that emotional upheavals may occur because of menopause. However, since menopause often happens during a time in a woman's life when there may be social changes such as children leaving home or changes in job status, it is difficult to attribute emotional changes specifically to menopause when these other life changes are occurring as well. Many women do experience night sweats that may disturb the sleep cycle and potentially affect their mood. It is important to remember that all women will experience menopause differently and will need individual attention and consideration.

Cause of Menopause

Menopause results from decreased production of the hormones oestrogen and progesterone by the ovaries. Through a complex system, the pituitary gland stimulates the ovaries to mature and release an egg every month. Oestrogen and progesterone help regulate this event. As a woman matures, the ovaries have fewer eggs to stimulate, and eventually oestrogen and progesterone production in the ovaries ceases.

Physiological Changes Associated with Menopause

- **Genito-urinary tract:** Most menopausal women will experience thinning of the skin of the vagina, vulva and urethra. These are referred to as atrophic changes.

- **Musculo-skeletal system:** All women lose bone density after menopause. This can lead to osteoporosis or brittle bones. A significant number of women experience fractures as a result of this change, especially hip or wrist fractures. Women with early menopause are at highest risk of osteoporosis.

- **Skin and hair:** Many women experience thinning of hair and skin. Skin may become loose, and thus lose some of its natural elasticity. Wrinkling of the skin however, is not specific to menopause: sun exposure, heredity, diet and smoking, all contribute to wrinkling. Some women experience abnormal hair growth after menopause, particularly on the face. Others may experience thinning of the scalp and pubic hair.

- **Weight gain:** An increase in body fat, especially around the abdomen, can occur during menopause, because of hormonal changes.

Heart Health after menopause: Women rarely die of heart disease before menopause because oestrogen provides protection against it – partially by helping to keep cholesterol levels in check. For reasons not completely understood by medical science, there is a relationship between hormone levels and the development of the plaque-like substance inside the blood vessels that can cause blockage and lead to heart disease. **A woman's risk of cardiovascular disease increases dramatically after menopause.** Surgical menopause (due to oophorectomy/total hysterectomy) also increases the risk for heart disease, even in young women.

Menopause itself is a risk factor for cardiovascular disease, along with high blood pressure, smoking, family history, poor diet, high blood cholesterol, diabetes, and obesity. Hormone replacement therapy (HRT) may help to promote cardiovascular health; but reducing the risk factors that are within your control can be equally important. Proper nutrition, regular exercise, maintaining your proper weight, and quitting smoking are key strategies for ensuring your cardiovascular health during midlife and beyond.

Maintaining Health Before, During and After Menopause

As is true throughout a woman's life, it is important to eat a nutritionally balanced diet which includes adequate amounts of calcium. Foods rich in calcium include milk, yogurt, cheese and broccoli. Three eight-ounce servings of milk or yogurt per day will provide a substantial portion of the daily calcium requirement.

Try to exercise at least three times a week for 20-30 minutes. Weightbearing exercises such as walking, jogging and aerobics are best. Good nutrition and exercise are two ways to help prevent both, osteoporosis and cardiovascular disease.

Many women feel more relaxed and enjoy their sexuality more after menopause, because the worry of pregnancy is gone. However, some of the changes in the skin and genital tract, can make intercourse or sexual stimulation uncomfortable. Vaginal lubricants and hormone replacement therapy may help with this problem.

As always, see your doctor once a year for a physical that includes a breast examination, pap smear, sonography of the pelvis, a pelvic examination, and to educate yourself about keeping a watch on any physical changes that indicate the onset of a disease, in order to catch it in its early stage.

Hormone Replacement Theraphy (HRT)

Every woman should learn about HRT in order to evaluate whether or not it is appropriate and necessary for her. HRT refers to the replacement of hormones that are no longer produced naturally, i.e. oestrogen, and if the uterus is intact, progesterone. The replacement hormones may be administered through pills, a skin patch, injections or a vaginal cream. There are different regimens for HRT, some of which cause monthly vaginal bleeding. This often disappears over time.

What are the benefits and risks? Although the studies

concerning HRT are limited, some clear benefits have been identified. They include:

1. Decreased dryness and thinning of mucous membranes and skin
2. Prevention of osteoporosis
3. Decreased frequency, intensity and duration of hot flushes and night sweats
4. Prevention of cardiovascular disease.

When replacement oestrogen was first administered, an increased risk of uterine cancer was noted, but when progesterone was added, that risk was reduced. There is also a concern about the **risk of breast cancer** with HRT. Study results are equivocal, with some indicating a slightly increased risk, and others showing no increased risk. Generally HRT is not recommended for women who have had breast cancer; it is not yet clear whether women with a strong family history of breast cancer should avoid HRT. Decisions should be made on an individual basis in consultation with a gynaecologist and/or an endocrinologist.

Conclusion

Menopause is a time of physical and emotional change for women. Good health habits such as eating a balanced diet with adequate sources of calcium, exercising 30 minutes three times a week, not smoking, avoiding excessive alcohol consumption, and seeing a doctor regularly are very important. Women should discuss HRT with their doctors as a possible method for alleviating the symptoms of menopause and preventing osteoporosis and heart disease.

Chapter 21

APHRODISIACS

Discussing the most popular sexual myth

The biggest and most popular myth that has survived down the ages is about aphrodisiacs. Centuries ago, people believed that aphrodisiacs had magical powers to open up the gates of divine sexual pleasures and fantasies. That belief exists even today. Almost in every corner of the world people still use aphrodisiacs to rev up their sex lives. It could be something as ordinary as banana or vanilla or as absurd as zebra tongue or tiger penis. All kinds of common and peculiar foods, beverages, drugs, magical potions, and chemical concoctions have been tried as aphrodisiacs to enhance sexual pleasure, energy and drive.

Named after Aphrodite, the Greek goddess of love, beauty and fertility, Aphrodisiacs are those substances that supposedly induce or boost sexual desire in a person. Several herbs, chemicals, plants, drugs, foodstuffs, and other substances are claimed to have positive effects on the human sexual function. However, there is no scientific evidence to back this up. Also, many so-called aphrodisiacs can be potentially toxic and thus be harmful. It is absolutely not advisable to try anything without scrupulously researching it first, although it may be difficult to find authentic and accurate information because of a lack of scientific evidence on the efficacy and safety of certain substances in human beings.

Non-prescription drugs, vitamins, plants, herbs and supplements that claim to enhance sexual function or alleviate erectile problems are mostly found to be ineffective.

Some of the popular foods that people have consumed as aphrodisiacs are oysters, bananas, asparagus, carrots, avocados, etc. People have traditionally endowed them with aphrodisiacal properties probably because of their resemblance to sexual organs. Garlic is another widely accepted stimulant. So are nutmeg and almond. According to stories, application of almond paste awakens passion in a female, just as the scent and flavour of vanilla is said to increase lust.

Chocolate is universally appreciated as an aphrodisiac. The two chemicals present in chocolate which are being closely studied are serotonin and phenylethylamine. They are believed to create feelings of ecstasy and unbridled bliss.

Plenty of references have been made to aphrodisiacs in ancient literature and history. In 19th century France, bridegrooms were served three courses of asparagus at their prenuptial dinner. The Aztecs referred to the avocado tree as the testicle tree and in Spain, Catholic priests forbade its consumption. Cleopatra, known for her beauty and amorous exploits, is believed to have used aphrodisiacs like cardamom, figs, aromatherapy and pearls to enhance her sexual prowess.

Most of the aphrodisiac claims are based predominantly on cultural myths than fact. Their fascination continues to this day, as people still experiment with them to boost their sex lives. Most of the existing evidence is very subjective and anecdotal.

In India, musk has long been held as a stimulating agent. In

Ayurveda, shilajit, the sap of minerals derived from the asphalt rock formations in the Himalayas is claimed to work like an aphrodisiac. Milk with a hint of saffron is given even today on the wedding night to supposedly set the libido on fire.

There are other more prized and deadly aphrodisiacs. For instance, the rhinoceros horns that bears a phallic symbol, is used in many cultures to perk up sexual performance. Zebra tongue and tiger penis is believed to boost your machismo.

What about Spanish Fly for Women?

The most famous and potent aphrodisiac of all is considered to be the Spanish Fly, a powder made of ground-up beetle. When consumed, the Spanish Fly is supposed to create an inimitable state of euphoria. This beetle is found in some parts of Europe. Spanish Fly makes the blood vessels around a woman's genitals dilate and throb, giving her the false sensation of sexual arousal. If a woman takes it internally, it causes inflammation and irritation of the urinary tract, which could result in permanent damage to her urinary system. Luckily, it is not available in India. What is available in the name of Spanish fly is a fake remedy.

Yohimbine chloridea standardised form of Yohimbine, one of the few drugs approved in the US for treatment of impotence, is found to be useful only in some cases of erectile dysfunction. Controlled studies in USA suggest that it is not always an effective treatment for impotence, and evidence of so-called increased sex drive is purely anecdotal.

There may be plenty of vibrancy and high spiritedness in the world of aphrodisiacs, but delve a bit deeper and all that you come across is disheartening delusion and deception. Aphrodisiacs don't perform miracles. Actually they don't perform at all because **there is no such thing as an aphrodisiac. There is no food or substance that exists in the world that can be called a sex tonic, sex stimuli, sex drug or aphrodisiac. All such claims are misleading.**

People should not be under the false impression that use of aphrodisiacs can set you on fire sexually or can solve all your bedroom problems.

Although countless research and studies are being done the world over about aphrodisiacs and their effect, nobody has been able to prove successfully that aphrodisiacs stimulate sexual desire in human beings. No scientific confirmations have been made yet about chemicals permeating the hypothalamic region of the brain. It is the hypothalamus, a complex region in the brain that controls sexual desire. Thus, it is wrong to make claims that aphrodisiacs work as stimulants and can increase your libido or solve all your sexual inadequacies.

Irrespective of whether or not aphrodisiacs act on the body, the power of suggestion, psychologically, is the key. If one greatly believes that using any particular substance (alleged aphrodisiac or not) will help boost his/her sexual capabilities, then it can help bring about sexual desire and arousal at least in the short-term, but this is more psychogenic and a self-suggestion, and the substance merely works as a placebo. Of course, a well rested body, adequate time, privacy, a conducive environment, confidence in your contraception, a relaxed state of mind, and an attraction for the partner may do just the same thing. Of course, as we always say, 'Love is the greatest aphrodisiac' that never fails, and that has been proven time and time again. What drugs cannot do… Love can. 'True Love' is the most powerful stimulant and aphrodisiac. If the couple does not feel for each other, they could consume all the world's oysters, tiger penis or Spanish Fly, but it will be in vain.

The second most important aphrodisiac, we tell our patients, is your health. If you are in good health, not suffering from high blood pressure, high cholesterol or other diseases, and you are relaxed, you can lead a healthy sexual life. Then you don't need an artificial agent to get aroused. You cannot isolate sexual health from the rest of your body. If you have a healthy diet and maintain good health, you will automatically have a satisfactory sexual life.

Our patients frequently ask us, "Doctor, which is the best diet for sex?" And we often repeat this line that "what is good for your heart is also good for your penis."

You'll be surprised to see the large number of ads for aphrodisiacs appearing in regional vernacular papers – all of them desperately wooing customers with promises of sexual bliss. These ads are published by fraudulent companies making cheap drugs, unscrupulous medical practitioners, quacks and others. After reading them, people come to us for advice on the use of aphrodisiacs. They get shocked when we debunk the aphrodisiac theory and tell them something as simple as good health ensures good sexual life. Eat the right food and lead a healthy lifestyle, and you will be naturally stimulated when required. Sexual desire or drive cannot be induced with the help of an outside agent, it has to come from within.

What about Viagra (Sildenafil Citrate)?

Effective drugs like Sildenafil citrate (Viagra) and Tadalafil (Tazzle), are now available in India for the complaint of inability to 'sustain' the erection. These drugs also cannot bring about an 'artificial' erection in a flaccid penis. They only help to sustain the existing normal erection longer. These drugs are useless in those who have difficulty in getting an erection. They absolutely do not enhance libido or induce sexual desire. They help only those who get an erection on their own but cannot sustain it long enough to perform satisfactory sexual intercourse. It is absolutely not advisable to take these drugs without a proper prescription by a qualified specialist. There are risks involved in taking them; and unless one is guided by a qualified expert, self-medication should strictly be avoided.

How does Sildenafil (Viagra) Work?

Nitric oxide (NO) is the principle neurotransmitter causing penile erection. Whenever there is sexual stimulation, Nitric Oxide (NO) is released from the nerve endings and endothelial cells in the spongy erectile tissue (corpus cavernosum) of the penis. NO increases the activation of cGMP (Cyclic Guanosine Monophospate) in the cavernosal smooth muscle cell, causing a relaxation of the arterial, arteriolar, and sinusoidal smooth muscle, which causes an inflow of blood into the penis, which then leads to an erection. cGMP is then hydrolysed back to the inactive GMP by PDE5 (Phosphodiesteras Type 5). This results in loss of the erection. Men who do not produce a sufficient amount of cGMP will have problems achieving an erection. Likewise, men with high levels of the enzyme PDE5 will have problems maintaining an erection.

Sildenafil (Viagra) works on an enzymatic level. Sildenafil suppresses the enzyme PDE5 in the penis. PDE5 is responsible for making the penis lose its erection and making it flaccid. On suppressing PDE5, the penis maintains its erection for a longer time.

Downside of Sildenafil (Viagra)

- Sildenafil is effective in only 70 per cent cases. Moreover, it takes up to an hour for the body to absorb it and show any effect.

- Sildenafil is contraindicated in those cases in which heartdisease medications such as nitrate drugs are being used. The combination of Sildenafil and nitrates can make your blood pressure suddenly drop to unsafe levels, causing dizziness, fainting, a stroke, or even a heart attack.

- In rare instances, men taking Sildenafil have reported a sudden decrease or loss of vision.

- Sudden decrease or loss of hearing has also been reported in people taking Sildenafil.

- Some men may experience a flushed face, altered color perception, bluish vision, blurred vision, upset stomach or a headache.

- If one has prostate problems or high blood pressure and is on medication such as alpha blockers, Sildenafil must be avoided.

- Priapism, a painful and prolonged erection that lasts for two to six hours, is a rare but potentially serious side effect of Sildenafil. A prolonged erection can permanently damage the tissues of the penis.

- The safety of Sildenafil has not been studied adequately for men above sixty five years of age.
- It is also not medically advisable to take it twice in one day.

Chapter 22

PARAPHILIAS: AROUSAL BEYOND THE NORMS

Discussing arousal variants

What Is Paraphilia?

The term Paraphilia was coined by Dr. Wilhelm Stekel in the 1920s. From its Greek roots, Paraphilia literally means love that goes beyond what is common, or what is expected. It was further popularised by Dr. John Money in the 1960s. Psychiatrists codified paraphilias as disorders in 1980 in the Diagnostic and Statistical Manual of Mental Disorders (DSM). The DSM describes paraphilias as conditions that are characterised by intense and recurrent sexual urges, behaviours or fantasies that involve unusual objects, activities, or situations, and cause clinically significant distress or impairment in social, occupational and other areas of functioning.

In simple words, it is a condition in which a person's sexual arousal and fulfilment depends on an unusual fantasy theme of an uncommon sexual experience that becomes the essential and primary focus of his/her sexual behaviour. A paraphilia can revolve around a specific object (clothes, shoes, children, animals, a certain body part etc.) or an unusual sexual act (exposing private parts in public places, wearing clothes of the opposite gender, inflicting injury on and causing pain to self or the other, making obscene phone calls etc.). The nature of a paraphilia is more often than not, quite specific and unchanging. Most paraphilias are significantly more common in men than in women.

The *Diagnostic and Statistical Manual of Mental Disorders* (DSM – 1980) provides clinical criteria for paraphilias. Some pharaphilias are as follows:

- **Exhibitionism:** The recurrent urge and/or behaviour of exposing one's genitals to an unsuspecting person. It can also be the recurrent urge and/or behaviour to perform sexual acts in a public place, or in view of unsuspecting persons
- **Fetishism:** The use of inanimate objects to gain sexual excitement. Partialism refers to fetishes specifically involving non-sexual parts of the body
- **Frotteurism:** the recurrent urge and/or behaviour of touching or rubbing against a non-consenting person
- **Pedophilia:** A psychological disorder in which an adult experiences a sexual preference for pre-pubescent children, or has engaged in child sexual abuse
- **Masochism:** The recurrent urge and/or behaviour of wanting to be humiliated, beaten, bound, or otherwise made to suffer for sexual pleasure
- **Sadism:** The recurrent urge and/or behaviour involving acts in which the pain or humiliation of a partner is sexually exciting
- **Transvestic fetishism:** Arousal from 'clothing associated with members of the opposite sex'

- **Voyeurism:** The recurrent urge and/or behaviour of observing an unsuspecting person who is naked, disrobing or engaging in sexual activities, or it may not be sexual in nature at all.

Fetishism

Fetishism by definition is an obsession or a fixation on a body part or an object that is not basically sexual in nature, and the compulsive need or demand for its use in order to experience sexual gratification. Fetishism is a non-coercive paraphilia. The object of a fetish is almost always habitually used by the fetishist during masturbation and may also be incorporated into the sexual act with a partner to bring about sexual arousal.

Fetishism is one of the most complex topics in sexology. It is not known how fetishes begin, though most likely they are a combination of one's genetic make-up (nature) and experiences one has had while growing up (nurture). Often a fetishist may find it very difficult to perform sexually, unless the fetish object is available; or may obsess over the fetish to the exclusion of other forms of sexual activity.

Psychotherapy can help fetishists to deal with their desires, to make positive life choices and to learn to accept themselves. It is worrisome only when the fetish is accompanied by other disturbing signs such as, very low frustration tolerance, obsessive-compulsive behaviour, weak impulse control or inability to function normally at work, home, or in society.

Exhibitionism

Exhibitionism is a form of paraphilia in which a person obtains sexual pleasure from exposing his or her genitals to strangers of the opposite sex, usually in a public place. The exhibitionist invariably suffers from the recurrent urge to expose his genitals to an unsuspecting person. Most exhibitionists are men and the victims are usually women, however, there are also some documented cases of female exhibitionists.

Exhibitionists are invariably not interested in touching women or having sex with anyone. They derive sexual satisfaction from the expression of shock or disgust on their victim's face. Exhibitionists often masturbate before exposing themselves, or later, by recalling the event while masturbating.

Sadomasochism

Sadomasochism can actually be divided into two different paraphilias – sadism and masochism. Sadists experience sexual pleasure and arousal from inflicting mild or mock pain on others. The majority of the time, this activity occurs with a willing partner. The counterpart to the sadist is the masochist. A masochist experiences sexual pleasure and arousal from receiving mild or mock pain. Sadomasochism, or S&M, is fairly common in its less extreme forms. Bondage and discipline, or B&D, is a type of S&M where one partner ties or restrains the other, and then pretends to punish or discipline the person who is in bondage.

Paedophilia

From its Greek roots, paedophilia implies love of a child (paidos + philia). Paedophilia is a disorder in which there is a predilection for sexual activity with pre-pubertal age children. A paedophile is a person who derives sexual pleasure from engaging in sexual activity with prepubertal age children. Paedophiles are almost always males. The children are more often of the opposite sex and are characteristically 13 years of age or younger.

Where Does It Begin?

During adolescence (Age 10 to 19 years), boys and girls start becoming sexually mature and start developing secondary sexual characteristics. During this phase of life, besides physically growing to become adults, a lot of psychological and emotional changes start happening rather rapidly. Strong sexual feelings and thoughts start crossing the psyche erratically. Unusual and unexpected sexual dreams, strong physical attraction for the opposite sex, overwhelming urges to associate, relate, connect and impress the opposite sex start occurring.

At this age, most people have sexual fantasies that serve a variety of functions and result in a wide range of responses within the individual. Some are pleasant or stimulating; others are confusing, embarrassing or even shocking.

The desire to know about something not yet experienced, forbidden or seemingly unattainable is often a key feature of sexual fantasies. Although it is only a make-believe excursion of the mind, fantasies do help young adults find temporary relief, excitement, adventure, selfconfidence and pleasure. Through fantasy, the real, unfavourable world can be transformed into whatever he or she likes, no matter how brief or improbable it might be. In this sense, in the growing years of early adulthood, it is a useful mechanism for sexual gratification. However, with every pleasure comes the very real possibility of a person getting obsessed with, or addicted to, and losing conscious control over, the phenomenon. The same device that was so useful when single can become an impediment and an obstacle once he or she is in a committed relationship.

Sexual fantasies occur in an astonishingly wide variety of circumstances and settings. Sometimes these imaginative interludes are intentionally called forth to enliven a boring experience, to pass the time, or to provide a sense of excitement. At other times, sexual fantasies float into awareness in a seemingly random fashion, perhaps triggered by feelings and thoughts of which we have little or no awareness.

Not all sexual fantasies are wilfully conjured up or pleasurable. Some fantasies recur over and over again despite being unwanted; other fantasies flood into the individual's awareness in a frightening fashion, producing inner turmoil or conflict and feelings of guilt and shame. Fantasies of this sort may either result in sexual arousal or may be so distressing that sexual feelings may shut off.

There are situations in which preferential fantasies may become troublesome. For some people, the repeated and exclusive use of such a fantasy may lead to a situation in which the fantasy becomes mandatory for sexual arousal. The person no longer responds sexually to one's partner since sexual arousal depends on fantasy alone. Sometimes, preferential fantasies can become obsessions that may interfere with behaviour or the thinking-feeling process.

CASES

One day, 13-year-old Vikas came out nude from his bathroom to his bedroom as always, and was accidentally exposed to a group of adolescent girls (friends of his 16-year-old elder sister) who had entered his room to access the internet on his PC. The sudden shock on their face and the undivided intense attention received unexpectedly from a group of teenage girls overwhelmed Vikas and gave him a sexual high as never before. He started masturbating regularly recalling the whole incident. As time passed he developed a full-fledged fixation for suddenly exposing himself to teenage girls and experiencing the sexual high. He had become an exhibitionist.

12-year-old Irfan was the eldest amongst eleven of his cousins. During the summer vacations, when the entire joint family would gather in their huge ancestral home for the holidays, Irfan would be given the responsibility of keeping all the younger children occupied in play etc. During such times, Irfan would often feel aroused while touching and holding his younger cousins while playing with them. Initially unknowingly, but subsequently knowingly, he started masturbating by rubbing himself against his younger cousins during play time. This was his initial and intense experience with sexual gratification in an otherwise orthodox family. He started masturbating recalling all such times and with time developed paedophilia.

13-year-old Peter had seen his parents engaging in intercourse and with time had started experiencing intense arousal watching them having sex. The day his mother discovered it, he was brutally beaten up and severely punished. He was confused when he experienced intense arousal when he was beaten up by his mother over this issue. He would often recall the whole incident related to watching them and the subsequent thrashing, and masturbate in privacy. By the time he completed his education and got married he had developed this fixation of being beaten up and getting sexually aroused. He had developed the paraphilia called Masochism.

Generally, imagination, creativity and playfulness are part of the act of fantasising. However if a fantasy becomes the controlling force in a person's life, the play element may get completely lost. A phenomenon that is found extremely prevalent with fantasising is that the person returns to a particular preferred fantasy again and again, and gets comfortable with or even addicted to it. Occasionally, minor variations may be played out in such a preferred fantasy, but by and large the central theme remains fixed.

Mental Health Implications

For almost half a century, psychoanalysts studied fantasies in depth. They viewed deviant sexual fantasies – those portraying anything other than heterosexual acts that led to intercourse – as immature expressions of the sex drive and as blocks to the development of more mature sexuality. Many psychoanalysts strongly believed that such fantasies were most likely to be forerunners of actual deviant sexual behaviour.

Medical science distinguishes between optional, preferred and exclusive paraphilias.

An optional paraphilia is an alternative way to sexual arousal. For instance, a man with otherwise routine and normal sexual interests might sometimes seek or enhance sexual arousal by wearing women's clothes. Optional paraphilias can disrupt otherwise stable relationships sometimes, when discovered by an unsuspecting partner. Open communication and mutual support can minimise or prevent such disruption in these cases.

In preferred paraphilias, a person obviously prefers the paraphilia to conventional sexual activities, but is also capable of engaging in conventional sexual activities. For instance, a man prefers to wear women's clothes during sexual activity. Preferred paraphilias often disrupt otherwise stable relationships.

In exclusive paraphilias, a person is unable to become sexually aroused in the absence of the paraphilia. Exclusive paraphilia almost always prevents normal courtship and committed romantic relationships, even when one desires such a relationship. Thus, loneliness or social isolation are common consequences.

In extreme cases, persistent or recurrent mental fixation with a preferred or exclusive paraphilia completely eliminates the more classical desire for real loving human relationships.

A Warning

Some popular magazines and even books written by sexologists suggest that if you are not turned on by your partner, you should fantasise about someone else while having sex. We personally do not agree with this suggestion. These things may work to improve one's sex life temporarily and on a superficial level. But beware of the great danger in superficial sexual remedies. As one becomes more and more dependent on outside stimulation, one decreases his/her natural ability to feel turned on by one's partner. You may feel turned on while being with your partner but not **by** her or him. Two people who are turned on **within** himself or herself, but not **by** the other person, are two people who are having sex, but not making love.

Chapter 23

CHROMOSOMES AND GENES

Discussing the microscopic building blocks

Each cell of our body contains a set of instructions called Genes that control the activities of that cell. We receive some of these genes from our father and some from our mother. It is genes that determine heredity. Each of the genes is a molecule of a complex chemical, called DNA (Deoxyribonucleic Acid). Although there are about 1.5 lakh genes in every cell, to fit them in, they are strung together in long chains that are coiled up in structures called Chromosomes (literally meaning coloured bodies). If viewed very closely, a chromosome appears like a tight coil.

Chromosomes are tiny rod-shaped structures in the nucleus of each cell. There are 23 pairs of them, making 46 chromosomes in total. An ovum and a sperm only have a single set of 23 chromosomes. When an ovum and sperm unite, they have the full set of chromosomes.

If a person's chromosomes are photographed under a special microscope, and images of the individual chromosomes are then cut up and arranged by size, we can see that there are 23 pairs. This procedure is called Karyotyping.

During Pregnancy, a sample of the amniotic fluid surrounding the fetus (baby) can be obtained via a thin needle inserted into the mother's uterus (womb). The amniotic fluid contains some of the baby's cells, whose chromosomes can be inspected through Karyotyping. This test is called Amniocentesis. It can reveal the baby's sex and any problems with the chromosomes.

Sex-Determining Chromosomes

A woman has 23 pairs of chromosomes, and the members of each pair are much identical. A man has 22 similar pairs and one pair consisting of two chromosomes that are different in size and structure. The 23rd pair in both the sexes are called sex chromosomes. The remaining pairs are called Autosomes. The two identical sex chromosomes in the female are called X chromosomes. One of the sex chromosomes in the male is also an X chromosome, but the other shorter one is called the Y chromosome. Each ovum produced by the female bears one X chromosome, but the sperm produced by the male can have either an X or a Y chromosome.

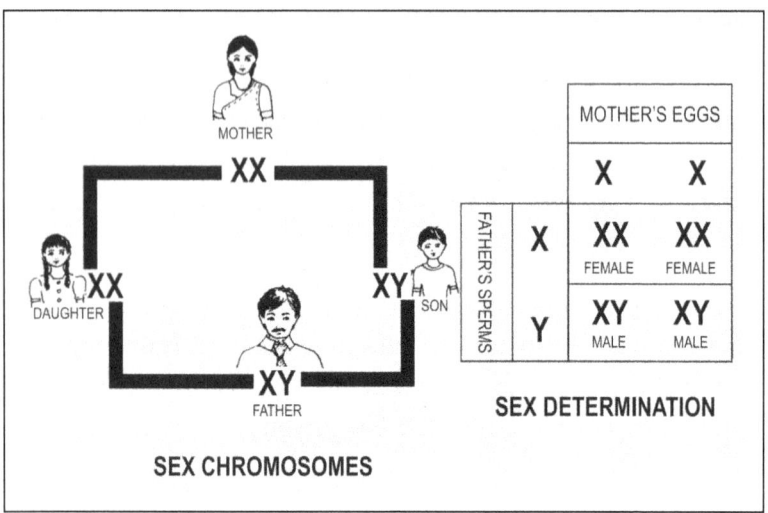

The union of an ovum, which always bears an X chromosome, with a sperm also bearing an X chromosome produces a female foetus – carrying XX chromosomes.

The union of an ovum with a sperm that contains a Y chromosome produces a male fetus – carrying XY chromosomes.

This is how the sex of a person is determined.

Identical Twins (Monozygotic/Uniovular Twins)

Identical twins or Monozygotic/Uniovular twins are produced when the zygote (the fertilised egg), splits into two. This division usually occurs within the first 12-14 days after conception when the egg gets implanted in the uterus. Even with recent advances in medicine and technology, medical science has still not figured out why the splitting of the single zygote occurs. Essentially, it results in the growth of two genetically identical babies sharing 100 per cent of their DNA. The creation of twins in this way ensures that they are always of the same sex, and accounts for the striking similarities in appearance usually exhibited by identical twins

Conjoined Twins (Siamese Twins)

These are identical twins which develop with a single placenta from a single fertilised ovum. They are the product of developing embryos that begin to split into identical twins during the first three weeks of gestation, but for some unknown reason stop part way, leaving the partially separated egg to mature into a fetus. Conjoined or Siamese twins are always of the same sex. They are rather uncommon, occurring once in every 40,000 births but only once in every 200,000 live births. Statistics suggest that between 40 per cent to 75 per cent, are either still born or die within 24 hours. Conjoined twins are more often female than male.

Non-Identical Twins (Dizygotic/Binovular/Fraternal Twins)

Twins that are not genetically identical are called dizygotic twins. This is simply two separate pregnancies that just happen to occur at the same time. Each embryo is in its own amniotic sac and has its own placenta. When twins are binovular, it means that two separate eggs have been impregnated by two separate sperms during ovulation. This results in the formation of fraternal twins. These infants have a different genetic make-up although they share the uterus during gestation. In contrast to monozygotic twins, they usually have different hereditary traits; genetically, they are no more alike than siblings born years apart. They do not necessarily look alike, and they can be either of the same or of different sex.

Chapter 24

SEXUAL ORIENTATION

Discussing the variations in orientation

What Is Sexual Orientation?

Sexual orientation is a term used to refer to an individual's primary physical, emotional, romantic and sexual attraction to individuals of a specific gender (male or female). The most commonly recognised sexual orientations are heterosexuality, homosexuality and bisexuality.

According to the American Psychological Association (APA) "it also refers to an individual's sense of personal and social identity based on those attractions, behaviours expressing them, and membership in a community of others who share them."

Homosexuality and Lesbianism

A sexual attraction to (or a sexual relation with) persons of the same sex is known as homosexuality. While homosexuality would technically cover same-sex preferences among both males and females, lesbianism is a term which specially implies female-female preference. Studies in the West have shown that about 4 per cent men and 2-3 per cent women are exclusively homosexuals, and 10 per cent men and women are bisexuals as they enjoy sex with both genders.

History of Homosexuality

Homosexuality has existed since ancient times. It has been admired as well as condemned throughout recorded history, depending on the culture in which it existed and the form that it took.

The first known mention of homosexuality in the print medium has been found in an 1869 German pamphlet by the Austrian-born novelist Karl-Maria Kertbeny.

In 1952, when the American Psychiatric Association published its first Diagnostic and Statistical Manual of Mental Disorders (DSM), homosexuality was included as a disorder. The American Psychiatric Association however removed homosexuality from the DSM in 1973, stating that homosexuality per se implies no impairment in judgment, stability, reliability, or general social or vocational capabilities.

The World Health Organisation listed homosexuality as a mental illness in 1977. This reference was subsequently removed on May 17, 1990 after the forty-third World Health Assembly.

In a detailed compilation of historical and ethnographic materials of Pre-industrial Cultures, strong disapproval of homosexuality was reported in 41 per cent of 42 cultures; it was accepted or ignored by 21 per cent, and 12 per cent reported no such concept. Of 70 ethnographies, 59 per cent reported homosexuality absent or rare in frequency and 41 per cent reported it present or not uncommon.

So far there has been no conclusive scientific evidence to believe that a person is born with a particular sexual orientation. There is no consensus among scientists about

the exact reasons that an individual develops a heterosexual, homosexual or bisexual orientation. Although much research has examined the possible genetic, hormonal, anatomical, developmental, cultural and social influences on sexual orientation, no findings have convincingly emerged, that permit scientists to conclude that sexual orientation is determined by any particular factor.

The American Psychiatric Association has stated that, to date, there are no replicated scientific studies supporting any specific biological etiology for homosexuality. The American Psychological Association has stated that there are probably many reasons for a person's sexual orientation and the reasons may be different for different people. However, the largest group of researchers believe that sexual orientation (Homosexuality, Heterosexuality or Bisexuality) is the result of an unconscious choice that a person makes during his growing years, due to various known and unknown factors, often beyond the conscious control of the person. It is the result of various factors such as the basic personality type, uncensored exposure to sex, sexual values in the environment, parental influence, moralistic/dogmatic upbringing which condemns sexual feelings, lack of correct and valuebased sex education, experience of direct or indirect childhood sexual abuse etc. However, if a person truly wishes to modify his/her sexual orientation at any age willingly, it is possible to help such a person through therapy. Such modification of course, cannot and should not be imposed on him/her. His/her self-motivation is imperative, as therapy is a collaborative process.

Functionality of a person is not connected to his/her sexual orientation. Thus, the homosexual/lesbian could very well be mentally sound, emotionally stable, intelligent, sharp, talented, efficient, hard working, faithful, trustworthy and socially well-adjusted like the rest of the (non-homosexual) population. As such, irrespective of one's sexual orientation, each individual deserves to be unconditionally accepted and respected as equals in the human society.

IN A LETTER TO AN AMERICAN MOTHER IN 1935, SIGMUND FREUD WROTE:

"Homosexuality is assuredly no advantage, but it is nothing to be ashamed of, no vice, no degradation, it cannot be classified as an illness; we consider it to be a variation of the sexual function produced by a certain arrest of sexual development. Many highly respectable individuals of ancient and modern times have been homosexuals, with several of the greatest men among them (Plato, Michelangelo, Leonardo da Vinci, etc.). It is a great injustice to persecute homosexuality as a crime, and cruelty too."

Coming out: Coming out in the open or declaring your homosexual orientation is necessary, especially if you want to take certain decisions that may require social approval. By and large, coming out in the open happens in three phases. The first phase is the phase of knowing oneself and the realisation or decision emerges that one prefers to same-sex relations. This could be described as an internal coming out. The second phase implies one's choice to come out to others e.g. family, friends and social circle. The third phase usually involves living openly as a homosexual or lesbian person with or without a partner.

What Is Homophobia?

Homophobia precisely means an irrational fear or aversion towards homosexuality, but the common usage of this term includes much more than plain simple fear. It is also an attitude of hatred, repulsion, disgust or rejection towards homosexuals based on the belief that homosexuality is morally wrong, disgraceful, disgusting and shameful. Homophobia also includes a fear of intimate relationships with the same sex. Unfortunately, this term is either loosely used by some people (that includes some social activists and legal experts working for the rights of homosexuals), or then the definition is not accurately understood by some.

Human Rights for Homosexuals

All human beings have equal worth and therefore, whether heterosexual or homosexual, everyone has the right to live with human dignity. We believe in equal human rights for homosexuals. They absolutely do not deserve to be treated like an inferior human species or second-class citizens of the world. **They are as much human as anyone else, and thus deserve to be treated humanely.**

However, as per the present Indian Penal Code Section 377, any sexual act (with the other) which is against the order of nature is punishable. Sexual activity such as Anal sex is thought to be against the order of nature and thus punishable. Anal sex is practiced by some homosexual partners. As per Section 377, anal sex is a punishable offence, even between husband and wife or any two hetero-sexual partners with mutual consent.

Being in the field of sexual medicine for over two decades, we have seen severe medical complications arising out of consensual sodomy or anal sex, whether between two homosexuals, or even when it has been compelled on a woman by a man. Therefore, while all human beings should be viewed and treated equally with the same human dignity by law and society, **all sexual acts done by anyone homosexual or heterosexual, if causing physical or emotional trauma to another, (whether minor or major), should also be equally viewed by the law of the land.**

CASES

Jagan a 19-year-old illiterate boy from a very poor family from rural India got a job in Mumbai as a domestic servant. His distant relative, a 37-year-old man Prakash who was working as a cook in a rich family, got him this much needed opening. The rich owners of the house would leave the house everyday in the morning and would return at 8 in the night. In their absence Prakash would use cooking oil as a medium and force anal sex on Jagan. Jagan was helplessly dependant on Prakash and could never gather courage to resist him and started consenting to the exploitation, till one day he developed a rectal prolapse, bled profusely, and had to be taken to the hospital.

Vinod and Swapnil, two 18-year-old boys were working as office boys in a private office. They would surf the net in the absence of senior employees and watch porn. One day they consensually attempted anal sex with each other and invited double trouble. While Vinod developed a bad tear in his rectum, Swapnil developed Paraphimosis – a painful surgical condition of the penile foreskin that needs an emergency circumcision surgery without which the penis could be permanently damaged.

Amit was a 20-year-old frail boy from a poor family. His father was dead and his mother was old and ill with two younger sisters at home to support. He got a job of a peon in a private office after a lot of struggle and a long wait. His boss, a 46-year-old rich married man fancied anal sex. He pressurised Amit to have anal sex with him after office hours in the privacy of his cabin. Amit felt helpless as this job was vital for him. He consented to the demands of his boss. A few months later, when he approached a doctor, he had developed infected painful fissures at his anus, and had partially lost control on the sphincter mechanism of the anal opening which was not functioning due to the injuries during anal sex. He had lost his job and had no courage to approach the police as he felt he had neither the moral right nor the legal standing as he was major and had consented to this act in privacy.

Amol, a 32-year-old married government employee was a bisexual. He would indulge in anal sex with some of his male office colleagues consensually for mutual pleasure. His wife was completely oblivious to this side of her husband. Amol also never felt that his secret parallel life would ever affect his marriage. During the second pregnancy of his wife, the obstetrician detected that she was not only HIV positive, but her tests for Syphilis, Hepatitis-B and Genital Herpes were also found positive. Amol too was tested positive for these four STDs. It was obvious that Amol had contracted all these STDs from his multiple homosexual contacts and now his wife and unborn child were also victims of these life threatening infections.

In all the four cases above, the involved individuals were adults and were engaging in anal sex with mutual consent in 'privacy'. These are just a few typical examples. Incidents such as these are rampant, and doctors are asked to treat several such cases in their private practice as well as in general hospitals.

Any sexual activity is strictly a matter of personal choice, but should be with genuine mutual consent (which has not been extracted under any kind of pressure/coercion). **It is strictly your personal choice to indulge in any act you enjoy as long as you are not causing any physical or psychological harm to each other.**

Medical Facts Related to Anal Sex

Medical science regards anal sex as high-risk behaviour. Physiologically, the anus is not designed for penetration by any hard object. The anal sphincter tightens ordinarily if stimulated, as a protective reflex action, and any attempt at penile insertion may be distressing, even if done slowly and gradually. If the penis is forced into the anus, injury is possible. The lining (mucus membrane) of the rectum is very thin, tears easily, does not heal fast and therefore is vulnerable to infections. Also, the tears can enlarge to a fissure or a crack leading to the outside of your body. These are painful and slow to heal. There is also a possibility that a fistula could open up, allowing faeces to reroute into the abdominal cavity or into the vagina. This can cause serious surgical complications. One may lose control over the anal sphincter, causing continuous involuntary leakage of faecal matter. There is also the increased risk of haemorrhoids, which are quite uncomfortable. Rectal prolapse, wherein the walls of the rectum protrude through the anus and hence become visible outside the body, is another surgical emergency that is seen resulting out of anal intercourse.

Some of the micro-organisms that are normally present in the anus of even a healthy individual are known for causing severe urinary infection if they enter the urethra and urinary tract. During anal sex the urethra actually enters the rectum, inviting infective bacteria into the urethra and thus the urinary tract. Repeated urinary infection can cause serious problems such as renal damage and even kidney failure.

Masters and Johnson in their book on *Sex and Human Loving* warn that because bacteria are naturally present in the anus, anything that has been inserted into the anus if subsequently put into the vagina, can cause severe vaginal infections. Therefore moving from anal intercourse to vaginal intercourse is extremely hazardous.

The rate of transmission of HIV (and other STDs) through anal sex is much higher compared to other penetrative sexual acts. It will be enlightening to know that **the condom, which is thought to be a means of so-called safe sex, is not designed for anal sex by the manufacturers. Anal sex involves a totally different kind of pressure dynamics, and the latex or polyurethane condoms are not manufactured keeping these pressure dynamics in mind. The condom is far more likely to get torn during anal sex (thus paving the way for the transmission of HIV/AIDS and other STDs). Therefore, it can be concluded that anal sex even with the use of a condom is definitely a high risk behaviour.**

While it is true that **as a society we need to learn to accept all persons with equal human rights irrespective of their choices, it is equally true that we reserve the right to reject certain behaviours that are injurious to the health** of those persons or others connected to them. Those choosing to be in loving same-sex relationships are no less human, and do not deserve any less respect, than anyone else. Talking in condescending terms to them or about them, or mollifying/placating them, both, reinforce a discriminatory attitude towards them. Therefore, an equal human approach must be adopted by the moral keepers of our society and by the law of our land.

What Is Gender Identity?

The sense of belonging to a particular sex, not only biologically but also psychologically and socially, is called gender identity. Sex refers to our biological sex, as determined by chromosomes and sexual organs. Sexual orientation refers to our attraction to others of the same or opposite gender. Gender identity, on the other hand, refers to an individual's identification with male or female gender roles and behaviours.

Gender Identity Disorder

(Transsexualism, Transgender, Gender Dysphoria)

Most biological men (XY) identify as male and most biological women (XX) identify as female. However, there are a minority of individuals who feel that their biological sex and their gender do not match.

Gender Identity Disorder (GID) or Gender Dysphoria or Transsexualism is a condition in which there is a strong and persistent cross-gender identification, i.e. a desire to live and be accepted as a member of the opposite sex. They believe that they should be the opposite sex. They are troubled with their sexual role and sex organs and may express a need to modify their bodies.

Transsexualism is a natural, medically recognised condition, though rare (about one in 30,000 individuals).

There is a persistent discomfort in transsexuals with his or her anatomical sex and a sense of inappropriateness in the gender role of that sex. For example, a person who is identified as male at birth, and has lived being perceived by others as a boy/male, may feel that his core sense of who he is, is a closer fit with a female or a woman. Commonly heard statements from transsexuals include, "I am a man in a woman's body" or, "I am a woman. I was born a woman, but unfortunately God gave me the wrong body." If this sense is strong and persistent, such people may decide to take steps to ensure that others perceive them as the core gender they believe they are. They often attempt to pass socially as the opposite sex. In other words, they may decide to transition to living as the sex that more closely matches their internal gender. They make every attempt to alter their physical appearance cosmetically and hormonally, and may eventually also decide to undergo a sex-change operation.

True transsexuals have normal XY (male) or XX (female) sex chromosomes appropriate for their physical gender. The vast majority of transsexuals have no identifiable physical abnormality. There is no laboratory test for Transsexualism. A transsexual person may have any sexual orientation i.e. s/he could be heterosexual, homosexual, bisexual, polysexual or even asexual. Thus, transsexual does not imply any specific form of sexual orientation.

Children with GID refuse to dress and behave in stereotypical ways in keeping with their anatomical gender. It is necessary to note that many children experience fantasies about being a member of the opposite sex. Such cross-gender behaviours generally become less obvious with time and by late adolescence, they are usually no longer present.

The distinction between these children and children with GID is that the latter experience significant disturbance in functioning because of their cross-gender identification. They may become socially withdrawn, severely depressed or abnormally anxious as they grow up.

Parents are more keen to bring boys (called sissies) to doctors for an evaluation, than girls (called tomboys). This is because there is more social acceptance of tomboys than there is of sissies.

The organic (biological) causes of GID are not known. According to one theory, a prenatal hormonal imbalance in the mother may predispose individuals to GID. Some others believe that sociological factors like problems in the individual's family dynamics, could also play a role in GID.

The Diagnostic and Statistical Manual of Mental Disorders, (the standard diagnostic reference for United States mental health professionals), describes the criteria for gender identity disorder as strong and lasting cross-gender identification and persistent discomfort with one's biological gender role. For classification as a clinical disorder, this discomfort must cause a significant amount of distress or impairment in the functioning of the individual.

The current edition of the *Diagnostic and Statistical Manual of Mental Disorders* (DSM-IV) has five criteria that must be met before a diagnosis of gender identity disorder (302.85) can be made:

1. There must be evidence of a strong and persistent cross-gender identification
2. This cross-gender identification must not merely be a desire for any perceived cultural advantages of being the other sex
3. There must also be evidence of persistent discomfort about one's assigned sex or a sense of inappropriateness in the gender role of that sex
4. The individual must not have a concurrent physical intersex condition (e.g., androgen insensitivity syndrome or congenital adrenal hyperplasia)
5. There must be evidence of clinically significant distress or impairment in social, occupational, or other important areas of functioning.

Gender identity disorder is usually diagnosed by a qualified expert in sexual medicine (with adequate training and experience in assessing and counselling such cases), or a psychiatrist (who has adequate training and experience in assessment of such cases) who conducts an interview with the person and takes the detailed social history. Family members are also interviewed during the assessment process.

Treatment for children with gender identity disorder mainly focuses on treating secondary emotional problems such as anxiety, confusion and depression and teaching them unconditional self-acceptance.

Sex Reassignment Surgery (Sex-Change Operation)

Transsexual adults often request hormone and surgical treatments to suppress their biological sexual characteristics and obtain those of the opposite sex. Usually sex reassignment surgery is not offered to anyone under the age of eighteen. Before the sex-change surgery can be considered, candidates undergo at least a year of psychotherapy with a specialist therapist who is trained and experienced in dealing with such cases. A real life test of living as a member of the desired gender for at least a year is suggested. A team of trained and experienced professionals, that includes the treating psychiatrist, sexologist, and surgeon, oversee this transitioning process. Because of the irreversible nature of the sex reassignment surgery, candidates for surgery are evaluated comprehensively and are often required to spend a period of time integrating themselves into the cross-gender role before the surgical procedure is undertaken.

Note: The concept of treatment for GID subjects has become greatly politicised, since some people fear that treatment of GID is actually a finely disguised attempt to curb or even reject homosexuality.

▪ An Educative Note for Medical Doctors

A male who has been cleared for sex-change surgery will have a vaginoplasty, i.e. a surgical technique for creating a 'neovagina.' The testes and penis are surgically removed. Surgeons also perform corrective plastic surgery on the larynx, and the growth of facial and body hair is suppressed with a drug like cyproterone acetate.

The surgery for changing a man into a woman is simpler than the surgery for changing a woman into a man. A woman who has been cleared for sex-change surgery will go through surgical removal of the breasts, uterus and ovaries. In some cases, a phalloplasty is also performed, creating a neophallus.

Significant social, occupational and personal issues arise from sex change surgery, and the person requires sustained psychotherapy and supportive counselling, before and after the surgery.

Transvestitism (Cross-Dressing)

Transvestitism, commonly referred to as cross-dressing, involves experiencing sexual pleasure and arousal from dressing in clothes normally used by members of the opposite sex. As compared to females, males are far more likely to engage in cross-dressing for sexual gratification. Female cross-dressers may be less obvious, since women commonly wear male clothing (trousers, shirts etc) in our society. In some people, cross-dressing may become a compulsion, or sexual arousal may be exclusively dependent upon cross-dressing. Most transvestites are heterosexual men whose behaviour pattern does not match with transsexualism. Other transvestites are homosexual men (drag queens), who often develop elaborate feminine personas.

Is Being Transsexual the Same As Being A Homosexual or a Transvestite?

Not at all! Homosexuals are sexually attracted to members of their own sex but are content with their bodies and have no desire to change their body or do not feel a misfit in their body. Their anatomical sex and gender identity is the same. Transvestites too are anatomical men with the gender identity of a man, but who are preoccupied with cross dressing in women's clothing largely for the purpose of sexual arousal and satisfaction. They are generally happy with themselves as men.

Eunuch

A eunuch is a castrated man; in particular, one who is castrated early enough to have major hormonal consequences. Castration is the process of removing the testes. Castration may also involve removal of the penis. There can be various reasons for castration.

If the testes are removed before puberty, the male will not develop all the secondary sexual characteristics of a normal male. If the male is castrated after puberty, the adult sexual characteristics already acquired will tend to become less prominent and diminish. Congenital bilateral undescended testes (Cryptorchism) can also lead to the same consequence.

The English word eunuch is derived from the Greek eune (bed) and ekhein (to keep), i.e. bed keeper. The term eunuch usually refers to those men who are castrated in order to perform a specific social function, as was common in many societies of the past.

In the Middle-Eastern countries and some Asian countries, it was necessary to have men to guard the harems, and as keeping a fox to look after geese is seldom desirable, it was considered imperative to ensure that these men did not take too good care of the women of the harem.

Till about 1825, little Italian boys used to be taken to the local barber by their mothers to be castrated and thereafter sold to the Turks, who paid a good price for them. Other advantages of castration were also discovered in Italy, for instance, the voice of castrated boys did not break upon reaching puberty, and therefore stayed high and melodious for singing.

Surgical removal of testes (Castration) is also done in some cases when a malignant growth of the testes is detected.

Mentally deficient and severely spastic children are sometimes castrated to avoid complications that could arise out of their sexual development.

Castration also used to be a punishment for sexual offences in some countries.

Hermaphrodite (Intersex)

This term is derived from the name of the son of Greek gods Hermes and Aphrodite. Hermes was the God of Intelligence and Wisdom, and Aphrodite was the Goddess of Beauty and Love. According to the legend, the son of these two Greek gods was half man and half woman, especially in regard to the sexual organs.

Hermaphroditism is ALWAYS used in connection with the anatomy of the genital organs. A hermaphrodite may have separate ovaries and testes, but more commonly, has an ovo-testis which is a gonad containing both sorts of tissue. This can be on one or both sides of the body. 60 per cent of hermaphrodites will have an XX karyotype and the remaining may have an XY karyotype or a mosaic (a mixture). There may be a uterus or more commonly, a hemi-uterus (half uterus) on the side where there is ovarian tissue. The person may be raised female or male, and often undergoes genital surgery. The ovo-testis is usually removed because of the risk of developing malignancy.

Every single cell in a man's body is male and every single cell in a woman's body is female. From a cellular viewpoint there is no such thing as a hermaphrodite. It is restricted to the anatomy of the genital organs only. Various types and degrees of hermaphroditism have been documented.

Klinefelter Syndrome (True Eunuch)

(XXY sex chromosomal configuration)

Normally, a human being has a total of 46 chromosomes in each cell, two of which (X and Y) are responsible for determining that person's sex. The combination of these two types of sex chromosomes determines the sex of a person. Males have one X and one Y chromosome (the XY combination) and Females have two X chromosomes (the XX combination).

Klinefelter syndrome is a condition in which one or more extra X chromosomes are present in a male. Most commonly, a male with Klinefelter syndrome will be born with 47 chromosomes in each cell, rather than the normal number of 46. The extra chromosome is an X chromosome. This means that rather than having the normal XY combination, the male with Klinefelter syndrome has an XXY combination. Because people with Klinefelter syndrome have a Y chromosome, they are all male.

Boys with Klinefelter syndrome appear normal at birth and have normal male genitalia. They enter puberty normally, but by mid puberty have low levels of testosterone causing small testicles and the inability to produce sperms.

Klinefelter syndrome is one of the most common chromosomal abnormalities, however it is not considered an inherited condition. About one in every 600 to 800 males is born with this disorder. The condition appears to affect all ethnic and racial groups equally.

From childhood, males with Klinefelter syndrome are taller than average with long limbs. Many males with Klinefelter syndrome have poor upper body strength and can be clumsy. Approximately one-third of males with Klinefelter syndrome have gynecomastia, with some even going for breast reduction surgery.

Children with Klinefelter syndrome frequently have difficulty with language, including learning to speak, read, and write. Approximately 50 per cent males with Klinefelter syndrome are dyslexic. They might also experience a tremor or shaking in the body.

Some people with Klinefelter syndrome have difficulty with social skills and tend to be shy, withdrawn, introvert, anxious or immature than their peers. They can also have poor judgment and are unable to handle stressful situations well. As a result, they often do not feel comfortable in large social gatherings.

Klinefelter Syndrome Variants

Diagnosis of Klinefelter syndrome is made by examining chromosomes for evidence of more than one X chromosome present in a male. Some men with Klinefelter syndrome go through life without being diagnosed.

Males with more than one additional extra X chromosome, such as 48 chromosomes (XXXY), are usually more severely affected than males with 47 chromosomes (XXY). The greater the number of X chromosomes present, the greater the disability; each extra X chromosome lowers the child's IQ by about 15 points.

Mosaic Klinefelter syndrome occurs when some of the cells in the body have an extra X chromosome and the others have normal male XY chromosomes. These males can have the same or milder symptoms than non-mosaic Klinefelter syndrome.

What Is LGBT?

LGBT (or GLBT) is an abbreviation referring collectively to Lesbian, Gay, Bisexual and Transsexual people. This abbreviation has been used commonly since 1990s.

Chapter 25

DE-STIGMATISING
SEX THERAPY

Discussing when to consult a sex therapist

Whenever we suffer an asthmatic attack or a lung infection we immediately go to a chest physician and promptly get ourselves treated. If our digestive system gets dysfunctional, we do not hesitate to go to a gastroenterologist. For a skin problem dermatologists are consulted promptly. Any chest pain and we rush for an electrocardiogram to a heart specialist. But whenever a man suffers from a sexual problem such as erectile dysfunction or premature ejaculation, where neither can he enjoy sex himself nor can he satisfy his wife, he either deliberately avoids going to a sex therapist, or then he is totally ignorant about the existence of a specialist who is trained in treating sexual problems.

If a woman suffers pain during intercourse or finds herself unable to reach an orgasm, she at the most, may visit her gynaecologist but would never even think of consulting a sex therapist.

Why Is it So

Why do we hesitate to consult a sex therapist? According to us, it's because of three main causes.

We have been taught to look down upon sex and sexual desire as something dirty, shameful, vulgar and condemnable for generations. A person feels guilty if he has a normal sexual urge. Those who consciously suppress their sexual desire and refrain from sex are respected and glorified in society. A young man feels guilty if he gets sexually aroused looking at a beautiful young woman. He feels like a sinner whenever he masturbates or gets a wet-dream. A woman too, condemns herself if she experiences normal sexual urges. It often happens that the husband either looks down upon his wife for her expression of a sexual urge or even starts suspecting her fidelity if she shows active interest in sexual gratification. This age-old condemnatory attitude towards sex and sexual desire comes in the way of consulting a sex therapist whenever one has a query or difficulty regarding his/her sexual desire, sexual capability or sexual satisfaction.

Another reason why people avoid consulting a sex therapist is that there are a number of quacks, who pose as sex specialists through advertisements. Many times, these people are unqualified and untrained. They do not even have a proper medical degree. They display either false degrees or unknown degrees. They deliberately propagate myths such as masturbation is harmful or wet-dreams is a disease. Due to lack of proper sex education in schools, colleges or for that matter anywhere in society, a common man falls prey to such fraudulent advertisements and lands up getting cheated by these quacks. We would like to enlighten readers that qualified medical practitioners are not allowed legally to publish or display any kind of advertisement. This simply proves that ALL those who give advertisements of their so-called sex clinics are frauds and cheats.

Serious Lack of Qualified Sex Therapists

Unfortunately, there is a serious lack of qualified sex therapists even in metropolitan cities. As compared to the number of cardiologists, child specialists, orthopaedic surgeons, skin specialists etc. we have less than 1 per cent truly qualified/ genuine sex therapists even in Mumbai, the commercial capital of our country. This lack of availability of genuinely practicing sex therapists makes it further difficult for a person to take the step towards getting his/her sexual problem treated correctly and in time.

The third reason why people either hesitate or completely avoid consulting a sex therapist is due to a lack of clarity about when to consult a sex therapist?

Women prefer visiting a gynaecologist whenever they have complaints related to their genital area. It is true that gynaecologists are trained in treating any organic (biological) problem related to the genitals. However, very often sexual problems are emotional, psychological or relational in origin and gynaecologists have no training in tackling such a problem. Women's sexual problems such as fear of intercourse, inability to relax and actively participate in the sexual act, frigidity, not being able to climax (orgasm), vaginismus etc. are not biological problems. Such problems are either emotional/psychological in nature or have their roots in the lack of proper pre-marital counselling and sex education for both husband and wife. Even qualified gynaecologists have no inkling or training in handling these problems. Sometimes some aware people consult a clinical psychologist or a counsellor for such problems. Unfortunately, clinical psychologists and counsellors are graduates or post-graduates in psychology from the arts stream, and totally lack the knowledge in medical science. This makes them completely incapable of helping those who require sex therapy.

Very often men tend to go to skin and VD specialists for their sexual problems. Skin and VD specialists are undoubtedly trained in treating skin diseases and sexually transmitted infections, but they are not trained in sexual problems such as erectile dysfunction (impotence) or premature ejaculation. They are utter aliens when it comes to treating cases that require sex counselling and sex therapy.

Therefore, one needs to understand when to consult a qualified/trained sex therapist.

Situations/Conditions When One Needs to and Should Consult a Sex Therapist

1 When s/he finds that s/he has no desire, low desire or altered desire for sex. When we say altered, it means a person experiences intense and recurrent sexual urges, behaviours or fantasies that involve unusual objects, activities or situations and cause clinically significant distress or impairment in social, occupational and other areas of functioning

2 When the sexual desire and need of married partners is mismatched most of the time

3 When a man either fails to attain or sustain erection in spite of appropriate sexual stimulation i.e. Erectile Dysfunction

4 When a man is unable to penetrate and perform intercourse during sexual intimacy with a willing partner

5 When a man ejaculates earlier than his own or his

partner's expectations persistently on a regular basis i.e. Premature ejaculation, resulting in a lack of sexual satisfaction for the partner

6 When a man takes excessively long time to ejaculate or is unable to ejaculate in spite of a proper sexual intercourse with a willing partner

7 When s/he has disturbing doubts and anxieties related to his/her sexual desire, arousal, capability (potency), stamina, performance or satisfaction

8 Whenever s/he has doubts or anxieties about the anatomy and physiology (functioning) of one's own or the partner's sex organs

9 When s/he has disturbing attitudinal issues regarding one's own or his/her partner's role in a sexual act. For e.g. who should take the initiative, what is the correct technique and duration of foreplay, what should be the correct frequency of intercourse, when and where intercourse should or should not be performed, who is supposed to be an active partner, should s/he fantasise about somebody else while having sex with the spouse

10 When s/he is obsessively preoccupied with sexual feelings, desires or urges that it is affecting his/her ability to perform essential human duties and responsibilities

11 When s/he has urges to engage in perverted sexual behaviours such as sadomasochism and anal sex

12 When intercourse is either not happening or it is painful in spite of mutual willingness, cooperation and active participation

13 When a woman is unable to achieve orgasm at any time or most of the times during willing sexual encounters with a loving partner in spite of mutual cooperation and active participation

14 Before the marriage for a proper sex education session

15 When a person is confused about his/her sexual orientation and sexual preferences

16 When a person is struggling with feelings of guilt/shame regarding sex.

This covers all possible situations and conditions when one should consult a genuine sex therapist for help.

To conclude, in spite of so many problems faced by so many people regarding their sexuality, it is unfortunate that they either do not acknowledge that they have a problem, or acknowledge but do not accept that they need to seek help to address the issue, or they accept but do not take the action of consulting a sex therapist because of the stigma attached to consulting a sex therapist.

It is important in this day and age when men and women are walking shoulder to shoulder in all the areas of life, and when women are gradually feeling more liberated about their sexuality, that mutual sexual satisfaction and sexual health be given the status that it deserves in a relationship, and this is where the sex therapist comes in.

Chapter 26

UNSAFE SEX

Discussing sexually transmitted diseases

The Facts

All plants and animals that reproduce sexually may develop Sexually Transmitted Diseases (STDs). They are also very common among human beings.

About **one out of four people (25 per cent) who have sex with another person, acquires a sexually transmitted disease.**

Sexually transmitted diseases (STDs) are diseases that are passed from one person to another by vaginal, oral and anal intercourse or other intimate contact. There are more than 30 such diseases. The most serious STDs are usually passed through penetrative sexual intercourse. The dark, warm, moist parts of our body are the common places where these infections originate and grow.

Millions of teenage boys and girls have STDs. But many of them have absolutely no symptoms at all and are not even aware that they are carrying the infection.

STDs can cause serious and permanent damage to an individual's health without displaying any symptoms or signs. Women and girls that are not treated for STDs may NEVER be able to bear children. Some STDs can be transmitted to the fetus during pregnancy and/or during childbirth. Some STDs can cause a lifetime of health problems and/or even death.

The most serious STD in humans is the Human Immunodeficiency Virus (HIV), which can cause AIDS (Acquired Immunodeficiency Syndrome). AIDS is the last stage of an HIV infection and is fatal. **There is no cure for HIV/AIDS.** A person can carry the virus (HIV) in the body for six to ten years or even more, before any signs and symptoms appear. During this period people with HIV can infect ALL their sex partners without even realising it.

Common symptoms or signs of STDs are blisters and sores on or around the sex organs or mouth; unusual discharges from the penis or vagina; itching, irritations, rashes and bumps on the sex organs and other parts of the body; and burning and pain during urination.

Many people, unfortunately, regard sexually transmitted diseases as a moral issue; hence the feeling of guilt and shame attached to it. The stigma results in people infected with STDs not acknowledging the problem, and thus their sexual health gets ignored.

Don't let embarrassment become a health risk. Many people find sex and diseases that involve the genitals very difficult to talk about. But when shame gets in the way of common sense, it keeps people from taking care of themselves and their sexual partners. It is necessary to speak frankly and openly with your doctor about your sexual health. Doctors on their own may or may not ask about your sexual well-being…so take charge and speak up.

Safer sex practices only allow a person to reduce (and not eliminate) sexual health risks. Safer sex is anything we do to lower our risk of contracting or transmitting sexually transmitted diseases. The basic rule for safer sex is to prevent direct contact with genitals and prevent the exchange of body fluids, such as semen, serum (blood), saliva and secretions at and around the genitalia.

If you or your partner has any of the following symptoms in the genital area, consult a doctor immediately.

- Abnormal or foul smelling discharges from the vagina, penis or rectum.

➤ Unusual bleeding	➤ Blisters
➤ Boils	➤ Buboes (a lymph node that is inflamed)
➤ Burning sensations	➤ Chancres (small, hard, painless nodule at the site of entry of a pathogen)
➤ Growths	➤ Itches
➤ Irritations	➤ Offensive odours
➤ Pus	➤ Painful intercourse
➤ Pain	➤ Polyps
➤ Rashes	➤ Swellings
➤ Sores (open skin infections)	➤ Tenderness
➤ Urinary changes	➤ Ulcers
➤ Vaginal yeast infections	➤ Warts

Some symptoms of STDs are similar to those of other infections. They may not even manifest in or around the genital area; but they could be serious. It is most advisable to seek medical advice if any of such symptoms listed below appear and/or persist.

- weight loss that is constant, rapid, or unexplained
- coatings of the mouth, throat, or vagina
- abdominal pain
- aching joints
- loss of appetite
- bowel problems
- chills
- diarrhoea
- coughs
- vomiting
- discoloured skin
- fatigue
- feeling exhausted
- fever
- general weakness
- growths
- hair loss
- hearing loss
- headaches
- jaundice
- light-headedness
- mental disorders
- muscular pain
- nausea
- night sweats
- sore throat
- swollen glands
- vision loss

Common Sexually Transmitted Infections

- Bacterial Vaginosis
- Chlamydia
- Cytomegalovirus (CMV)
- Genital Warts
- Gonorrhea
- Hepatitus B Virus (HBV)
- Herpes
- Human Immunodeficiency Virus (HIV)
- Molluscum Contagiosum
- Pelvic Inflammatory Disease (PID)
- Pubic Lice
- Scabies
- Syphilis
- Trichomonal Vaginitis infection (Trichomoniasis)
- Urinary Tract Infections

Now let us learn about some important STDs.

Chlamydia

Chlamydia trachomatis is a bacterium that can cause an STD. Chlamydia is the most common STD and the number of persons infected with it is on the rise. It is transmitted through sexual contact (vaginal, anal, or oral sex) with an infected person. It is thought to affect approximately one in 100 sexually active people under the age of 25. The bacteria infect the cervix, urethra, rectum, throat and eyes. Symptoms usually appear one to three weeks after infection.

About 75 per cent women and up to 50 per cent men infected with Chlamydia have no symptoms. Because of this, a substantial number of infections do not manifest, and therefore, remain unknown and undiagnosed. In women, symptoms could include lower abdominal pain, bleeding after sex, bleeding between periods, and unusual vaginal discharge or pain when passing urine. Symptoms in men could include, discharge from the penis and pain on passing urine. If you have a rectal infection you may have discharge, pain, inflammation and sometimes bleeding from the anus. Men can develop testicular pain and Reiter's syndrome (arthritis).

Chlamydia can be easily treated and cured with antibiotics. Because men and women infected with Chlamydia often also have gonorrhoea, treatment for gonorrhoea is often provided as well. It is important to make sure that your sex partner also receives treatment in order to prevent infecting each other again. Avoid having sex while being treated. This reduces the chance of re-infection and/or transmitting it to someone else.

If left untreated in women, it can spread into the pelvic area and infect the uterus, fallopian tubes, and ovaries – leading to pelvic inflammatory disease (PID). PID can be a very serious condition and requires immediate medical care. It may cause permanent damage to the woman's reproductive organs and can lead to infertility, chronic pelvic pain, and an increased risk of ectopic pregnancy.

Chlamydia can cause early labour and delivery, and can be passed from mother to baby during birth. Chlamydia infection in newborns can cause neonatal conjunctivitis (an infection of the baby's eyes) and pneumonia. Without prompt medical treatment, the infant's eyes can be seriously and permanently damaged.

In men, untreated Chlamydia can affect the testicles, leading to swelling and pain. Related complications can also lead to infertility.

The primary risk factors for chlamydia include:

- Engaging in unsafe sex
- Having sex with more than one partner
- Being in a sexual relationship with someone who has/had multiple sex partners

Gonorrhoea

Gonorrhoea is a bacterial infection caused by the bacteria Neisseria gonorrhoeae. It is transmitted through sexual contact (vaginal, anal, or oral sex) with an infected person. Gonorrhoea is similar to chlamydia but less common. Women aged 16-24, and men aged 20-24 are at the greatest risk.

About 50 per cent of women and up to 20 per cent of men infected with gonorrhoea have no symptoms. Gonorrhoea passed on during oral sex does not usually cause symptoms, even though the infected person is a carrier of the infection, and can continue to infect others through sexual contact without his own knowledge.

Gonorrhoea can lead to infection of the urethra, cervix, rectum, mouth and throat.

The symptoms, complications and primary risk factors of Gonorrhoea are identical to that of Chlamydia. On rare occasions, Gonorrhoea can even cause inflammation of the heart, a certain type of liver disease and also life-threatening meningitis.

Gonorrhoea can be easily treated and cured with specific antibiotics. Because men and women infected with Gonorrhoea, also often have chlamydia, treatment for chlamydia is usually provided as well. If untreated, this infection can cause infertility in women and in men. Gonorrhoea can be passed from mother to baby during birth, infecting the baby's eyes, and without prompt treatment, the infant's eyes can be seriously and permanently damaged.

Syphilis

Syphilis is an infectious systemic disease that may be either congenital or acquired through sexual contact. It is caused by the spirochete bacterium Treponema pallidum. It is a complex systemic disease with protean variations that can mimic many common infections or illnesses. It manifests in both, an acute and chronic form, and it causes a range of symptoms at different stages of infection affecting most of the body's organ systems. The variety of symptoms makes it easy to confuse Syphilis with less serious diseases and ignore its early signs. If left untreated, Syphilis can have many serious complications.

Syphilis is transmitted through sexual contact (vaginal, anal or oral) with an infected person. In particular, the syphilis bacterium is transmitted through direct contact with syphilis sores, which mainly occur in the genital area of both men and women. Because the sores are often painless, the infected person may not know that s/he is infected.

If contracted before or during pregnancy, it can be passed from mother to infant, resulting in congenital Syphilis. Babies with congenital Syphilis may suffer from blindness, other severe organ damage, and even death (still-born baby).

What Are the Risk Factors for Syphilis?

The primary risk factors for Syphilis include:

Engaging in unsafe sex
Having sex with more than one partner
Having sex with someone who has multiple sex partners

Acquired Syphilis has four stages (primary, secondary, latent, and tertiary) and can be spread by sexual contact during the first three of these four stages.

Primary symptoms: The first symptom of Syphilis infection is usually a small painless sore (chancre) in the area of sexual contact (penis, vagina, anus, rectum, or mouth). The sore usually appears about 2-4 weeks after exposure, and disappears even without any treatment within 4-6 weeks.

Secondary symptoms: Soon after the sore heals, a pinkish rash all over the body including soles of the feet and palms of the hands, swollen lymph nodes in the groin, fever, headache, loss of appetite, loss of weight, hoarseness of voice or prostration (extreme physical exhaustion) may be observed. The rash does not cause any burning or itching. These symptoms also disappear within 3-6 months without any treatment. Even though the initial symptoms resolve on their own, the Syphilis bacterium remains in the body if not treated. After this stage the disease remains in a latent stage for some time.

Latent symptoms: During the latent stage of Syphilis there are no symptoms, but the bacterium is still in the body. During this stage, the bacteria spread in the eyes, the nervous system, the cardiovascular system, and even the bones. After this the disease manifests ultimately in its tertiary stage, in the form of serious diseases of the nervous system, cardiovascular system, dementia, blindness and ultimately death.

Syphilis can be diagnosed in several ways. A sample from the Syphilis sore can be examined under a microscope. In addition, a blood test (VDRL and/or TPHA) can be used to diagnose Syphilis.

Syphilis is treated and cured effectively with the antibiotic penicillin. People who have had Syphilis for less than one year can be cured with one dose of penicillin. For people who have had Syphilis longer, more doses of penicillin are required.

It is important to make sure your sex partner(s) also receives treatment in order to prevent getting infected again. Avoid having sex while being treated to reduce the chances of getting the infection again or transmitting it to your partner.

Herpes

Herpes is a viral infection caused by two different but closely related viruses – Herpes Simplex Virus Type 1 (HSV-1) and Herpes Simplex Virus Type 2 (HSV-2). Both are easily transmitted. Brief, direct contact is all that is needed to pass the virus. Both have similar symptoms, and can occur on different parts of the body. When the infection is on the mouth, it is called oral herpes. When it is on or near the sex organs, it is called genital herpes.

Symptoms of herpes are usually tingling or itching on or around the genital area (penis, vulva, vagina, cervix, buttocks or anus), and/or on the lips or inside the mouth, followed by the appearance of small and painful blisters i.e. cold sores or fever blisters. Symptoms may last several weeks and go away, but the virus stays in the body, and can flare up and cause sores again. These sores may return in weeks, months, or years. Symptoms are more painful and last longer in women or men with illnesses that weaken the immune system – like leukemia and HIV.

The first episode of symptoms of a genital herpes infection is called primary herpes. Primary herpes usually begins two to three weeks after the virus enters the body, though it could also happen earlier, or even take much longer.

The symptoms of later episodes are usually less severe than the first.

Herpes is easily spread by casual touching, kissing, and sexual contact, including vaginal, anal, and oral sex. It can be passed from one partner to another and even from one part of one's own body to another. It is also possible, to get herpes from someone who does not even have sores.

If a pregnant woman is infected; contact with herpes sores during delivery can lead to severe damage of the nervous system of the baby and even death.

A special blood test can detect if you have been exposed to the Herpes virus – even if you do not have any obvious symptoms.

Is there a cure for herpes?

No complete cure is available as yet for herpes, but an anti-viral drug such as Aciclovir, can reduce the severity of the first and recurrent episodes, as well as the duration of the first episode. In most cases, the frequency and intensity of the outbreaks reduces over the course of a few years.

Genital Warts

Human Papilloma Virus (HPV) infection

Genital warts or Venereal warts are caused by the Human Papilloma Virus (HPV) infection. HPV infection is also known as acuminate warts, condyloma acuminata, verruca acuminata or genital warts. They are fleshy growths found on or around the genitals and anus. Sometimes they can be found in the mouth or in the throat. The warts are usually painless, but can itch, get inflamed and may even bleed. Warts are not always visible, especially if they occur inside the vagina particularly on the cervix, or in the anus. There are about 70 variations of HPV, all of which can result in warts, or flat lesions that appear on or around the genitalia. The highest rate of infection is among women aged 20-24 and men aged 25-34. HPV is spread by unprotected sex with someone who is infected with the virus, and is one of the extremely common STDs. Many people who have HPV have no symptoms. These people (carriers) can pass the virus to others unknowingly. Condoms do not provide a complete protection against HPV transmission, and therefore there is no way to absolutely ensure that you will not get the virus if you have sex with someone who has it. In those infected persons who manifest symptoms like warts or lesions, the symptoms usually appear 3 weeks to 8 months after contact with an infected individual. HPV infection is rampant because the most dangerous period for transmission is before any visible signs and symptoms appear, and therefore transmission takes place without the knowledge of the infected person.

HPV is the MOST important risk factor for cancer of the cervix in women. Practically all cases of cervical cancer are caused by HPV. A regular Pap Smear examination can help early detection and treatment of pre-cancerous cell changes which can then prevent cervical cancer. HPV infection can NEVER be completely cured/eliminated. The treatment is primarily aimed at removing the warts by freezing or applying a lotion, reducing the number of viral particles and possibly stimulating the immune response to help control the viral infection. The virus can remain in the body and be passed on to a sex partner even though the warts are removed.

Pap Smear

A Pap Smear test is used for screening women for changes of the cervix that could lead to cervical cancer. A sample is taken during a routine gynecological examination. Cells are collected from the cervix, put onto glass slides, and looked at under a microscope for any abnormalities. The Pap Smear may indicate that pre-cancerous cells are present. If the test is positive, the woman may need a repeat Pap smear test or may need additional/advanced tests. Pre-cancerous cell changes usually cause no symptoms. If a Pap Smear does lead to detection of pre-cancerous cells at an early stage, the outcome of the treatment is more likely to be positive. That is why it is very important for a woman to have a regular Pap Smear test.

Vaccination to Prevent HPV

Vaccination for HPV infection is now available. It

can help to prevent Cervical Cancer before it occurs. This vaccination acts by producing antibodies against the Human Papilloma Virus. These antibodies then protect the cervix from an HPV infection, by fighting the virus. By protecting the Cervix from an HPV infection, vaccination offers protection against Cervical Cancer.

The Vaccine is given in three injections over a period of six months. It is best given as early as possible to teenage girls, as this is when the best immune response to the Vaccine is achieved. However, since all women remain at risk of Cervical Cancer, the Vaccination can be given at any age.

Hepatitis B

Hepatitis B is a serious liver infection that is caused by the Hepatitis B virus (HBV). HBV is extremely infectious and is spread through contact with the blood and other body fluids (including semen, vaginal secretions, and breast milk) of infected individuals. A person gets infected with HBV either by blood-to-blood contact (blood transfusion, sharing of needles and syringes, use of contaminated razors or tattooing needles, use of unsterilised surgical and dental equipment, or even equipment used in invasive cosmetic procedures) or by sexual contact (vaginal, oral or anal). HBV is much more infectious than HIV. Although HBV can infect people of all ages, adolescents and young adults are at greater risk. HBV directly attacks the liver and can lead to severe illness, liver damage, and in some cases death.

Although there is no cure for the HBV, there is a safe and effective vaccine that can prevent Hepatitis B. This vaccine has been available since 1982 and is given in a series of three injections. It provides protection against HBV in 90-95 per cent of vaccinated individuals. Getting vaccinated is the best way to 'reduce' your risk of contracting HBV, however, it does not completely eliminate the possibility of HBV transmission.

Many people with Hepatitis B have only mild or no symptoms. However, some people experience flu-like symptoms or may develop yellowing of the skin (jaundice). The majority of individuals have selflimiting infections, experience complete resolution, and develop protective levels of antibodies.

The bodies of a small number of infected individuals (5-10 per cent) are unable to clear the infection and become 'chronic carriers'. Of the chronic carriers, 10-30 per cent develop chronic liver disease and/or cirrhosis. In addition, chronic carriers can infect others throughout their lives, and their risk for developing liver cancer is 200 times higher.

Pregnant women with Hepatitis B can transmit the virus to their babies. Most infected babies (who are not treated promptly) become chronic carriers and face an increased risk of cirrhosis, liver failure and liver cancer. Therefore, all pregnant women should be tested for HBV, and if the test is positive, a gynaecologist and obstetrician should be consulted.

Hepatitis B can be diagnosed by blood tests. Routine blood tests, which include liver function tests, may indicate an infection. In addition, a specific blood test (Australia Antigen/ Hepatitis B Surface Antigen) for the virus can give a definitive diagnosis of Hepatitis B.

There is no specific treatment or cure for acute Hepatitis B and no drugs have been known to alter the course of infection once someone develops symptoms. However, for individuals with chronic Hepatitis B, interferon therapy may help.

Chapter 27

THE AIDS PANDEMIC

A detailed discussion on HIV infection

What Is Aids/HIV Infection?

Acquired Immune Deficiency Syndrome (AIDS) is caused by the Human Immunodeficiency Virus (HIV). It is a serious disorder of the immune system in which the body's normal defences against infections break down, leaving it vulnerable to a host of life threatening infections, including unusual malignancies.

HIV is found in the blood and other body fluids (particularly semen, pre-ejaculatory secretions, vaginal secretions, saliva and breast milk) of persons infected with the virus. A person can be infected with HIV and not know it. It is currently believed that most people infected with HIV will develop AIDS over a period of time depending on their general health and natural defence mechanism of the body. However, they can be infected with HIV for many years (often more than 10 years) before they develop AIDS. AIDS is the most advanced stage of the HIV infection.

HIV/AIDS has been one of the most feared diseases ever since human beings began efforts to control and prevent major diseases. History is witness to several successful attempts of mankind in controlling, eradicating and preventing major causes of disability or death.

Control of diseases such as measles, polio, tetanus etc. through vaccines, and the eradication of smallpox are examples of our triumph over many killer diseases. Although a large number of health problems continue to defy human efforts to control them, none of them presents a challenge greater than the control and prevention of HIV/AIDS. This is mainly because at the moment there is neither a scientifically proven cure, nor a vaccine to prevent HIV/AIDS.

Key Events in the History of HIV/AIDS

1981 – First case of AIDS was detected in Los Angeles (USA).

1982 September – The Centers for Disease Control and Prevention (CDC) coined the term AIDS and started using it.

1983 – The Human Immunodeficiency Virus (HIV) was identified at the Louis Pasteur Institute, Paris (France).

1986 April – The first cluster of HIV positive individuals (sex workers) was detected in India at Madras (Chennai).

1986 May – The first person with AIDS in India was detected in Mumbai.

1988 December – World AIDS day was observed for the first time on December 1st.

How Many People Have HIV/AIDS?

An estimated 4.03 crore people worldwide were reported to be living with the HIV infection in the year 2005.

An estimated 3.34 crore people worldwide were reported to be living with the HIV infection in the year 2008.

South Africa is reported to have the largest population living with HIV/AIDS, at well over 5 million people infected, followed by Nigeria in second place and India being the third largest population of HIV infected with more than 2.31 million people reported.

According to the United Nations Programme on HIV (UNAIDS) and the World Health Organisation (WHO) estimates, 11 people around the world were infected per minute during 1998 (i.e. around 6 million).

As per the statistics for the year 2005, 4.9 Million (10 per minute) people were newly infected with HIV in 2005 and 3.1 Million (6 per minute) people died of AIDS in 2005.

As per the statistics for the year 2008, 2.7 Million (6 per minute) people were newly infected with HIV in 2008 and 2 Million (4 per minute) people died of AIDS in 2008.

Presently, every 10 seconds one person (6 per minute, 8640 per day, 31.54 lakhs per year) is speculated to be getting newly infected with HIV in the world, and every 15 seconds, one person (4 per minute, 5480 per day, 20 lakhs per year) is speculated to be dying of AIDS in the world.

More than 95 per cent HIV-infected people are in developing countries.

HIV/AIDS in India

India has the world's third largest HIV infected population after South Africa. In India over 1 crore people are estimated to be HIV positive presently, though the official figure is 4.58 million for 2002, 5.1 millions for 2003, 5.134 million for 2004 and 2.31 million for 2007.

According to the National AIDS Control Organisation (NACO), there has been a 15 per cent rise in the HIV infected population from 2002 to 2003 in India. NACO estimated that the number of Indians living with HIV increased by 500,000 in 2003. Around 38 percent of these people were women.

The number of people with the HIV infection in India is difficult to determine. India's prevalence estimates are based solely on sentinel surveillance conducted at public sites. The country has no national information system to collect HIV testing information from the private sector, which provides 80 per cent of health care in the country.

Although the HIV prevalence rate is low (0.9 per cent), the overall number of people with the HIV infection is very high according to estimates by UNAIDS. Given India's large population, with most of the Indian states having a population greater than a majority of the countries in Africa, a mere 0.1 percent increase in the prevalence rate would increase the number of adults living with HIV/AIDS by over half a million people.

Maharashtra accounts for close to 50 per cent (which is the maximum) of all reported HIV and AIDS cases in India, followed by Tamilnadu and Manipur.

The prominent mode of transmission of HIV infection in India is found to be through heterosexual contact (74.17 per cent), followed by blood transfusion and blood product infusion (8.15 per cent) and injectable drug use (7.05 per cent).

Structure of HIV

HIV is of two types: HIV 1 and HIV 2. The subtype C is common in Asia.

HIV has a coat of fatty material known as the **viral envelope**. Projecting from the viral envelope are about 72 little spikes, which are formed from the proteins **gp120** and **gp41**. Just beneath the viral envelope is a layer called the **matrix,** which is made from the protein **p17**. The **viral core** (or caspid) is usually bullet-shaped and is made from the protein **p24**. Inside the core are three enzymes required for HIV replication called reverse transcriptase, integrase and protease. Held within the caspid is the genetic material of HIV which consists of two identical strands of RNA.

HIV: A Retrovirus

In medical terminology, HIV is a Retrovirus.

HIV can copy its genetic material RNA into DNA using a unique enzyme called reverse transcriptase. Normally viruses make RNA out of DNA. In HIV it is the reverse, thus the name retrovirus. HIV inserts its DNA copies into the DNA of the cell of the immune system, turning them into HIV factories.

Most viruses carry their genetic blueprint as DNA, making vaccine development comparatively straightforward.

As HIV is a retrovirus, it carries its genetic code in the related RNA molecule. No RNA-virus vaccine has been created so far.

How Does HIV Affect the Body?

HIV destroys a particular variety of White Blood Cells (WBCs) that are essential for destroying disease-causing germs. There are several varieties of WBCs in the body. Of these, Lymphocytes form about 25 per cent of the total WBC count (i.e. around 1000 to 2750/c.mm.) They normally increase in number in response to any infection.

There are two types of Lymphocytes

- B cells
- T cells (T-helper cells/T-lymphocytes/CD4)

When B cells come in contact with a disease-causing agent such as a bacteria or virus, they secrete large volumes of antibodies – chemical substances that can destroy the germs.

When disease-causing germs enter the body, the T cells produce several new copies of itself. Each T cell contains a chemical substance that can destroy the specific germ.

HIV destroys T cells which are a part of the body's defence system, thus breaking down the immune system – our body's shield against disease. The body is then open to attack from infections or cancers that it would otherwise be able to resist. These are called opportunistic infections.

When Do Symptoms Appear?

Some people (70 per cent) develop the primary symptoms shortly after being infected.

Most of the HIV infected people develop symptoms of AIDS after about 6 to 12 years.

There are several stages of the HIV disease. The first symptom is often swollen lymph glands in the throat, armpit, neck or groin. Other early symptoms include low-grade fever, headaches, fatigue, muscle aches, and swollen glands. They may last only for a few weeks. Then there are usually no symptoms for several years.

How Does HIV Infections Progress?

HIV infection progresses in four stages

Primary infection: Infection with HIV results in rapid proliferation of the virus in the blood and lymph nodes. Two to six weeks after the first entry of the virus in the body, 70 per cent people suffer from flu-like symptoms such as fever, headache, enlarged lymph nodes and a general feeling of being unwell. The effect of the HIV infection on the lymphatic system, results in a rapid decline in the number of CD4 T cells (CD4 lymphopaenia) in the bloodstream by 20 to 40 per cent. By the time the flu-like symptoms appear, the normal defense mechanism of the body fights back with the killer T cells and the antibodies produced by B cells. As a result, the HIV levels in the body reduce dramatically and the total number of CD4 T cells may go back to 80-90 per cent of the original levels.

Early immune deficiency (CD4 count more than 500/ml): During this phase the immune system has controlled the virus, which is largely restricted to the lymphoid tissue. In this phase, damage inflicted by the virus is limited to the regenerative capacity of the immune system and people with HIV are usually without symptoms.

Intermediate immune deficiency (CD4 count 200 to

500/ml): Viral replication is very high and CD4 turnover is rapid. Subtle signs and symptoms indicating compromise of the immune system begin to appear.

Advanced immune deficiency (CD4 count less than 200/ml or 14 per cent of all lymphocytes; or when viral load is above 100,000 copies/ml): The virus which proliferates throughout the body overcomes the immune system. Major opportunistic infections and malignancies become increasingly common. Death follows soon.

What Are the Later Symptoms of the HIV Disease?

The symptoms at the later stage of HIV infection (AIDS) are primarily the result of conditions that do not normally develop in individuals with healthy immune systems. Most of these conditions are infections caused by bacteria, viruses, fungi or parasites that are normally controlled by the immune system that HIV severely damages.

Opportunistic infections are very common in people with AIDS. HIV attacks virtually every organ system. People with AIDS also have an increased risk of developing various cancers such as Kaposi's sarcoma, cancer of the cervix and cancers of the immune system known as lymphomas.

- A thick, whitish coating of the tongue or mouth (thrush) that is caused by a yeast infection and sometimes accompanied by a sore throat
- A MAJOR opportunistic infection in AIDS patients is Pulmonary Tuberculosis
- Severe or recurring vaginal yeast infections

- Chronic pelvic inflammatory disease (PID) or severe and frequent infections like herpes zoster
- Rapid loss of weight i.e. more than 10 per cent of body weight (about 5 Kgs/10 pounds) lost without increased physical exercise or dieting
- Long-lasting bouts of diarrhoea
- The appearance of discoloured or purplish growths (Kaposi's sarcoma) on the skin or inside the mouth
- Recurring fevers and/or night sweats
- Periods of extreme and unexplained fatigue that may be combined with headaches, light-headedness, and/or dizziness
- Swelling or hardening of glands located in the throat, armpit, neck or groin
- Periods of continued, deep, dry coughing and increasing shortness of breath
- Unexplained bleeding from growths on the skin, from mucous membranes, or from any opening in the body
- Recurring or unusual skin rashes
- Severe numbness or pain in the hands or feet, the loss of muscle control and reflex, paralysis, or loss of muscular strength
- An altered state of consciousness, personality change, or mental deterioration.

After the diagnosis of AIDS is made, the current average survival time with Anti-retroviral treatment is estimated to be more than five years, but because HIV continues to evolve resistance to treatments and because new treatments continue to be developed, estimates of survival time are likely to continue to change.

Without antiretroviral therapy, death normally occurs within a year. Most patients die from opportunistic infections or malignancies associated with the progressive failure of the immune system.

WHO (World Health Organization) Disease Staging System for HIV Infection and AIDS

In 1990, the World Health Organization (WHO) introduced a staging system for patients infected with HIV-1. An update took place in September 2005. Most of these conditions are opportunistic infections that are easily treatable in healthy people.

- Stage I: HIV infection is asymptomatic and not categorised as AIDS
- Stage II: includes minor muco-cutaneous manifestations and recurrent upper respiratory tract infections
- Stage III: includes unexplained chronic diarrhoea for longer than a month, severe bacterial infections and pulmonary tuberculosis
- Stage IV: includes toxoplasmosis of the brain, candidiasis of the oesophagus, trachea, bronchi or lungs and Kaposi's sarcoma; these diseases are indicators of AIDS.

How Is HIV Transmitted?

HIV is transmitted through direct contact of a mucous membrane or the bloodstream with bodily fluids containing HIV, such as blood, semen, pre-ejaculatory secretions, vaginal secretions/fluids, saliva and even breast milk. This transmission can come in the form of vaginal, oral or anal sex, blood transfusion, contaminated hypodermic needles and other instruments, and transmission from mother to child during pregnancy, childbirth, or breastfeeding.

HIV is commonly spread by —

- Having unprotected penetrative sexual intercourse (vaginal, oral or anal) with someone who is infected with HIV.
-Sharing needles or syringes with someone who is infected with HIV.
- Being pierced with a hypodermic needle or surgical instrument contaminated with HIV.
- Receiving transfusions of blood products donated by someone who is infected with HIV.
- Getting HIV-infected blood, semen, or vaginal secretions into open wounds, sores or infected skin.

HIV can also be passed from a woman to her foetus during pregnancy or childbirth. **15 to 30 percent of babies born to women with HIV are also infected.** However, the use of the anti-viral drug Zidovudine can reduce the risk of transmission by two-thirds. It should be noted that all infants born to women who are HIV positive will test positive for HIV at birth because of the presence of the mother's antibodies in their blood. Antibodies testing, 18 months after the childbirth, can more accurately determine the HIV infection. Because the HIV virus can also be transmitted through breast milk, HIV-positive mothers are advised not to breastfeed their newborns.

Note: A person cannot get infected with HIV from:

- Ordinary social or casual contact.
- Shared clothing.
- Touching.
- Shared food, dishes, or eating utensils.
- Dry kissing.
- Hugging.
- Shaking hands.
- Sharing wash rooms, toilet seats.
- Insect bites.
- Coughing or sneezing.
- Swimming pool, Jacuzzi.
- Self Masturbation.
- Living or working with an HIV-infected person.

How Can You Protect Yourself from Getting HIV Infection?

The surest way is to abstain from sexual intercourse with anyone besides your spouse who is HIV negative i.e. long-term monogamous relationship with an uninfected person. Your chance of becoming infected with HIV can be reduced by avoiding highrisk behaviours. The best way to prevent HIV infection is to abstain from unsafe sexual and drug using practices. Refrain from sharing needles or any instruments that touch the blood of a person.

Don't share personal items that may be contaminated with blood. This includes toothbrushes, razors, needles for piercing or tattooing, and blades for ritual cutting or scarring.

Be tested and treated for sexually transmitted infections every year. Women and men with open sores from herpes and other infections get HIV more easily than other people.

Stay in charge. Good judgment and self-control are the basis of safer and healthier sex. Alcohol and drugs weaken both. Don't risk your good judgment and self-control with alcohol or other drugs.

HIV Risk Comparisons

Here are some common sexual behaviours grouped according to relative risk

No Risk

- Self masturbation
- Fantasy
- Intercourse with a partner who is truly HIV negative.

Low Risk

- Using sex toys
- Mutual masturbation

- Touching – massage
- Erotic massage – body rubbing
- Dry kissing

Moderate Risk

- Oral sex on a man with a condom
- Vaginal intercourse with a male condom or female condom
- Anal intercourse with a condom
- Wet kissing

High Risk – Millions of reported cases due to these behaviours

- Vaginal intercourse without a condom
- Oral sex without a condom
- Anal intercourse without a condom
- Deep kissing (with blood letting)

How and Where to Get Tested for HIV?

There are blood tests to determine if a person is infected with HIV. Tests are available at clinical laboratories, health clinics and hospitals. Local, state, and central government health departments offer free testing. Some medical centres have anonymous HIV counselling and testing facilities.

HIV infection can be detected by a **direct test** (testing for antigen) or **an indirect test** (testing for antibodies).

More commonly, the diagnosis of the HIV infection is made by detection of antibodies to HIV by a test called ELISA and confirmation by another test – the Western Blot. Because these tests look for antibodies rather than the actual virus, it is possible that during the time between transmission of infection and when levels of antibodies are high enough to be detected, an HIV test will be negative, even if the person is actually infected with HIV. This window period varies from person to person. Therefore, persons who think that they might be infected should wait for a period of 3-6 months since their last possible exposure before getting tested.

There are other blood tests p24 antigen testing, **Polymerase Chain Reaction** i.e. PCR, plasma HIV-1 RNA measurement (viral load) or DNA test that can look for the actual presence and amount of virus in the blood (direct test). However, these tests are very expensive and are used primarily in treatment decisions for persons already known to be HIVinfected.

Counselling before and after testing should be an integral part of the HIV testing procedures. During counselling, vital information is made available to those who test positive to prevent subsequent transmission to their partner(s), to prevent acquiring other STDs, to identify links to social and health resources, and to receive guidance for maintaining health through a healthy lifestyle. For those who test negative, counselling information can be critical in helping to prevent future infection. Testing can make a critical difference in the lives of those who test positive, as knowing they have HIV, empowers them to take appropriate action in planning their lives ahead, and in getting the services they need.

Privacy and Testing

You can be tested confidentially or anonymously. Anonymous testing means your name is not used i.e. your identity is kept undisclosed.

Is There a Treatment for HIV Infection or AIDS?

Currently, there is **no cure** for HIV infection or AIDS. However, a variety of new treatments – combinations of medicines – offer hope. With the combined use of new antiviral drugs (known as combination therapy) as well as drugs to prevent opportunistic infections, many people with HIV infection and AIDS have extended and improved the quality of their lives and delayed the progression of HIV infection to full blown AIDS. These drugs can cause a number of side effects that may require a person to switch to other drugs, or stop taking them. In addition, combination therapy requires taking a large number of pills on a complicated schedule. These drugs are also very costly and unavailable to many people in many parts of the world, where the majority of individuals with HIV infection and AIDS exist. While there is increasing hope for people with HIV, there is still **no cure.**

Prognosis

Some people have lived with AIDS for many years. New treatments and increased knowledge may help many more people live with AIDS even longer.

Without anti-retroviral treatment, the net median survival time after infection with HIV is estimated to be 9 to 11 years (depending on the HIV subtype), and the median survival rate after diagnosis of AIDS in resource-limited settings where antiretroviral treatment is not available ranges between 6 and 19 months. In areas where it is widely available, the development of **Highly Active Anti-Retroviral Therapy** (HAART) as effective therapy for HIV infection and AIDS reduced the death rate from this disease by 80 per cent, and raised the life expectancy for a newly-diagnosed HIV-infected person to about 20 years.

Condom and Safe Sex

While it is believed that the use of condoms is effective in reducing the risk of STD transmission, the degree of risk reduction varies depending on the STD. For STDs that cause genital ulcers, such as syphilis, herpes, and chancroid, and for HPV infection, the degree of protection that condoms provide is lower, since these infections are transmitted through contact with genital skin and mucosal surfaces. This contact can occur in areas that the condom does not cover.

It is probably safe to have sex without a condom when both partners are free of STDs (including HIV) and they are not having sex with other partners. Remember, it is necessary to have an HIV test six months after engaging in risky sexual behaviour to be sure that you are HIV negative. In addition, some STDs do not have symptoms for a long time, and therefore it is impossible to know for sure if you are infected unless you are tested. However, getting a partner's sexual history could be difficult and unreliable. People may not be honest because of fear or shame. Sometimes a partner may have an STD or HIV but is unaware of it because he or she does not have any symptoms.

The most reliable way to avoid transmission of STDs, including HIV, is to **abstain from sexual intercourse** – vaginal, oral, or anal sex – or to be in a long-term, mutually monogamous (sexually exclusive) relationship with an uninfected partner.

GLOSSARY

Abstinence
The voluntary decision not to engage in sexual relations of any kind; in some cases, the decision not to engage in penetrative sex

Abortion
Termination of pregnancy before the foetus has become capable of sustaining an independent life outside the uterus; an abortion can occur either spontaneously (spontaneous abortion), or it can be brought about by deliberate intervention (induced abortion)

AIDS
Acquired Immune Deficiency Syndrome(AIDS); it is a serious disorder of the immune system caused by the Human Immunodeficiency Virus (HIV) in which the body's normal defences against infections break down, leaving it vulnerable to a host of life threatening infections, including unusual malignancies

Anal sex (Sodomy)
Sexual activity characterised by anal penetration or stimulation with penis, finger or inanimate objects

Anorgasmia
Persistent or recurrent absence of orgasm following a normal, willing, participative sexual act

Bartholin's glands
Two small glands on either side of the vaginal opening that secrete a mucus-like fluid during sexual arousal, providing vaginal lubrication

Benign prostatic hyperplasia (BPH)
Non-Cancerous enlargement of the prostate that causes urinary difficulties

Bestiality (Zoophilia)
Sexual contact with animals

Bisexual
A sexual orientation in which one feels attracted to both males and females

Blue Balls
Slang expression for a painful testicular sensation felt when a man becomes sexually aroused repeatedly or persistently without release through ejaculation.

Bondage and discipline
A sexual act involving elements of Masochism and Sadism in which a submissive partner is bound or restrained, and then disciplined, punished or chastised physically or mentally by the dominant partner

Castration
The surgical removal of the gonads (testes or ovaries); in popular use, also refers to the amputation of the penis.

Celibacy
Abstinence from all sexual activity and sexual relations

Cervix
The tapered, lower end of the uterus that opens into the vaginal canal and allows passage of menstrual flow from the uterus and passage of sperm into the uterus

Circumcision
The surgical removal of the retractable foreskin (prepuce) covering the glans penis in men

Clitoris
An erectile, hooded organ at the upper joining of the labia minora that contains a high concentration of nerve endings and is very sensitive to stimulation; it is the only anatomical organ in women whose sole function is providing sexual pleasure

Coitus
(sexual intercourse, copulation, vaginal intercourse)

It is a peak response to sexual excitement when the erect male penis enters the female vagina and after reaching a climax of excitement ejects the semen into the vagina. This can result into conception (pregnancy)

Coitus interruptus
(Withdrawal)

One of the oldest known methods of contraception in which the man withdraws his penis from the vagina before ejaculation; it has a very high failure rate

Condom
A flexible sheath (usually made of thin latex or polyurethane)

designed to cover the erect penis (male condom) or vulva (female condom) during sexual intercourse to protect against sexually transmitted infections and/or unwanted pregnancy

Cowper's glands
A pair of pea-sized glands at the base of the penis under the prostate gland that secrete a clear alkaline fluid into the urethra during sexual arousal

Cunnilingus
(oral sex on a woman)
Oral stimulation of the female genitalia for sexual pleasure

Cybersex
Using a computer and internet in some way to experience sexual pleasure

Dyspareunia (Painful intercourse)
It is painful sexual intercourse, due to biological or psychogenic causes

Ejaculation
The expulsion or squirting of semen from the penis

Epididymides
Tightly coiled tubes at the back of the testicles, where sperms mature and are stored until they are released during ejaculation

Episiotomy
A surgical cut made through the skin, tissues and muscles of the vagina and perineum to enlarge the vaginal opening during childbirth

Erection
The firm and enlarged condition of penis in men; it can happen when a person is aroused by a sexual thought, feeling, fantasy or by the sight or memory of someone one finds sexually attractive or when the penis is touched stroked or caressed

Erectile dysfunction
Recurrent or persistent inability to achieve or maintain a penile erection

Erogenous zones
Erogenous zones are areas of the body that are particularly sensitive to sexual stimulation if touched in a special manner.

Erotic
Marked by strong sexual desire or being especially sensitive to sexual stimulation.

Estrogen (Oestrogen)
A female sex hormone secreted in the ovaries that stimulates the development of secondary sexual characteristics in females.

Eunuch
A man who has been castrated

Exhibitionism
The persistent and recurrent urge or behaviour to expose one's private parts (genitalia and/or breasts) to an unsuspecting person

Fallopian tubes (oviducts)
A pair of tubes that extend from the upper lateral corners of the uterus toward the ovaries, but not touching them. The egg

(ovum) travels through fallopian tubes, from the ovaries toward the uterus every month, where fertilisation of the ovum could occur.

Fellatio (oral sex on a man/blow job)
Oral stimulation of the male penis for sexual pleasure

Fetishism
A fixation (or an obsession) on a body part or an object that is not basically sexual in nature, and the compulsive need or demand for its use in order to experience sexual gratification

Foreplay
Mutual sexual stimulation such as kissing, touching, caressing, fondling etc usually preceding sexual intercourse

Foreskin
A loose, retractable sheath of skin that covers the glans-penis

Frottage
Sexual stimulation derived by rubbing one's body against another person without her or his consent

G-spot (Grafenberg spot)
An area of increased sensitivity within the vagina, with maximum potential for sexual arousal; it is supposed to be located on the upper vaginal wall about two inches from the external vaginal opening. However, as studies have shown, it may not be present in all women

Gay
A person who identifies himself as homosexual

Gender
Refers to what a person, society or legal system defines as male or female

Gender roles
The set of culturally or socially defined attitudes, expectations, behaviours, and responsibilities considered appropriate for women (feminine) and men (masculine)

Glans penis
The head of the penis that is normally covered by the foreskin

Hermaphrodite
A person with both male and female primary sexual characteristics

Heterosexual
A person who identifies himself or herself as sexually oriented to persons of the opposite sex

HIV (Human Immunodeficiency Virus)
A virus that is responsible for Acquired Immuno Deficiency Syndrome (AIDS)

Homosexual
A person who identifies himself or herself as sexually oriented to persons of the same sex

Hymen
A thin membrane that partially covers the vagina; it may or may not be present at birth.

Hysterectomy
The surgical removal of the uterus

Impotence

Inability to achieve and/or maintain erection sufficient for satisfactory sexual performance

Incest

Sexual activity among blood-related family members such as brother-sister, mother-son or father-daughter; it is not permitted morally as well as legally irrespective of the willingness of participants

Intercourse (Coitus, copulation)

It is a peak response to sexual excitement when the erect male penis enters the female vagina and after reaching a climax of excitement ejects the semen into the vagina; this can result into conception (pregnancy)

Infertility

The inability of a couple to conceive a child (get pregnant) after one year of unprotected sexual intercourse

Lesbian

A female who identifies himself as sexually oriented to persons of the same sex.

Libido

Sexual desire

Masochism

The recurrent urge and/or behaviour of wanting to be humiliated, beaten, bound, or otherwise made to suffer for sexual pleasure

Mastectomy
Surgical removal of the breast

Masturbation
Self-stimulation of the genital organs for sexual pleasure

Menarche
The beginning of menstruation in women

Menopause
The end of a woman's menstruation cycles

Menstruation
Periodic flow of blood out of the uterus and through the vagina approximately every 28-30 days, usually lasting 3-5 days

Mons pubis
A pad of fatty tissue over the pubic bone that protects the internal reproductive organs in women

Necrophilia
Sexual activity with a corpse

Nymphomania
A term used to refer to a sexually hyper-active woman, often meaning uncontrollable or excessive sexual desire; this term is often pejorative and reflects gender biases in which women are expected to be without active sexual desire i.e. sexually naïve

Orgasm
An orgasm is the intense feeling of physical pleasure that one experiences at the climax of sexual stimulation

Ovaries

The Ovaries are two oval-shaped sex glands (gonads) located on either side of the uterus at the end of each fallopian tube; the ovaries produce ova, and release one ovum per month from menarche to menopause. The ovaries also produce hormones responsible for the development of secondary sexual characteristics in females

Ovulation

The monthly release of an ovum from the ovary

Paraphilia

Conditions that are characterised by intense and recurrent sexual urges, behaviours or fantasies that involve unusual objects, activities, or situations, and cause clinically significant distress or impairment in social, occupational and other areas of functioning

Paedophilia

A psychological disorder in which an adult experiences a sexual preference for pre-pubescent children, or has engaged in child sexual abuse

Pederasty

Sexual relations between an older man and an adolescent boy outside his immediate family

Penis

It is a cylindrical organ in males with the ability to be flaccid or erect; it provides a passage for both urine and semen. It can be a source of pleasure in response to sexual stimulation and is the organ that penetrates the vaginal canal during sexual intercourse

Perimenopausal

Characterising the years both before and after the menopause (last period); this term is interchangeable with the term climacteric

Perineum

A diamond-shaped area on the inferior surface of the trunk, located between and surrounding the vagina and anus in women, and the penis and anus in men

Peyronie's disease

The formation of a plaque or hardened scar tissue (fibrosis) beneath the skin of the penis that causes pain, curvature, and distortion, usually during erection

Postmenopausal

The one to two year period after completion of menopause (last period)

Premature ejaculation (PE)

A condition in men characterised by recurrent or persistent ejaculation with minimal sexual stimulation before, during, or shortly after penetration

Progesterone

A female sex hormone produced by the corpus luteum in the ovaries that has a major role in menstruation and pregnancy

Prostatectomy

Surgical removal of the prostate gland and some of the tissue around the gland in men

Prostate gland

A walnut-sized gland that lies just beneath the urinary bladder in men; it secretes about 30 per cent of the fluid that makes up semen

Rape
It is an assault by a person upon another person involving penetrative sexual intercourse (vaginal, oral or anal) without that person's consent using physical force, threat, or coercion

Refractory period
The time immediately following orgasm, during which men cannot achieve another erection

Retrograde ejaculation
Ejaculation in which semen is discharged back into the urinary bladder rather than out through the penis

Sadism
The recurrent urge and/or behaviour involving acts in which the pain or humiliation of a partner is sexually exciting

Sadomasochism
The consensual use of domination or pain for sexual arousal and/or stimulation; playing out or fantasising dominant and submissive roles; the sadist is the partner who dominates and/or inflicts pain, and the masochist is the partner who is dominated and/or receives pain

Scrotum
A pouch of loose skin hanging directly under the penis that contains the testes and functions to maintain the temperature necessary for the production of sperms by the testes

Seminal vesicles
The pair of glandular sacs that secrete approximately 60 per

cent of the fluid that makes up semen in which sperm are transported

Sex toys
Objects used for or designed for enhancing sexual pleasure e.g. vibrators, dildos

Sexually transmitted infections (STIs)
Infections usually passed from one person to another through sexual contact, although some STIs can be passed on by other means (e.g., through needle-stick injury). Also called sexually transmitted diseases (STDs)

Sexual orientation
An individual's primary physical, emotional, romantic and sexual attraction to individuals of a specific gender (male or female)

Swinging (mate swapping, wife swapping)
Exchanging partners for sexual recreation

Testes
Paired, egg-shaped glands located in the scrotum that produce sperm and testosterone

Testosterone
A sex hormone responsible for the development of secondary sexual characteristics in males and for the sexual desire (libido) in men and in women

Transvestism (cross-dressing)
Transvestitism, commonly referred to as cross-dressing, involves experiencing sexual pleasure and arousal from dressing in clothes normally used by members of the opposite sex

Uterus

A hollow, thick-walled, pear-shaped, muscular organ located between the rectum and bladder; it is the structure that sheds its lining monthly during menstruation, and the site for implantation of the fertilised ovum (zygote), the location where the foetus develops during pregnancy

Vagina

A muscular, highly expandable, tubular cavity leading from the vestibule to the cervix of uterus

Vaginal intercourse (coitus)

It is a peak response to sexual excitement when the erect male penis enters the female vagina and after reaching a climax of excitement ejects the semen into the vagina. This can result in conception (pregnancy)

Vaginismus

A sexual dysfunction in women characterised by difficulty in achieving penetration due to involuntary spasm of vaginal muscles

Vasa deferentia (singular: vas deferens) are the paired tubes 45 cms (18 inches) long that carry mature sperms from the epididymis to the urethra.

Vestibule

The area covered by the labia minora that includes the openings to the vagina and urethra, as well as the Bartholin's glands

Voyeurism

The sexual interest in or practice of spying on people engaged in intimate behaviours, such as undressing, sexual intimacy, or other activity usually considered to be of a private nature

Vulva

The external female genitals include the mons pubis, the clitoris, the labia majora and the labia minora. Together, along with the vaginal opening, they are known as the vulva

ABOUT The AUTHORS

Dr. (Prof) RAJAN B. BHONSLE, MD
Consultant in Sexual Medicine & Counsellor

- Hon. Professor and Head of the Department of Sexual Medicine at KEM Hospital and Seth GS Medical College, Mumbai (India)
- Diplomate, American Board of Sexology and The American College of Sexologists
- Member, International Society for Sexual Medicine and Asia Pacific Society for Sexual Medicine
- Fellow, Council of Sex Education and Parenthood International

Dr. Rajan Bhonsle is an Hon. Professor and Head of the Department of Sexual Medicine at KEM Hospital and Seth GS Medical College, Mumbai (Largest Hospital and Medical College in

Southeast Asia). The Department of Sexual Medicine at the KEM Hospital, is the only one of its kind in the country.

Dr. Rajan Bhonsle is the Founder Director of Heart To Heart Counselling Centre and Dean of the Institute of Human Technology. He is a senior Consultant in Sexual Medicine & Counsellor, practicing in Mumbai since 1986.

Dr. Rajan Bhonsle passed his MBBS from Grant Medical College, Mumbai in 1981. He stood first in the MD examination of Bombay University in the year 1985.

He has authored five books on *Sex Education*. His Marathi Best Seller *Samagra Kaamjeevan* is in its Ninth edition since its first release by the Health and Education Ministers of Maharashtra. Dr. Bhonsle has also edited and contributed to a Q&A book on *Sexuality* published by NDTV.

Dr. Bhonsle started India's first full-fledged Pre-Marriage Counselling Centre in Mumbai. He has been conducting Training programs for Sex Educators in English, Marathi and Hindi. He is the first and the only one in India to conduct such intensive training programs for the adult community (Teachers, Social workers, Doctors, Parents etc) to train them to become Sex Educators. He has also been leading various AIDS awareness campaigns for the youth in India.

He has been writing very popular Question-Answer columns – Ask the Doctor and Expert Speak for *Bombay Times* (A Times of India group publication), Let's Talk Sex for *DNA*, Heart 2 Heart for the *Afternoon*, Intimacy Issues for the popular magazine *New Woman,* Teen Talk for *JAM*, Sex Talk for *Maharashtra Times* (the largest read Marathi Daily from Mumbai), a column Baat Ban Jaye for *Navbharat Times* for several years.

Dr. Bhonsle has appeared as an expert panelist on several popular TV shows on various TV channels such as NDTV, Times Now, CNN IBN7, Aaj Tak, Zee TV, Star TV, IBN Lokmat, Alfa TV, ETV, Mumbai Doordarshan, Me Marathi etc.

About the Authors

Dr. (Prof) MINNU BHONSLE, PhD
Consulting Psychotherapist and Counsellor

Dr. Minnu Bhonsle has done her Doctorate in Psychotherapy and Counselling and has been working in this field for several years.

She is a qualified Trainer in the Robert Carkhuff model of counselling (which is an offshoot of Carl Rogers' Client-centered Therapy) as well as Cognitive Behavior Therapy and conducts intensive, practical training programs in counselling for those in the helping profession.

She has had Advanced Training in Albert Ellis' Rational Emotive Behavior Therapy (REBT) and is a Member of the Association of REBT (UK). Her papers have been published in various journals including the British Journal of REBT.

She has had Advanced Training in Stress Management (Multimodal approach) conducted by the Centre for Stress Management (UK).

She is also a Member of the Council of Sex Education and Parenthood International and was given a special award for her contribution in the field of Counselling and Psychotherapy by the said Council in the year 2001.

She has conducted several training workshops in various national and international organizations, forums and institutes such as Tata Institute of Fundamental Research (TIFR), National Institute of Industrial Engineering (NITIE), Post Graduate Department of Mathematics – Mumbai University, SNDT University, Rajiv Gandhi

National Institute, Commonwealth Youth Programme etc.

She has trained more than 2000 doctors, psychiatrists, counsellors, psychologists, social workers, teachers, HRD personnel, Management trainees (MBA students) etc in various models of counselling.

Her module on *Humane Management* (Management with a Human Touch) which helps increase the Sensitivity Quotient (SQ) of participants and trains them in the much required people skills in the corporate world, is extremely popular with leaders in Management and management trainees alike.

She has been writing articles and features on relationships and psycho-social issues for prominent publications and internet sites such as *India Today, New Woman, Complete Well-being, Life Positive, Parenting, Express Healthcare Management, Health Screen, Economic Times, Mumbai Mirror* etc. She has been writing very popular Q&A columns – Expert Speak for *Bombay Times* (A Times of India group publication), Heart Talk for *My World* (a woman's magazine by Future Media group), Lifeline – Mind for *Life Positive,* Heart 2 Heart for the *Afternoon,* the column Baat Ban Jaye for *Navbharat Times* for several years.

www.ingramcontent.com/pod-product-compliance
Lightning Source LLC
Chambersburg PA
CBHW050552170426
43201CB00011B/1660